Chapter Four is silent_____
of the Lawton team in demonstrating how SBTs
(and QTech) provide an American Edge for North
American Tires. As you know all to well, it is not
as easy as it first appears to make SBTs an
effective competitive advantage. It has been a
pleasure working with the Lawton team.

Dan Klein

The American Edge

Leveraging
Manufacturing's
Hidden Assets

Janice A. Klein Editor

Jeffrey G. Miller Editor

McGraw-Hill, Inc.

New York San Francisco Washington, D.C. Auckland Bogotá
Caracas Lisbon London Madrid Mexico City Milan
Montreal New Delhi San Juan Singapore
Sydney Tokyo Toronto

Library of Congress Cataloging-in-Publication Data

The American edge: leveraging manufacturing's hidden assets / edited
 by Janice A. Klein and Jeffrey G. Miller.
     p.   cm.
 Based on the Boston University Roundtable held in 1990.
 Includes bibliographical references and index.
 ISBN 0-07-035040-X
   1. United States—Manufactures—Congresses. 2. Industrial
 management—United States—Congresses. 3. Competition,
 International—Congresses. I. Klein, Janice Anne. II. Miller,
 Jeffrey G.
 HD9725. A69   1993
 685'. 00973—dc20   93-25092
                                                CIP

1 2 3 4 5 6 7 8 9 0 DOC/DOC 9 9 8 7 6 5 4 3

ISBN 0-07-035040-X

*The sponsoring editor for this book was Philip Ruppel, the editing supervisor
was Frances Koblin, and the production supervisor was Suzanne W. Babeuf. It
was set in Palatino by McGraw-Hill's Professional Book Group composition
unit.*

Printed and bound by R. R. Donnelley & Sons Company.

Contents

Part 3. Outsiders

Part 4. Technologies

Part 5. Conclusion

Contributors

Sheila H. Akabas is a Professor of Social Work, Chair of the World of Work Field of Practice, and Director of the Center for Social Policy and Practice in the Workplace at Columbia University School of Social Work. She is a graduate of Cornell University, with a Ph.D. in Economics from New York University.

Lyn Tatum Christiansen is a founding partner of The Argos Executive Group in Auburndale, Massachusetts. She was previously a member of the General Management faculty at the Harvard Business School. She received her B.A. in economics from Wellesley College and her M.B.A. and D.B.A. degrees from the Harvard Business School.

Jane Fedorowicz is an Associate Professor of Management Information Systems in the School of Management at Boston University. She received her M.S. and Ph.D. degrees in Systems Sciences from Carnegie-Mellon University.

Kasra Ferdows is a Professor of Business Administration at Georgetown University and a Visiting Professor of Technology Management at INSEAD. He holds an M.S. in Mechanical Engineering, an M.B.A., and a Ph.D. in Industrial Engineering from the University of Wisconsin.

Lauren B. Gates is the Director of Research at the Center for Social Policy and Practice in the Workplace at Columbia University School of Social Work. She holds a doctorate and master's in City and Regional Planning from the University of North Carolina and an M.S. in Environmental Psychology from the University of Massachusetts.

Julie H. Hertenstein is a founding partner of The Argos Executive Group in Auburndale, Massachusetts and a Visiting Associate Professor at Northeastern University. She received her M.B.A. and D.B.A. degrees from the Harvard Business School, where she was also a member of the faculty in the Management Control area.

Janice A. Klein is a Visiting Associate Professor in the Operations Management area at M.I.T.'s Sloan School of Management. She holds a B.S. in Industrial Engineering from Iowa State University, an M.B.A. from Boston University, and a Ph.D. in Industrial Relations from M.I.T.'s Sloan School of Management.

Robert T. Lund is Professor of Manufacturing Engineering and Research Professor of Technology and Policy at Boston University's College of Engineering. He holds a B.A. and an M.B.A. from Harvard University.

Marion E. McCollom is Assistant Professor of Organizational Behavior at Boston University's School of Management. She holds an A.B. from Radcliffe College, an M.P.P.M. and a Ph.D. in Organizational Behavior from the Yale School of Organization and Management.

Jeffrey G. Miller is Professor of Operation Management at Boston University's School of Management. He received his Ph.D. in Industrial Management from Purdue University and his M.B.A and B.A. from the University of California at Los Angeles.

James E. Post is Professor of Management and Public Policy at Boston University. He received his Ph.D. in Management from SUNY at Buffalo and a J.D. from Villanova University.

Wickham Skinner is the James E. Robison Professor of Business Administration, Emeritus, at the Harvard Business School. He holds a degree in Chemical Engineering from Yale University and an M.B.A. and D.B.A. from the Harvard Business School.

Pieter A. VanderWerf is Assistant Professor of Management Policy at Boston University's School of Management. He holds a B.A. in Economics and Mathematics from Dartmouth and a Ph.D. in Management of Technology from M.I.T.'s Sloan School of Management.

Preface

"Why do we always copy the Japanese?" "Isn't there something in America that is worth elevating as a way to resolve our competitiveness problem?" These questions were raised by the industry members of the Boston University Manufacturing Roundtable in 1990 as they considered the future of American manufacturing. Bob Badelt of Northern Telecom, a member of the Roundtable, noted: "The basic knowledge and techniques are often developed in the United States, but our paradigms do not allow us to implement them as successfully as other societies, cultures, or environments. What is it about U.S. paradigms that does not allow U.S. manufacturing companies to successfully implement programs as well as others? It appears that we are better teachers than learners. Why?"

Having raised these questions, the Roundtable asked us to assemble a team to address them. *The American Edge* is the result of our efforts to answer the questions posed by the Roundtable.

The Roundtable's assignment became known as the "Paradigm Project" because we began our journey by identifying paradigm shifts (i.e., changes in individual, group, or organizational thought patterns, rules, and procedures) that have influenced, and would continue to influence, American manufacturing and its competitive abilities.

As leaders of the Paradigm Project, which included members of both the industrial and academic community, we organized a yearlong seminar series that brought together some of the best U.S. and international thinkers on manufacturing for debate and discussion. The members of the project team concluded that the prevailing paradigm now influencing much of domestic manufacturing is a negative one. It is rooted in the belief that America has lost its competitive advantage and that the Japanese and Germans have found a better mousetrap.

As we explored the implications of this finding, we became concerned that this "woe is me" attitude was blocking the creativity of managers and companies. This concern led us to explore what we had begun to call "America's secret weapons"—the fundamental elements of American society, infrastructure, and management methods that form the core competencies of the nation's manufacturing competitiveness. They were secret, in our view, not because they were unknown, but because no one seemed to be looking for them. For a competency to qualify as a secret weapon, it had to meet the following criteria:

- The United States must be in a particularly good position to exploit the competency, due to geography, social characteristics, or previous investments.

- The competency has to be one that is not generally acknowledged by "big manufacturing" as an advantage.

- The competency has to be one that has not yet been exploited to its full potential by the majority of U.S. manufacturing firms, but could be.

It is important for the reader to understand that this book is the result of a team effort, a unique feature of which is the caliber of the contributors—Sheila Akabas, Lyn Christiansen, Jane Fedorowicz, Kasra Ferdows, Lauren Gates, Julie Hertenstein, Bob Lund, Marion McCollom, Jim Post, Wick Skinner and Pieter VanderWerf—and the breadth of multidisciplinary perspectives each brought to the project. Each contributor drafted his or her respective chapter, which became the agenda for one of our monthly seminars. These discussions became the basis for individual chapter revisions and the forum for generating linkages between the individual weapons.

As we examined the list of weapons we had assembled, we began to understand that the American edge was more than just a list of disconnected secret weapons. The American edge is the whole cloth, while the individual secret weapons are the warp and the woof that knit it together. The aim of our book is, therefore, to help shift America's paradigm to a more balanced perspective. Those readers who are looking for 10 secret things to do tomorrow to improve their manufacturing competitiveness will be sadly disappointed with this book. *The American Edge* is not a cookbook.

Over the years, a number of CEOs and manufacturing executives have thanked us for helping their companies improve their manufac-

.turing competitiveness. We thanked them for the recognition, but typically responded that the major contribution we had made was to say, "See that young man or woman or team over there. Listen to them. They have the answers to your problems." At a gut level, we knew all along what the American edge was. But, it was only after completing our research that we were able to articulate that the American edge is American workers using the unique resources of U.S. society to achieve their utmost. To them, we dedicate this book.

Acknowledgments

The intellectual effectiveness of the initial Paradigm Project was based on the work of a number of colleagues who served as "provocateurs." The Boston University faculty who played this role included Peter Arnold, Simeon Chow, Robb Dixon, Moshi Hagigi, Tim Hall, John Henderson, Jay Kim, Tom Vollmann, Phillip Bell, and Ron Klinberg. Three special visitors—Stan Davis, Roland Van Dierdonk, and Chan Hahn—helped shape our view of the future and how those overseas view us.

The industrial members of the Manufacturing Roundtable helped the team stay firmly planted in the "real world." We acknowledge them all for their financial support and their review and critique of the project. Particular thanks go to Bob Badelt and Jerry Dehner from Northern Telecom, Steve Denker from DEC, Bob Downing from Rohm & Haas, and Stu Christy from Johnson & Johnson, as well as Roundtable Directors Dick D'Entremont, Fred Scott, and Steve Rosenthal.

Linda Angell, Janelle Heineke, Andy Donkin, and Nancy Clark provided outstanding assistance throughout the project.

Lastly, we thank Deans George McGowen and Lou Lataif of Boston University for their support of the Roundtable.

Individual contributors would also like to acknowledge inputs to their respective chapters. In particular, Pieter VanderWerf is indebted to Don Ruiz, an insightful and meticulous researcher, for much of the material in his chapter. He also attempted to draw on the considerable knowledge and insight into Japanese society of Dr. Shuichi Matsuda, which was graciously shared with Pieter over the years. Pieter also thanks Piet Delagaye for key ideas and pieces of information about Europe. Jane Fedorowicz is indebted to her research assistant, John Storck, for her chapter title and also for his creative assistance in developing the ideas in her chapter. James Post is grateful for the research assistance of Jennifer W. Griffin, doctoral candidate at the Boston

University School of Management. Lyn Christiansen and Julie Hertenstein thank the managers interviewed for their chapter, who generously gave their time and thoughts to them.

Jan Klein
Jeff Miller

PART 1
Introduction

1
Balancing the Debate

Somewhere along the line Americans have lost confidence in the nation's ability to compete in manufacturing. They point to the declining number of manufacturing jobs, the industries where foreign competitors are now powerful, and the technologies that are developed elsewhere. Perhaps the most negative manifestation of this loss of confidence is the prevailing assumption that American manufacturers do things wrong and others, particularly the Japanese and Germans, do things right.

The defeatist tone is a dangerous element in the continuing debate over how U.S. manufacturing industries should best maintain and increase their competitiveness. This is an important debate because American business is in a serious fight with global competitors. The assumption that American manufacturing is losing and that the country's strengths should be overlooked in favor of foreign "best practices" frames the debate in defensive terms, when the nation should be taking the offensive.

It does not make sense for America to assume it is failing competitively when it is, in fact, winning on a number of fronts. In the haste to emulate foreign competitors, it is also foolish to neglect what America does well. Until the successes of American manufacturing are clearly understood, and the nation's strengths are valued in equal terms with its weaknesses, the debate will be unbalanced and will do a disservice to the country.

The Competitiveness Debate

Why has the competitiveness debate gotten out of balance? Why have the nation's strengths in manufacturing been neglected? Certainly one reason is the general tendency to criticize the status quo and to "hunt down the culprits" and expose them. The nation's press exemplifies this proclivity most clearly, but the tendency extends to much of society.

Another reason is the failure to appreciate that many of the competencies that the United States may now use to compete globally have been very painful to acquire or are still in development. For example, U.S. manufacturers have struggled with diversity issues for so long that it is difficult to recognize that many foreign competitors, particularly in Germany and Japan, are just now being confronted with those problems the United States has been coping with for years.

Perspectives on national advantages are also clouded by the country's widespread fear of economic and political decline. The people of the United States can see that the country's superpower status is declining. With the fall of communism in Soviet and Eastern European countries, and the rise of regional alliances like the European Community, America's military prowess provides fewer immediate advantages. Defense spending has been drastically reduced, as have the economic rewards of military supremacy. Economic warfare has now taken center stage.[1]

The failure of the manufacturing sector to generate high-paying jobs has had a great negative impact on outlooks over the last decade. Employment and manufacturing competitiveness are not the same thing, however. To the contrary, the loss of traditional manufacturing jobs has occurred, in part, because American industry has become much more productive and competitive. If there is a failure in manufacturing, it is a failure in communication, bred by unrealistic expectations and an oversimplification of tremendously complex issues. The failure in generating jobs should be appropriately placed on the country's financial system and economic policies, which have failed to create new businesses and new industries at a fast enough pace to absorb employment displacements.

The majority of America's population was reared during the apogee of the industrial age. In the 1950s and 1960s, economic growth and prosperity were driven by an increase in the number of jobs in traditional manufacturing. Though traditional manufacturing is now clearly in decline in advanced nations around the world, old mind-sets which teach that success means more high-paying jobs in traditional industries still prevail. In reality, industrial success requires higher productivity, which, in turn, means fewer jobs as the traditional industrial sector matures.

Because the U.S. manufacturing sector has *not* produced jobs at the rate it did 10 or 20 years ago, U.S. manufacturing has been spectacularly successful in regaining its competitive position in recent years. The volume of U.S. exports has grown by 90 percent since 1986, and the country's market share of total exports has continued to grow, exceeding that of Japan. The overall rate of productivity growth in U.S. manufacturing since the early 1980s has far exceeded that of Japanese and German manufacturers when both labor and capital productivity are taken into account.[2] At the same time, U.S. manufacturers have begun to regain market share in several key industrial sectors that many assumed had been lost to the Japanese, such as automobiles and semiconductors.

The competitiveness success story indicates that the United States does have success factors worth considering. The purpose of this book is, therefore, to balance what has become a lopsided debate about where American manufacturers should look for answers to the question of how to compete in the future. Our objective is to explore those elements of American society, technology, and management that can provide U.S. manufacturers with a global competitive advantage. We do not deny that our manufacturers have problems. We are aware and concerned about the current shortcomings of the country and its manufacturers, and have done our share of writing about them elsewhere. But we believe that the debate about the nation's competitiveness in manufacturing is out of balance, and we want to set things straight.

A considered assessment of America's competitiveness must include a realistic evaluation of its strengths. Indeed, successful organizations are particularly adept at identifying and exploiting their key strengths, or as they have come to be called, their *core competencies.* Core competencies are those skills central to an organization's identity that distinguish it from its competitors and lay the foundation for future success. They define a company's competitive edge.

America must look beyond the competitive edge of its individual companies to find an overarching American edge. In other words, the nation, like its corporations, must consider the future in terms of the nation's core competencies and then consider the country's problems and liabilities. Moreover, America must consider its strengths in terms of future requirements for competition.

Global Forces for Change

Enormous changes in the global competitive environment are placing new requirements on manufacturers in both mature and developing businesses. Mastery of the practices that led to foreign success in manufacturing, such as lean production, will be insufficient responses to these changes. If the American edge is to ensure U.S. manufacturing competitiveness in the future, it must address today's forces for change. Let us consider these forces and the new competitive requirements they are creating.

Political events rank first among the forces that drive global change. The world is moving toward the acceptance of capitalism and the development of regional alliances. The fall of communism in Eastern Europe and in Russia and the movement toward a single European market have fundamentally changed the nature of future global political confrontations. Moreover, they have set the stage for further expansion of global trade.

Another major force for change is economic. The goal of U.S. foreign policy at the end of World War II appears to have been achieved: There is something akin to economic parity among the major industrialized countries of the world, and economic trade has developed to the extent that each major country counts the others as major trading partners. An interesting paradox has developed. Economic interdependence has increased among the nations of the world, and the companies in them, at the same time that competition between them has grown. U.S. manufacturers depend on growth in Germany; Japanese manufacturers depend on U.S. economic growth. A manufacturer in any country can look for financing from bankers in any other country. At the national level, Japan, the United States, and Germany find they must cooperate in developing policies to stabilize currencies and to promote global growth.

Technical forces are also shaping the future. New product designs and process technologies require significantly less of the traditional labor inputs typically associated with manufacturing. Communication technologies have developed to the point where it is possible to instantly communicate face-to-face with customers, coworkers, and suppliers around the globe.

Societies in developed nations have advanced to the point where the basics of life, such as food and shelter, are virtually guaranteed for very large segments of the population—certainly for those who work for manufacturing organizations. Once these basic needs are assured, factors affecting the quality of life become more important—how employees and customers feel emotionally about their work, the quality of the air they breathe, the water they use. A significant portion of the industrial world's population is now secure enough in its daily needs to think long term about the health of the planet.

The effects of these global forces on industry and industrial management have been enormous, and they will continue to be a significant influence in the future. One result is that most manufacturing companies find themselves competing against a larger number of competitors from many more countries. This increased competition has intensified the fight to gain the customer's attention.

Another result is the employment shift from traditional smokestack industries to knowledge-based industries, such as computers, telecommunications, biotechnology, and related services. Alvin Toffler, John Naisbitt, Stan Davis, and other futurists have concluded that we are moving from the industrial age into the information age. Davis compares the shift from industry to information in this century to the shift from agriculture to industry in the last century. He notes that the percentage of the American work force engaged in agriculture which was 50 percent in 1870 was 3 percent by 1970. He projects a similar reallocation of the nation's human capital from manufacturing to the information industry by the year 2020.[3]

These changes mean that organizations must learn faster than their competition. They must continuously improve their products and processes through the multiplicative effect of thousands of small incremental changes identified by those who are closest to the work at hand. More radical leaps in improvement are also required to respond to emerging needs and knowledge. Knowledge gained from outside the organization, from customers, technical and other partners, and even competitors, is critical and must be integrated into existing knowledge bases. Lastly, organizations must examine what they have done in the past in an effort to learn how to learn better. This learning implies that organizations, and the individuals in them, must become aware of what helps and what hinders learning and work to accelerate the rate at which ideas for improvement are identified and communicated.[4]

Requirements for Competitiveness

Peter Senge points out that the common effect of all of these forces is a vastly increased level of interdependency between regions, nations, organizations, functions, and work groups.[5] One has only to look at the interest in alliances and teams to see that his observation holds merit. Other writers and thinkers such as Peter Drucker and Richard Pascale have identified the new requirements for organizations who must adapt to this increased level of interdependency.[6] The common theme in these requirements is *integration*—global, functional, and technical.

Global Integration

Global integration requires that manufacturers develop the means and mechanisms to understand and work with customers, workers, suppliers, and partners on a global basis. This requirement is more stringent than simply being able to manage foreign nationals, to sell to foreigners, or to negotiate with foreign partners with home-grown management systems. It requires that firms understand how to integrate their organizations with others for best effect, that is, to create new management systems that draw from and merge with the best of different cultures and situations.

Functional Integration

Whereas global integration requires incorporating knowledge from across the world, functional integration means uniting knowledge that already exists within organizations. To compete for the attention of the customer, organizations must reorient their focus horizontally so that action is directed along business process linkages to customers. There must also be less emphasis on vertical relationships from superior to worker and a move away from traditional work systems, which assume that managers have all the knowledge and that workers are merely hired to perform preplanned tasks. Shortened design-to-market cycles cannot tolerate the red tape associated with traditional bureaucratic structures. This means flatter organizations that put more and more reliance on cross-functional teams.

Technical Integration

Technology has always been a critical ingredient in manufacturing, and it will remain so in the future. However, the emphasis is shifting from discovery and mastery of a single technology, such as transistors, to integrating technologies into complex social-technical systems. The new requirement for competition is typified by the work of modern computer manufacturers attempting to develop technological platforms for multimedia computer systems. Here, companies must bring together numerous technologies and the requirements of multiple customers linked with other technologies to invent and manufacture viable solutions.

It is important to note that mastery of these new requirements is as critical for our foreign competitors as it is for American-based manufacturers. Some would say that the international experience and orientation of European multinationals may give them an edge in developing global integration skills. The Japanese have led the way in implementing continuous improvement through the 1980s, and some give them the nod on functional integration. Americans still lead in many key technologies and have the most experience in social-technical integration. However, these "leads" attributed to regions were developed in the past and must be viewed with skepticism. The economic, social, political, and technological forces fostering ever greater competitiveness and integration are changing the context in which these new requirements for competitiveness must be exercised. The race will go to manufacturers who can master all three integration requirements—and we believe that American manufacturers gain some important advantages in doing so.

America's Secret Weapons

This book is the result of a yearlong seminar series that brought executives and academics together for debate and discussion on the current paradigm in manufacturing. (A paradigm is defined as the way in which a group of people agree to organize their thinking around complex subjects.[7]) After concluding that the prevailing paradigm was negative, we decided to turn the tables and seek potential American advantages.

Our search uncovered 10 "secret weapons" available to U.S. manufacturers. They are secret not because they are unknown, but because no one seems to be looking at them. These weapons are unique to America due to the country's culture, political and legal systems, and previous investments. In total, they strike at the core of the fundamental competencies and opportunities for the nation and the manufacturers who produce here. As shown in Figure 1-1, we have grouped these secret weapons into the three categories: *Administrative heritage* comprises the managerial inheritance manufacturers have to build upon, the nation's *outsiders* enhance the skill base and force companies to look at the world from different perspectives, and the country's *technologies* provide a foundation to explore new opportunities.

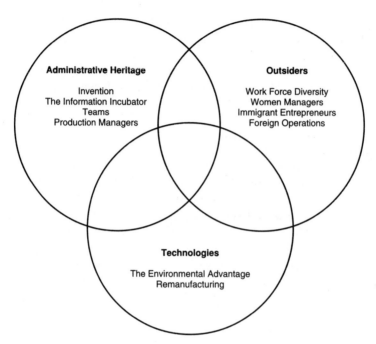

Figure 1-1. The "secret weapons" of the American edge.

Administrative Heritage

American management methods have been roundly criticized in recent years. The management system is seen as being too short term, overemphasizing the extensive division of labor, and being too focused on financial as opposed to customer needs. These negative characteristics of the American management approach are aspects of its administrative heritage, rooted in the development of a unique brand of capitalism and the way American companies have grown and developed since the turn of the century. But there are positive aspects of the American administrative heritage as well—attributes that can work to its advantage. Part 2 of the book shows how the U.S. administrative heritage provides the foundation for manufacturers to exploit the American edge by identifying four positive elements that have been neglected: (1) invention, (2) information, (3) teams, and (4) production managers.

Invention

In Chapter 2 Pieter VanderWerf identifies an extremely important part of the American administrative heritage, the nation's ability to invent.

He acknowledges that it would be to the advantage of the United States if it were equally adept at commercialization. He emphasizes that there are a number of ways to exploit the country's inventive abilities to a greater extent—methods that the United States is beginning to use to advantage with high-definition television, semiconductors, and other emerging technologies.

Information

There is a substantial information technology infrastructure in American industry that is continuously expanding. Use of computers is much more pervasive in the United States than in other developed countries; for example, the PC penetration (number of PCs per population) is 19 percent in the United States compared with 7 percent in Europe and 6 percent in Japan. This advantage is not in the hardware itself, but in the information it makes readily accessible. U.S. culture allows wide accessibility to data, and it promotes innovative uses of this data in all aspects of life. This ease of access and innovativeness give the United States the capability it needs to increase performance. In Chapter 3 Jane Fedorowicz argues that integration of information and flexibility of infrastructure combine to provide the country with an opportunity for enhancing performance and measuring it more effectively.

Teams

While most managers recognize the power of "Yankee ingenuity," many tend to underestimate the ability of their organizations to effectively utilize it, especially in the workplace. Many managers think the Japanese make the best use of teams, but in fact, the Japanese notion of teams is a restrictive one. The United States has led the world in the broad-scale introduction of self-managed work teams that are empowered to work on a broad range of issues. In Chapter 4 Jan Klein illustrates how American firms have mastered and expanded the team concept.

Production Managers

Chapter 5 might be called "the lighted fuse" or "the cake in the oven" or "seeds in a field in late spring." Wick Skinner argues that the manufacturing sector is currently experiencing an extraordinary burst of ideas, experiments, innovations, plagiarisms, equipment and process technologies, cultural attitudes, hungry and talented consultants, involved directors, literate and demanding consumers, and discontented middle managers. This explosion has set the stage for a new wave of American managers of production to shape the future.

Outsiders

The people of any nation provide the central underpinning of its competitiveness. For this reason, the original label for this category was "people." Upon reflection, however, we recognized that all four chapters in Part 3 had one key aspect in common: They are about people who are *outside the mainstream of traditional manufacturing*.

Outsiders provide different perspectives; they are less bound to traditional paradigms. They also provide a steady stream of fresh ideas. But, what is it that makes these "outsiders" secret weapons for American manufacturers? More importantly, how do successful companies set about managing these outsiders to make the best use of their abilities and ideas? Part 3 addresses these questions from the following points of view: work force diversity, women managers, immigrant entrepreneurs, and foreign operations.

Work Force Diversity

The United States is a potpourri of cultures and ethnic groups. United States laws encourage managers to fully utilize all segments of its population—women, minorities, those with disabilities, and senior citizens. Some managers complain of the difficulty in managing this diversity. Companies in Germany and Japan are only now being forced to react to demographic and political changes that undermine their homogeneity. Their cultures do not lend themselves to readily dealing with diversity. In Chapter 6 Sheila Akabas and Lauren Gates show how United States manufacturers and their employees can use their head start in learning how to manage diversity to competitive advantage.

Women Managers

Women form a larger proportion of managers in the United States than in any other advanced economy. Possessing extensive education and experience, women managers bring skills and talents to the workplace that address needs central to revitalizing U.S. manufacturing. In Chapter 7 Lyn Christiansen and Julie Hertenstein present specific cases of women managers building teams, creating cross-organizational linkages, and leading manufacturing organizations through turn-arounds.

Immigrant Entrepreneurs

The United States has attracted and continues to draw people from around the world looking for political freedom and economic opportunity. Unlike Germany and Japan who rely on "guest workers" to supplement their work force, the United States embraces the immigrant as a member of society. Problems with immigration are well publicized: drains on public services, competition for jobs, racial, and ethnic tension. In Chapter 8 Marion McCollom argues that the United States benefits significantly from the typical entrepreneurship of first-generation arrivals. She points out that the immigrant experience is a potent force that can help manufacturers shape their competitive response.

Foreign Operations

In Chapter 9 Kasra Ferdows suggests that if someone were to compile a list of the 100 companies most admired for their ability to manage international networks of factories, a large number of American companies would be on that list—far more than any other country—even after adjusting for the size of the economy. This, he argues, is not an accident. There are good reasons why American companies have an advantage in managing factories outside the United States. And, these foreign operations afford an additional source of "outsider" perspectives.

Technologies

In discussions of competitiveness, no topic has received more attention at public policy levels than technology. These discussions have focused on whether the United States is ahead or behind in certain key technologies like semiconductor design, magnetic imaging, or advanced composites. An alternative view of technology, and one that we take here, focuses on the integration of the country's installed base of technologies rather than on individual technologies themselves. For example: What does the nation's prior use of numerous discrete technologies in attacking environmental issues buy it? How can the United States capitalize on its enormous durable goods resource base? Our authors demonstrate the potential of two of America's secret technological weapons: the environmental advantage and remanufacturing.

The Environmental Advantage

In Chapter 10 Jim Post explains how America has an environmental advantage over the rest of the world in at least three aspects. American companies have an edge in environmental technology and in managing environmental systems for waste and toxic materials reduction. Most importantly, there is a "mind-set" advantage—large companies know they have to adapt to these new realities, and new entrepreneurial companies are springing up daily to meet these needs. America is spawning a new generation of companies founded on values of sustainable development.

Remanufacturing

As global industrial development and population growth put increasing demands on the world's natural resources, the share of these resources the United States can claim must necessarily decrease. Do Americans have a secret weapon that can prevent the declining standard of living this implies? In Chapter 11 Robert Lund presents the case for making the country's "durable" goods live longer. In addition to describing design approaches for longer product lifetimes, he introduces us to remanufacturing, a little-known but large sector of American industry. Remanufacturers can keep products alive indefinitely. Remanufacturing illustrates the kind of thinking that can be applied to exploit the country's base of capital goods.

Is There an American Edge?

As one of our authors observed at the midpoint of this project, "After 389 beginnings, 675 outlines, and 94 pages of wasted typing, I now believe that I can write something positive, honest, true, believable, and realistic. Thanks for your patience. My problem is that I haven't written anything optimistic for 29 years!" It is difficult for Americans to take a positive view. But it is time for the country and its manufacturers to examine the weapons at their disposal. It's not sufficient to merely espouse the virtues of foreign competitors. It is self-defeating to focus only on problems. By doing so, the country misses the opportunity to differentiate itself from other nations.

To improve America's competitiveness, the country's strengths must help manufacturers meet the new requirements for global, functional, and technical integration. We believe they do. The authors of the 10 chapters that follow show how their secret weapons can help America in its quest to maintain its industrial prowess. One key question remains, however: Do these 10 secret weapons add up to something more fundamental—Is there an American edge? We believe there is such an edge and will address this subject in the final chapter. But we challenge the reader to first consider the important messages in each chapter.

References

1. Lester Thurow, *Head to Head: The Coming Economic Battle Among Japan, Europe, and America,* William Morrow, New York, 1992.
2. Dirk Pilat and Bart van Ark, "Productivity Leadership in Manufacturing: Germany, Japan, and the United States 1973–1989," Institute of Economic Research, University of Groningen, Netherlands, 1991.
3. Stan Davis, *Future Perfect,* Simon & Schuster, New York, 1988.
4. Chris Argyris, *Overcoming Organizational Defenses: Facilitating Organizational Learning,* Allyn and Bacon, Boston, 1990.
5. Peter M. Senge, *The Fifth Disciple: The Art and Practice of the Learning Organization,* Doubleday Currency, New York, 1990.
6. Peter Drucker, "The New Society of Nations," *Harvard Business Review,* September–October 1992; Richard Tanner Pascale, *Managing on the Edge,* Simon & Schuster, New York, 1990.
7. Thomas Kuhn, *The Structure of Scientific Revolutions,* University of Chicago Press, Chicago, 1970.

PART 2
Administrative Heritage

2
Invention

Pieter A. VanderWerf

*Assistant Professor of Management Policy,
Boston University*

What has become of America's industrial hero: Technological innovation? At one time we were confident that the United States was more innovative than any other country in the world and that this made us strong. By linking new technologies to human needs we led in the creation of new industries and the overhaul of old ones. We were at the forefront of applying internal combustion to travel and took the world's greatest share of the auto industry. Applying chemistry to fibers and electronics to calculation gave us head starts that led to long-term, worldwide superiority in the synthetic fabric and computer industries.

But now that same innovation is a symbol of our decline. A common current view is that other nations do as much innovation as we do. Even when we are first and have borne the development cost, other countries reap the commercial benefits of the new idea.

There is some truth to this view, but there is also some danger. The danger is that we may overlook the very great strength we do have. Simply put, the United States still generates radical inventions at a pace far beyond that of any other country in the world. Although it is true that others have exploited many of our inventions better than we have, we confuse the historical observation that we *have not always* benefited from our inventions with the belief that we *can not* benefit from them. We do benefit all the time, and with some thoughtful management, we can become considerably better at exploiting our inventions.

The American Edge

The United States produces a disproportionately large share of the world's radical product inventions—the application of technologies to new uses. This proficiency results from the relatively diverse, individualistic, nonhierarchical U.S. culture. That culture is an excellent incubator for radical invention. And, because cultures are slow to change, the U.S. capacity for radical invention is likely to remain the world's greatest for decades.

Where we have failed to match the rest of the industrialized world is in the other major component of innovation—incremental improvement on existing products. This has resulted in our commercial demise in many modern industries: steel, autos, consumer electronics. When we offer a new product or a better version of an existing product, the product attracts interest for a while. However, buyers are quick to abandon the inventor when a competitor makes the same product better.

Sharpening the Edge

One approach to this situation is to hone our skills of product improvement and let radical invention fend for itself. This boils down to playing catch-up with the Europeans and Japanese. Another option is to leverage our unique strength in radical invention. Correctly wielded, radical invention enables a firm to lead all competitors in product performance or cost—and commercial success—*even if the firm is inferior at product improvement.*

This last point is difficult for many to accept now that the business press is focused on the benefits of incremental improvement. However, some firms—and even entire societies—successfully employ radical invention to maintain superiority over competitors that are better at improvement. They do it with a few clear strategies that we can analyze and adapt to other situations. But to understand these strategies we must first clarify the activities involved in achieving a commercial product and assuring its success, and we have to understand global differences.

Commercial Product Development

The first step in understanding the strengths and weaknesses of the United States in applying technology to commercial products is to

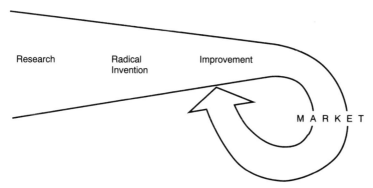

Figure 2-1. Technical activities contributing to the success of a commercial product.

ditch the word "innovation." It is too broad to be useful. Innovation includes the whole range of activities involved in bringing a product to market. The United States is good at some of these activities and it is not good at others. Some activities are important for one strategy and some are important for another. To get down to specifics, we have to distinguish three distinct activities included in innovation. These are research, radical invention, and improvement.

Research lays the groundwork by providing basic technologies that can be applied to a range of human needs. Radical invention applies the technologies to create products so different from and better than existing products that they rearrange the competitive landscape. Improvement is the continuous process of raising the performance or lowering the cost of the product. In practice, these three activities are interrelated. The path to commercial success for any given product is fraught with false starts, new insights, and steps backward to redo things formerly considered resolved. In all, it resembles a sort of "funnel" that somewhere along the way weeds out all but the very best projects. Figure 2-1 depicts the process.

Research

The search for new physical phenomena and the explanations for them is conducted mostly in universities and government-sponsored laboratories. The scientists doing the work are interested in shedding light on broad areas and usually do not know exactly how the results will be used. For example, the early experimenters in combustion processes, electronic switching, and polymer technology were either indifferent to the ultimate commercial applications or incorrect about what they would be. The most promising phenomena attract a lot of attention, and scientific researchers start to put more effort into refining understanding of them. Biotechnology went through this phase a decade ago. High-temperature superconductors are going through the refinement stage now. If interest continues long enough, understanding becomes so good that nonscientists can exploit these phenomena. About this time they come to be called "technologies."

Radical Invention

The application of a technology to a particular use for the first time is the stuff new industries spring from: the first automobile, the first synthetic fiber, and the first electronic computer. Some radical inventions are colossal failures. Where are the hovercar and the capacitance disk player now? But in some cases the sharply different technology gives the new product strong performance or cost advantages over anything else that went before. It also, incidentally, requires a dramatically different set of skills for design, production, and maintenance. The automobile, for example, replaced horse-drawn carriages. But its speed, power, and endurance were a quantum leap higher, and a whole new type of engineer, craftsman, and mechanic arose to design, build, and fix it.

Radical invention is usually the work of engineers or inventors different from the original scientists, laboring long after the scientific discoveries on which the invention is based. They work more often as independents or in corporate laboratories than in universities or government labs.

Improvement

Once a new product is born, inventors and engineers improve it over time. This is extremely important. James Utterback of MIT has commented that the improvements in a product may eventually add up to an increase in its performance or reduction in its cost that is as big as the original jump the product made over older products when it first came out.

Improvement involves many small steps—what are sometimes called "incremental inventions"—that accumulate over time. A powerful contributor to this process is market feedback. Putting the product into users' hands provides precise information on what to change and how to change it. This sets up a snowball of progress. The more we sell a product, the more we learn about how to improve it; then the more we improve it, the more we sell. But over time efforts to improve the same invention run into diminishing returns. Improvement becomes more costly and incremental, as engineers use up the best available ways to tweak the basic technology. We are now confronting such constraints in automobiles. Maximum speeds of cars using internal combustion engines have been stuck at a little over 200 miles per hour for decades; advances in fuel economy are requiring massive levels of development unheard of in earlier years.

Technical Proficiency and Market Success

Despite the adage about "building a better mousetrap," originating a radical invention is no guarantee of commercial success. It is generally the party that offers the best product that gets the sales, and this party may or may not have any connection to the original scientists and inventors.

In the first place, even if a new type of product takes off, some inventors find that they have pursued a commercial dead end. Since there is almost always more than one technology that can provide a given function, different inventors often adopt different technologies to fill the same market need. The result is that they end up competing for the same customers with distinctly different inventions. A clear example comes from the early days of the automobile, when proponents of the internal combustion, steam, and electric engine competed in the marketplace. The products that ultimately sell best will be those based on technologies that best meet customers' needs, while the rest will flop or grab a specialty niche. Which technology best meets customers' needs depends on a combination of which has the best physical characteristics (i.e., which one can be improved the fastest and the most) and which one attracts the most effort to improve it. Typically, one of the physically "better" technologies eventually attracts so many firms to work on it that it gets improved to a level of performance or cost far beyond that of competing technologies. At that point backers of the other technologies are scared off by the big gap that they would have to cover just to catch up. Back to our example, work on steam and electric cars all but stopped once the internal combustion engine gained a big lead in function and cost. Most of the firms behind these alternative technologies went out of business.

Within the technology that prevails, those companies that can provide a superior version of the product on a large scale tend to take the lion's share of the new market. Providing the superior version depends on a combination of starting work on the invention early and improving it rapidly. Firms that can do one of these two tasks well have a chance for success, even if they are not so good at the other.

Inventors have an advantage at commercializing their own products, namely lead time. They have exclusive access to the invention for a while, during which they can get ahead in the process of improving it. If the inventor is an established firm with experience at improving products, or if it can gain this experience before more adept competition enters, the inventor can *stay* ahead.

There are other potential victors, however: firms that are especially strong at product improvement. Their skills may enable them to overtake competitors that got an earlier start.

Industry Leadership

Even after a few market leaders have emerged, innovation continues to influence which company is most successful. Forces of improvement tend to preserve the leaders' position for a time, but in the long run radical invention threatens it again.

Once a few firms have taken industry leadership—in the form of superior products and higher sales—they have advantages that tend to let them keep it. Two of the most important advantages are greater access to market feedback and investment funds. These are important because they help the firms to continue improvement of the products at a rapid pace, thereby keeping their leadership position. As noted earlier, market feedback provides important information for product improvement. Since the sellers generally have greater access to this feedback, they are in a better position to carry out improvement. They also have the revenue to do the improvement. Industry leaders get substantial revenue from selling the product, and they can put that revenue back into improving it. Anyone trying to enter the industry from outside must raise speculative investment funds or take profits from other product lines, leaving those product lines vulnerable.

These advantages allow market leaders to build up a product edge that can be commanding. Would-be entrants face a daunting level of investment just to catch up. The persistent dominance of the Big Three in the U.S. auto industry was for many years a telling case in point.

The leaders' dominance can disappear, however, when the next radical invention supersedes their product. The Swiss watch industry dropped by half in a couple of years after introduction of the quartz watch. Except for IBM, the major producers of mechanical and electrical calculators failed to make the transition to electronics. No one even recalls the major carriage makers anymore.

In fact, Arnold Cooper and Dan Schendel at Purdue University found that compared with firms entering from outside, the leaders of an industry usually fared *worse* in their attempts to commercialize a new, technically different product that was a replacement for their traditional product.[1] It has since been documented time and again that the firms dominant in the old product either underfund their development effort for the new one or handle it badly. A variety of things appear to explain this. The traditional leaders' specialized product skills are irrelevant or even *inappropriate* for the new invention. Management is skeptical about the potential of the new product because they have lived through many other highly touted inventions in the industry that failed. And the organizational change necessary to shift a dominant firm to the new technology raises internal opposition. The result of all of these factors is that firms outside the traditional industry leadership often ride a new technology to dominance while the old guard watches almost helplessly.

Thus the appearance of a radical invention brings competition for a market full circle. Alternative technologies compete, and one or two emerge dominant. In exploiting them, the inventors have an edge in lead time, and others may have an advantage with their proficiency at improvement. Leaders emerge and build up specialized advantages. But at the next radical invention they become vulnerable to outside competitors again, beginning the process anew.

Global Differences in Technical Proficiency

The major industrial regions of the world have very different levels of proficiency at the technical activities necessary for commercial product success. Figure 2-2 summarizes the situation.

In research, the United States and Europe are about even. Japan's research output is far lower. In radical invention the United States excels, even compared to Europe. Japan again has a low level of output. But in the case of improvement, the pecking order turns upside down. U.S. proficiency, compared to the other two regions, falls sharply. And Japan rises to the lead, in dramatic contrast to its showing in the other activities. Some simple measures confirm this.

Research

As an indicator of research output, take the number of Nobel Prize winners from each region. Table 2-1 totals the winners in the natural

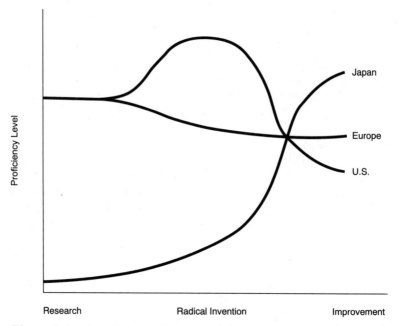

Figure 2-2. The relative proficiencies of Japan, Europe, and the United States at the three technical activities necessary for commercial success.

Table 2-1. Nationalities of Nobel Prize Winners in the Natural Sciences, 1980–1990

| Region of Nationality | Discipline | | | |
	Chemistry	Medicine and Physiology	Physics	Total
United States	10	12	10	32
Europe	6	9	13	28
Japan	1	1	0	2
Other	4	3	2	9
Total	21	25	25	71

SOURCE: Data from Bernard S. Schlessinger and June H. Schlessinger, *The Who's Who of Nobel Prize Winners,* Oryx Press, Phoenix, 1991.

sciences since 1980. Scientists from the United States and Europe dominate. Japan has roughly one-fifteenth the number of winners as either of the other two.

Radical Invention

To measure relative regional proficiencies at radical invention, consider the respected study by Jewkes, Sawers, and Stillerman.[2] They compiled a list of major modern inventions and carefully researched their histories. Table 2-2 lists the product inventions and their originators. Nearly all of the inventions were the work of people in the United States or Europe. But the share by each of these two groups shifts over time. In the 1800s the United States accounts for about one in ten product inventions. This rises so that by the 1940s one-half of the product inventions come from Americans. If we look at where the work was being done, instead of at the nationality of the inventors, the U.S. share in later decades is even higher. By the 1940s it is up to 75 percent.

To bring our measurement of invention up to date, consider an industry in which the United States is supposed to be an also-ran: consumer electronics. U.S. companies' share of the consumer electronics market is the lowest of all three regions. Nonetheless, the United States has been a proficient inventor in the field. As evidence, consider flat panel displays and high-definition television. These are two high-potential products so new that there are still multiple competing technologies for each product. Each of these products is widely expected to account for multiple billions of dollars in sales by the end of the century. Flat panel displays are sometimes called "the TV you hang on your wall." Simply put, they are electronic screens a couple of inches thick and up to several feet on diagonal that can function as television or computer screens. Simple versions are already used in laptop computers. High-definition television (HDTV) is a version of TV with a much sharper picture and sound. Most HDTV technologies depend on a novel design of the electromagnetic signal that carries the picture and sound along with some changes in transmitting and receiving hardware.

Table 2-3 lists every distinct technology employed for flat panel displays. A quick count shows that U.S. organizations dominate the list of inventions. This is true despite the generally recognized lead that Japanese firms have in improving and selling them. In fact, Americans originated the approach that the Japanese are most vigorously pursuing (the active liquid crystal matrix). Moreover, U.S. domination of

Table 2-2. Origins of Major Product Inventions

Invention	Inventor	Region
1800s		
Ballpoint pen	John J. Loud	United States
Diesel-electric locomotive	Indeterminate	Indeterminate
Fluorescent lamp	Becquerel	France
Gyrocompass	Foucault	France
Magnetic recording	Valdemar Poulsen	Denmark
Methyl methacrylate polymer	Fittig	Germany
Radio	Marconi	Italy
Synthetic detergent	Krafft Co.	Germany
Titanium	Nilson and Petterson	Sweden
Zipper	Whitcomb L. Judson	United Kingdom
1900s		
Automatic drive	H. Fottinger, Vulkan Shipyard	Germany
Bakelite	Leo Hendrik Baekeland	Belgium*
Safety razor	King Gillette	United States
Silicone	Dr. F. S. Kipping, Nottingham University	United Kingdom
Stainless steel	Various	France, UnitedKingdom, United States
1910s		
Cellophane	Jacques Brandenberger	Switzerland†
Cotton picker	Price-Campbell Corp.	United States
Helicopter	Various	Europe
Tungsten carbide	Coles and Donaldson Voigtlander and Lohman Co.	United States Germany
1920s		
Crease-resistant fabric	Tootal Broadhurst Lee Co.	United Kingdom
Insulin	Dr. Frederick Banting, University of Ontario	Canada
Neoprene	Arnold M. Collins, DuPont	United States
Penicillin	Alexander Fleming, University of London	United Kingdom
Power steering	Harry Vickers, Vickers Inc.	United States
	Francis W. Davis,	United States
Rockets	Dr. R. H. Goddard	United States
Sulzer loom	Rudolf Rossman, Deutsche Wolle Co.	Germany

Table 2-2. Origins of Major Product Inventions (*Continued*)

Invention	Inventor	Region
1920s (*Continued*)		
Television	Vladimir Zworykin	Russia*
	Philo Farnsworth	United States
Tetraethyl lead	Thomas Midgely, General Motors Corp.	United States
1930s		
Cyclotron	Dr. Ernest Lawrence, Yale University	United States
DDT insecticide	Paul Muller, J.R. Geigy Co.	Switzerland
Jet engine	Sir Frank Whittle, Power Jets Ltd.	United Kingdom
Nylon	Dr. Wallace Carothers, DuPont Corp.	United States
Polyethylene	Imperial Chemicals Industries Ltd.	United Kingdom
Radar	Various	Europe and United States
Xerography	Chester Carlson	United States
1940s		
Long-playing record	Dr. Peter Goldmark, Columbia Co.	United States
Streptomycin	Dr. Selman Waksman, Rutgers Univ.	Russia*
Terylene	Whinfield and Dickson, Calico Printers Association	United Kingdom
Transistor	Bardeen, Brittain and Shockley, Bell Laboratories	United States

*The inventor was working in the United States at the time.
†The inventor was working in France at the time.
SOURCE: Data from John Jewkes, David Sawers, and Richard Stillerman, *The Sources of Invention,* Macmillan, London, 1960.

radical invention continued even after the Japanese began heavy investment in flat panels in the early 1970s.

A similar count of technologies applied to HDTV (Table 2-4) again reveals a U.S. plurality. For this product, the regions' invention totals are closer together—four and a fraction for the United States, three and a fraction for Europe, and three for Japan. But the simple totals are misleading. First of all, two of the European approaches actually

Table 2-3. Origins of Flat Panel Displays

Approach	Year	Inventor	Country
Plasma display	Early 1950s	Burroughs Corp.	United States
Flat cathode ray tube	1957	West Coast Electronics	United States
Electroluminescent display	1958	RCA Labs	United States
Vacuum fluorescent display*	1960s	Stanford Research Institute (phenomenon)	United States
	1973	I se Electronics Corp. (prototype)	Japan
Electrophoretic display*	1961	RCA Labs (phenomenon)	United States
	1973	Matsushita Corp. (prototype)	Japan
Passive liquid crystal	1964	RCA Labs	United States
Laser display	1965	Rome Air Development Center	United States
Light-emitting diodes	1966	IBM Electronic Systems Center	United States
Active liquid crystal matrix	Late 1960s	Westinghouse	United States
Electrochomic display	1970	DuPont Corp.	United States
MicroCurl devices	1981	MicroCurl Display Technology	United States
Deformable mirrors	1980s	Texas Instruments	United States

*In some cases the party that originally conceived of an approach and demonstrated its scientific feasibility in the laboratory was different from the party that produced a working prototype. In these cases we have listed both parties.

came from the U.S. subsidiary of Philips N.V. of the Netherlands. Second, the totals fail to take account of the radicalness of the approaches. The development of HDTV can be traced to CBS Laboratories in the 1950s, which conducted work to refine the original analog broadcasting techniques. Japanese firms picked this up in the 1960s. They refined the analog technology further and applied it in three distinct ways over the years, as listed in the table. The most strikingly different technologies have come from the United States: the open architecture receiver, which would merge signals of all types, and all-digital transmission.

Table 2-4. Origins of Versions of High-Definition Television

	Year	Inventor	Country
Receiver Approaches			
Improved definition TV	1983	North American Philips	Netherlands*
Open architecture	1983	MIT	United States
Transmitter Approaches			
Enhanced definition TV	1988	Various (concept)	United States, France, Netherlands†
	1991	Faroudja Laboratories (prototype)	United States
NTSC-compatible HDTV	1988	Various	United States
Augmented Signal Approaches			
Augmented analog	1988	NHK	Japan
Hybrid	1988	North American Philips	Netherlands*
Terrestrial Simulcast Approaches			
Analog	1986	NHK	Japan
Hybrid	1988	Zenith	United States
Digital	1990	General Instruments	United States
Satellite Simulcast Approaches			
Analog	1981	NHK	Japan
Hybrid	1986	Philips and Thomson CSF	Netherlands and France

*North American Philips is the U.S.-based subsidiary of the Dutch electronics company Philips N.V.

†The developers of enhanced definition television include Faroudja Laboratories, a U.S. company headed by French-born Laurent Faroudja, and the Advanced Television Research Consortium, which includes Thomson/CSF of France and Philips of the Netherlands as well as three United States organizations.

Improvement

A useful way to measure relative regional proficiencies at technical improvement is with patent applications. In truth, patent applications may cover radical inventions as well as smaller improvements. But there are so many more improvement inventions that they swamp the totals. What we are doing is a little like comparing the total number of motor vehicles in different countries to see which country has the most four-wheeled cars and trucks. The motor vehicle totals include trucks with six or more wheels, but there are so many more four-wheeled vehicles that comparing the totals gives proportions that accurately reflect the differences in vehicles with four wheels.

Table 2-5. Worldwide Patent Applications by Region

	Year	
Region of Applicant	1988	1990
United States		
Total applications	146,904	164,558
Per $1 billion Gross Domestic Product	31	31
European Community		
Total applications	323,267	334,762
Per $1 billion Gross Domestic Product	73	66
Japan		
Total applications	345,239	376,371
Per $1 billion Gross Domestic Product	190	173

SOURCE: Data from Organization for Economic Cooperation and Development, *Main Science and Technology Indicators 1992*, OECD Publications Service, Paris, 1992.

Counts of the patent applications by parties from each region are in Table 2-5. As expected, Japan holds the greatest total, and the United States holds the smallest. Moreover, Japan's share—in each region and worldwide—has been growing.

Determinants of Global Technical Proficiencies

The relative strength of the United States and Europe in research is not a chance event or a temporary phenomenon. Nor is the U.S. proficiency at radical invention or the Japanese proficiency at improvement a chance occurrence. They all rest on ingrained social practices and cultural characteristics. As a result, the pecking order in each of these activities can change only over decades.

Research

The high rate of research in the United States and Europe is the output of a well-funded and well-organized system of scientific inquiry. The government and paying students subsidize the training and work of scientists through various means. The scientists train their successors and organize themselves into professional associations that review one anothers' work. None of these supports or institutions exists to nearly the same degree in Japan. The emphasis in Japan is on engineering. We get a quick verification of this difference from the total research expenditures of each region, as shown in Table 2-6.

Table 2-6. 1981 Regional Expenditures for Research in the Natural Sciences and Engineering
(Billions of 1981 U.S. Dollars)

Region	Total research expenditures
United States	17.1
European Community	12.6
Japan	4.5
Total	34.2

SOURCE: Data from Organization for Economic Cooperation and Development, *OECD Science and Technology Indicators*, OECD Publications Service, Paris, 1986.

If, say, Japan were to decide to become a leading producer of scientific research, it would have to redirect government spending toward this area and foster the development of a research community. Experience tells us that major government spending shifts are slow. Building a research community would probably take about two generations: one to train teachers and establish institutions, and one to teach a body of researchers.

Radical Invention

Radical invention is dependent on access to a large body of high-potential research results and on the act of linking this research with human needs. Access to research results is important because it lets one adopt the latest technologies sooner than the competition. Firms in societies without research communities may require a couple of years to locate and translate technical information before they are in a position to use it for invention. And in invention a delay of two years can mean the difference between dealing with new technology and improving on established technology. Obviously, linking a technology with a new application is vital—it is the essence of a radical invention. Those that cannot do it well must usually watch others do it and react.

Greater U.S. and European access to cutting-edge research is guaranteed by their research communities, described above. It is thus unlikely to diminish in a short time.

But even if all regions had equal access to research, the United States should still account for more than its share of radical inventions. As Scott Shane of the University of Pennsylvania has verified, there is a link between a nation's culture and its inventive output.[3] U.S. culture has characteristics that encourage linking technologies and needs in new ways. Specifically, the United States has population diversity, it gives people practice in exploration of novel ideas, and it provides individuals with independence—and even support—for pursuing their ideas.

The *diversity* of the U.S. population is well documented in other parts of this book. Immigration—past and current—gives this country perhaps the broadest range of cultural diversity in the world. In addition, for all our shortcomings, the diverse cultures interact more freely than in many other nations. In Europe and Japan most immigrants are "guest workers" that fill specific, temporary voids in the labor force; they do not become citizens and must return to their homelands.

The importance of diversity to invention is clear from research on small groups. In experiments, groups of people have been given broadly defined problems to solve, such as how to survive in the wilderness with only a bag full of common household items. In these sessions, far and away the largest number of solutions, and the most exotic solutions, come from those groups with the most diverse membership. On reflection this makes sense. The more points of view there are and the more different they are, the more proficient we would expect the group to be at generating ideas.

The amount of *practice* that Americans get at thinking up new, useful solutions to problems is also far greater. This difference is clearly reflected in the schools and in scientific and commercial laboratories. Schooling in most of Europe and Japan is directed heavily toward the assimilation and memorization of facts and formulas that have been established by others. Common U.S. assignments like "make up a story" or "design a moon rocket" are rare. Laboratories abroad are relatively hierarchical organizations: an individual researcher is expected to contribute rather than originate. In many U.S. labs, in contrast, an individual staff member—even the most junior—might be considered deficient if he or she could not design and execute an original project.

The *independence* afforded Americans to pursue their ideas is also reflected in our schools and laboratories. A good example of this independence occurs in the business community. Per capita venture funds and new business foundings are several times as great in the United States as in Japan or most European countries. Even in established companies the latitude for individual action is generally greater in the United States than in other regions.

The upshot of all of this is that for Europe or Japan to become as proficient at radical invention as the United States would require fundamental changes in their society and culture. These changes would include such major steps as increasing the diversity of their populations, reorienting their education systems, and making a quantum increase in the individual independence afforded their citizens. But greater diversity would be virtually impossible for them: there is not enough room to put immigrants, and they are already experiencing bad social reactions to influxes of outsiders. Our own experience shows reorienting an educational system is a decades-long endeavor. Increasing independence is probably an even greater task. Therefore, the differences in radical invention proficiency, like those in research, could probably not change to any degree before the middle of the next century.

Improvement

Proficiency at improvement depends on skills that are almost the opposite of those conducive to invention. Continuous technical advance, and the other commercial activities associated with it, are complex endeavors requiring the coordination of large numbers of people toward relatively well-understood goals. These endeavors benefit from discipline and attention to detail, which tend to be stronger in groups that are relatively homogeneous, with members drilled in standard information and procedures.

Again, research on groups demonstrates this point. Researchers have measured the success of different groups at carrying out a defined task. The findings are always the same. The groups that are the most homogeneous execute the narrowly defined task most efficiently.

This relationship makes sense. People who are more alike have to do less communication to understand one another and coordinate. Practice at originating new ideas and experience with individual freedom do *not* help. Once direction is established, a person who has had a lot of practice at thinking up new directions could be frustrated. Furthermore, an organization that allows great individual freedom can more easily stray from the established direction.

Changing a country's proficiency at improvement would require policy and cultural shifts similar to those necessary to change invention abilities. Should the United States, as a nation, want to become as good at product improvement as the Japanese, it might have to make major changes that conflict with its culture.

Traditional Competitive Strategies

Because each region of the world has different technical proficiencies and weaknesses, the business environment and competitive dynamics are different in each. To fit with their situations, firms in each region tend to adopt different competitive strategies.

The United States

When it appears that applying new technology to a particular human need has high potential, U.S. society bubbles up large numbers of inventions to meet the need. The inventors will likely employ many different technologies—good, bad, and weird. The different technologies then have the opportunity to slug it out in the market for supremacy. In fact, in the end it may happen that more than one technology is successful. The survival of both the MS-DOS and Macintosh standards for personal computer operating systems is a good example.

The firms that enter the fray at this early stage are the ones that have more to gain by moving early. Start-ups, for example, often depend on lead time to build their organizations so that they are competitive with larger firms. It is to the advantage of many more established firms to wait and watch, however. Bringing a new product to market implies risk; the originator could spend great sums on a technology with low potential or on one that not enough other firms end up working on to keep its rate of improvement competitive. In these cases products based on another technology will probably shoot ahead and the investment is wasted. On top of that, switching to the winning technology can be even harder than if the firm had never worked on any of the technologies at all for the same reasons that industry leaders have trouble adapting to a new radical invention. As a standard or dominant technology does emerge, however, many of these cautious firms will seriously consider a quick entry.

U.S. government policy supports this pattern of events. Consistent with the national value of independence, the government is slow to establish standards that might precipitate convergence on one technology. The government also restricts coordination among firms, which might let them agree on a single technology and concentrate on it.

Europe

The strategic approach of European firms reflects a society somewhat less proficient in radical invention, but more proficient in improvement. With this skill, they must often catch up to outside inventors. This is often done with a sustained effort over a long time. European firms, with their patient investors and management, often take this approach. Catch-up can also be accomplished by improving much more rapidly than others, which is possible if the firms involved concentrate their resources on the dominant technology. In Europe, large government efforts to coordinate development are popular methods of concentrating resources. A good example is the European development of the Concorde. The Europeans followed this approach again, somewhat more successfully, to break into the commercial aircraft market with Airbus Industrie.

The result is that European firms are particularly strong in industries based on long-established technologies: mechanics, chemistry, and so on. They are also competitive in those select newer industries in which they have successfully caught up through coordinated effort.

Japan

After WWII the situation in Japan was similar to that in Europe, but even more extreme. Domestic firms were far behind in most important industries, and the Japanese had little capacity for radical invention with which to supersede the leaders. Instead they used a proficiency for improvement to catch up. To concentrate resources, the government helped coordinate the activities of the firms.

But the Japanese went a step further. They found a way to lead new industries from the *beginning* through a process we can call "convergence." As radical inventions to meet some human need begin to appear, the major Japanese firms in the field evaluate the alternative technologies quickly and converge on *one* of these as having the best prospects. This convergence is often facilitated by cooperative R&D and standard-setting bodies. As Michael Porter has observed, these groups actually do little to advance any of the technologies other than to foster agreement on the most promising one.[4] The result is that nearly all the major firms in the relevant industry concentrate on the same technology. They thus get so far ahead that it is too expensive and too risky for competitors to try to catch up with the same or any alternative technology. The Japanese virtually eliminate the risk of backing the wrong technology, which is such a deterrent to jumping in early for U.S. firms, with their nearly unanimous support for improving *one* technology. Even if another technology is physically superior (i.e., it can be improved more rapidly with the same effort), the big lead of the Japanese scares off potential competitors.

Examples of Traditional
Strategies

The development of flat panel displays and HDTV offer good examples of typical strategic behavior by firms of the different regions. U.S. inventors and firms have long recognized the technical and commercial potential of flat panel displays. They have invented several versions, each employing a slightly different technology. Various U.S. start-ups have even manufactured and sold the devices. But large firms—many of which invented one or more of the versions—have waited on the sidelines. Granted, there is plenty of uncertainty to keep a firm from acting. It is always possible that it will prove too hard to drive the cost low enough, or get the picture sharp enough, to be competitive with conventional screens. A firm that puts the time and money into developing the displays might thus find out it was all a waste. On top of that, no one knows which technology will be the best. Each technology has some technical and marketing obstacles that may or may not be difficult to overcome.

European firms have largely watched the progress and maintained exploratory work in their laboratories. Japanese electronics firms, in contrast, converged fairly early on a single technology. They are all working to improve the active liquid crystal matrix (ALCM) approach, which was originated in the United States. As a group they have invested over a billion dollars in the devices to date. Their screens are now competitive with conventional screens in some uses.

In the case of HDTV, a sharper television format has been clearly possible for decades. There were, however, no strong indications that anyone would attempt to commercialize such an invention or, if they did, what technology would be used. U.S. firms took little action, and what they did take was restricted to exploratory research. In contrast, Japanese firms picked up the conventional analog technology and altered it to improve its sharpness. By the early 1980s they could seriously propose their refined version as a replacement for the standard transmission. After this, interest in Europe and the United States renewed. The Europeans organized large technical development and standards-setting efforts to produce their own version of HDTV. Their inventions had some novel features and potential advantages over the Japanese technology. They are in the process of trying to get all affected areas of European industry to agree to a single standard. In the United States, companies and independent inventors have produced an array of new approaches, some bordering on the bizarre.

The U.S. Federal Communications Commission is now near the end of a multiyear process to evaluate competing approaches and select one as a standard for broadcast television in the United States. It is most likely that the winner will be one of the all-digital approaches originated in the United States because of their greater technical merits. This is much to the chagrin of the Japanese firms that originally entered the evaluation with analog approaches. They and the Europeans now confront the possibility that much of the market will fall to the U.S. digital approach, or something like it. However, the FCC standard will apply only to broadcast television. Being unregulated, U.S. cable, satellite, and closed-circuit television may adopt whatever new transmission method or methods they choose.

U.S. Strategic Options

The more frequent occurrence of radical invention in this country gives U.S. firms a major competitive advantage in the form of relatively quick access. Regardless of their diligence, foreign firms that want to adopt inventions from the United States must lose more time and expend more resources than their U.S. counterparts to locate these inventions and translate them into the language and culture of their own organizations.

This advantage makes it possible to succeed with several competitive strategies that are not readily available to foreign firms. An understanding of these strategies can help U.S. firms become industry leaders in a wider set of industrial situations. One major constraint on the choice of a strategy exists, however. This is the trade-off between radical invention and improvement.

The Radical Invention and Improvement Trade-off

Earlier in the chapter we uncovered a critical trade-off in the design of a successful commercial strategy: doing the kinds of things that will improve one's radical invention proficiency tends to reduce one's improvement proficiency, and vice versa. For society as a whole, this is a long-term trade-off because a shift would take several decades. Therefore, an individual firm operating in a region would have to accept the general proficiency levels as a given.

However, this trade-off can also occur within a firm. To foster radical invention, a firm hires diverse personnel and gives them great independence—the same things that cause invention proficiency in society as a whole. To maximize its improvement proficiency, a firm hires people with a common understanding and drills them in the corporate goals. Since these are nearly opposite courses of action, building one proficiency will normally reduce the other.

Of course trade-offs can be shifted over time. It is possible to learn clever ways to become good at two things at once. As early as 15 years ago, a group at the Harvard Business School, among others, recognized that this particular trade-off exists and began investigating methods of reducing it. But this problem will likely require much time to solve, if it can be solved at all. The fact that the group at Harvard is still working on the problem after 15 years gives us an idea of how tough a nut it is to crack.

For the U.S. firm this trade-off has two major corollaries for strategy. The first corollary is that strategies that require "doing everything well" are not always realistic. Choices must be made, at least between these two key proficiencies. The second corollary is that strategies based heavily on an improvement proficiency require some swimming upstream. U.S. society does not naturally provide the type of personnel and mentality best suited to high improvement. Extra effort at recruitment and training may be necessary. Thus it may be unrealistic to expect to surpass foreign competitors at this proficiency in less than a decade or two.

Within the constraints of this trade-off, there are three distinct strategies that employ the inventive edge to give U.S. firms leadership in at least some situations.

Improvement-Improvement

One of the most popular responses to our recent failures has been to emulate the Japanese. That is, to attempt to become better at improvement. In some industries a concerted program of "improvement-improvement" may be the *only* workable strategy. Where there is no potential for radical invention in the near future, the most successful firms will tend to be those most skilled at improvement of the current technology.

However, even in industries marked by regular radical inventions, improvement-improvement can be part of a successful strategy. The key is not to overdo it; concede that foreign competitors will always be somewhat faster at improving a product, and leverage the faster access to radical inventions to make up for this deficiency. Specifically, faster access provides lead time that allows the firm to get market feedback and start snowballing its industry leadership before the competition. The principle is a little like two drag racers, one of whom accelerates more slowly but has a one-second head start. The slower racer will likely stay ahead until the finish. Likewise, a U.S. firm that adopts radical inventions early may lead until the next radical invention, when the process begins anew.

An interesting example of this approach comes from Nucor—the U.S. minimill steel producer. It has vigilantly searched for new steel technologies, first adopting electric arc furnaces, and more recently thin casting. In segment after segment it has taken share from less quick but better-funded competitors, foreign and domestic.

The managerial challenges to adopting this strategy are to move quickly on risky new technologies and to avoid the organizational resistance to adoption that traditionally plagues industry leaders. Adopting risky technologies requires, first, assiduously monitoring for promising inventions. Second, it requires comprehensive technical and market evaluation of each invention to separate the dead ends from the winners. In fact, a firm following this strategy may simply have to accept that occasionally it will release a losing product and so must learn how to catch this early to minimize the losses.

Overcoming organizational resistance requires that a firm organize technology evaluation procedures to free them from political pressures. It means funding mechanisms that give support to new technologies without interruptions due to internal opposition or profit squeezes. And it typically means setting up the new businesses as fairly independent units, so that they cannot be squashed or forced to do business the traditional (and perhaps inappropriate) way.

A good example of the kind of organization that works is Johnson & Johnson's new Ethicon subsidiary. J&J is the traditional market leader in surgical suture supplies. But their business was threatened when U.S. Surgical introduced laparoscopic surgical tools. These allow the surgeon to work through very small openings in the body, drastically reducing the number of stitches and the recovery time. Quick to move, top management of J&J assigned a small team to start a new subsidiary totally separate from the sutures subsidiary, ordered them to capture 50 percent of the market within five years, and told them "not to come back five years from now and say you failed because you didn't ask for enough money."

Stairstepping

Another firm operating in an industry with high potential for radical improvement might succeed by concentrating its efforts at the opposite end of the proficiency spectrum—that is, on radical invention. Such a

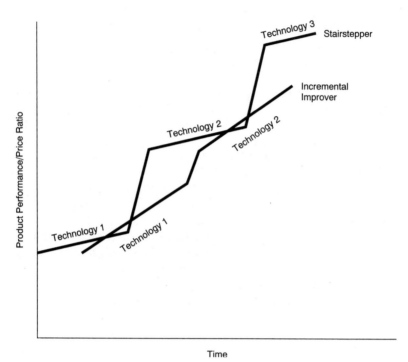

Figure 2-3. Increases in product performance under alternative strategies.

firm is following the "stairstep strategy," a name that derives from the frequent, sharp jumps in product attributes it attempts to make.

Like the firm following a strategy of improvement-improvement, the stairstepper is counting on periodic quantum leaps in product attributes to maintain its industry leadership. In contrast, it may be relatively poor at improvement. To stay ahead it depends on the extra lead time it gets by originating many of the inventions itself and on a greater frequency of radical invention.

Figure 2-3 depicts how a stairstepper can continuously offer products of superior attributes despite the ability of competitors to improve existing products at a much higher rate. The competitor's product catches up rapidly, but as it closes the gap, the stairstepper jumps to a new level.

A good example is the historical behavior of Cray Research, Inc., world leader in supercomputers. Cray long had the top-performing supercomputers, which employed vector processing. Fujitsu, NEC, and Hitachi worked to develop improved vector processing machines, but before they could catch up Cray had invented parallel processing.

Cray is not quite first to commercialize the newest technology—massively parallel processing. But as the U.S. supercomputer industry moves to it, the leap still represents something of a stairstep for the U.S. supercomputer industry as a whole: it comes just as the Japanese firms begin delivering supercomputers with performance comparable to Cray's more basic parallel processing machines.

The stairstep strategy is more effective when the firm originates the next successful radical invention. This adds to its lead time. But the firm cannot always count on this, so it must typically keep watch for competitors' developments, just like an improvement improver.

The stairstepper also depends on being in a product area that has potential for frequent radical advances. But the firm can *make* this happen to some extent because it is set up to generate radical inventions itself. The supercomputer industry, for example, would probably not generate new products as rapidly as it has were it not for Cray Research. In addition, a firm can try to foster invention activity through partnerships with start-up firms or by rewarding inventors that sell inventions to the company.

The other managerial challenges facing the stairstepper are the same as those facing the improvement improver: locating potential advances, picking the winners, and overcoming organizational resistance.

The new threat to the improvement-improvement and stairstep strategies is the Japanese strategy of convergence. Just as a U.S. firm using either of these two strategies is about to move to a new technology, several Japanese firms may also move to it in unison or move to yet a different technology. In either case, a U.S. firm acting in isolation will quickly be left far behind.

U.S. firms might hope to counter a convergence strategy with one of their own. The result would be coordinated, regional efforts dueling with one another to lead a new market. But U.S. culture and laws are not conducive to this kind of approach. There is a more promising response from U.S. firms that draws on the region's proficiency at radical invention. Some firms are trying this new strategy in select situations. We call it "the moonshot."

The Moonshot

In the card game hearts, the safest strategy is to try to take the jack of diamonds while avoiding all hearts and the queen of spades. However, once the other players have visibly committed to this strategy, the alternative of doing *exactly the opposite* may become extremely low risk. And the payoff for "shooting the moon" is far higher.

U.S. firms have an analogous opportunity to take the lead over foreign firms converging on a new technology for a product. By waiting until foreign competitors have committed to an approach, U.S. firms may have the opportunity to gain a greater share of the business at lower cost by selecting one of the *ignored* options.

Early convergence, or the jack-of-diamonds strategy, is the foreign firms' potential weakness. After the foreign firms are squarely on the path of improving their chosen technology, a physically better technology may appear. Either someone originates a new, superior invention based on another technology, or new evidence suggests that one of the other existing technologies would actually work better. In such a situation U.S. firms would normally not act anyway because massive development funds would still be necessary to catch up. But if U.S. firms concentrate their efforts on the most promising alternative technology, they might shoot the moon. That is, they might rapidly improve their version of the product to the point that it is higher in performance and/or lower in cost, with lower investment. The result is a big chunk of the market for the U.S. contenders.

Individual companies have already adopted this strategy successfully. Richard Foster of McKinsey cites the example of Celanese versus DuPont in the tire cord market.[4] In the early 1950s, tire makers used mostly rayon for the cord of their product. But nylon looked like it could be better than rayon if it were refined, and DuPont committed to developing it as a replacement. DuPont had actually produced strong sales for nylon by the early 1960s. But in the meantime Celanese was investigating polyester, and had good indications that it could be made into a better tire cord than nylon with less effort. Celanese succeeded in making a superior product with half the investment. Needless to say, the Celanese cord was also a big hit with tire makers. DuPont had access to polyester all along, but could never bring itself to put much effort behind it because of the same inertia factors that afflict firms dominant in an old technical approach.

The HDTV industry may be an example of a moonshot in the making. Japanese producers adopted an approach early and improved it assiduously. Yet when substantial commercial potential appeared, the U.S. generated an array of alternatives, some of them superior. It looks as though substantial resources will get behind one of those alternatives, and U.S. firms will have a bigger chunk of the resulting industry than they would have had otherwise.

In theory the flat panel industry could give rise to another moonshot. Japanese production of the ALCM is reportedly running up against difficult problems that may ultimately limit the performance and price of the devices. Several alternatives might have better performance and cost characteristics. And some U.S. firms have paired up to push the alternatives; for example, Coloray and Micron Technology are developing the vacuum fluorescent display. The possibilities of a successful moonshot look somewhat more remote here, however. Even if the returns to development effort on an alternative like the vacuum fluorescent technology are greater, it might take half a billion dollars or so to equal the progress resulting from the Japanese investment of a billion dollars in the ALCM. Two firms the size of Coloray and Micron could hardly marshal such resources and larger U.S. firms have generally steered clear of taking a big risk in this industry.

We might worry that foreign firms could themselves adopt a moonshot strategy. This would be unlikely to succeed, however, because the situation is asymmetric. For one thing, U.S. firms do not readily converge on an approach. If foreign firms wait until one approach wins in the U.S. market, they will either wait forever (in cases when multiple approaches survive) or enter after the U.S. firms that backed the right approach have built up a substantial lead. For another, since foreign firms require extra time to adopt an invention originated in the United States, they must select their technology from those that were applied to the product at least a couple of years ago. U.S. firms can draw on the newer approaches as well. This gives them a wider range of alternatives to search to find one capable of supporting a moonshot.

A separate reason for concern about the moonshot is that it may require coordination between firms. Even when the moonshooters find an alternative invention that can be improved rapidly, it may take a concerted effort to overtake the foreign group with a large lead. The flat panel display industry is an example. Any firm or group of firms that musters only a modest development effort in this business is likely to end up with a half-baked, uncompetitive product.

As noted above, fielding coordinated efforts is not a traditional strength of U.S. society. However, joint activity becomes less threatening if U.S. firms and the government recognize that effective coordination only requires agreement on a single technology and the establishment of incentives to pursue it. U.S. firms have, indeed, managed to do much more than this; for example, cooperative research organizations such as Sematech and the Microelectronics and Computer Technology Corporation (MCC) have been in existence for years and met with some success.

Government has generally shied away from "picking winners" among alternative industrial technologies. This would appear to eliminate one potential mechanism for achieving coordination. However, there are exceptions of a sort to this, too. The FCC's insistence on reviewing alternative HDTV systems has had the effect of slowing adoption of the earlier Japanese analog systems and giving domestic firms time to develop alternatives. In fact, the backers of digital systems have formed teams. They have thus taken advantage of the time to converge on a few approaches among themselves.

There is also an important pattern in these examples of U.S. cooperation. Specifically, resistance to coordination falls when there is a threat of losing an industry. All of the joint efforts mentioned arose in reaction to a sharp fall in competitiveness within an industry. And this is exactly the situation in which a moonshot is needed. When foreign firms target an industry and converge to take it, the moonshot is a logical strategy, and U.S. firms and the U.S. government are most likely to cooperate to accomplish it.

Conclusion

There are some things that U.S. industrial corporations are unlikely to change much in the short run. These include the informal U.S. school system, the great independence exercised by the country's citizens, and government opposition to coordination among firms. We are accustomed to bemoaning these particular traits because they hinder our ability to emulate the business strategy that has proved to be the runaway most successful strategy in many industries: continuous, incremental improvement based on a thorough understanding of current customer needs. To the extent that dissatisfaction brings about change, it may be beneficial. It may be that without the ability to engage in the strategy of incremental improvement in at least certain situations, U.S. industry cannot maintain a strong enough competitive position to preserve the national standard of living.

However, dissatisfaction will not improve the competitive position of U.S. businesses in the short run, when we must play the cards we are dealt. We do hold one long suit that is easy to overlook. The people of the United States are especially prone to conceiving of the radical, the drastic, the bizarre. They do this as surely as they do not excel at the incremental, because both characteristics—propensity for the radical and inability in the incremental—result from the same cultural causes.

For industry, an important manifestation of this American proficiency is the origination of radically different technological inventions. The greater access that this gives U.S. business to radical inventions can be leveraged to compensate for the deficiency at incremental improvement. Radical invention is not sufficient to make domestic firms competitive in every industry or every segment, but it probably is sufficient in several sectors that involve sales of a few trillion dollars a year.

The trick is to take competition out of the realm of improvement of existing technologies based on the measurable needs of existing customers and turn it into more of a betting game. The bets are inventions employing new technologies that perform functions people cannot yet fully conceive.

This is a gutsy leap for an individual firm. A wrong decision will often result in complete failure of the organization. But there are ways to make the leap, and bearing the risk may be preferable to a long, slow decline. When some coordination among firms is permissible—as it more often is when the loss of the industry to foreign competition is imminent—some of the risk *declines*. It does not just get spread out, it declines. Several firms acting in unison can shape an industry into a more inventive mode, and simultaneously increase the probability that the inventions they are pursuing will prevail in the market.

Radical invention is the long suit of the United States. If U.S. business develops ways to play the cards of this suit better, it should suddenly find itself winning against those holding a different type of hand.

References

1. Arnold C. Cooper and Dan Schendel, "Strategic Responses to Technological Threats," *Business Horizons*, 19(1), 1976, pp. 61–69.
2. John Jewkes, David Sawers, and Richard Stillerman, *The Sources of Invention*, Macmillan, London, 1960.
3. Scott A. Shane, "Why Do Some Societies Invent More than Others?" *Journal of Business Venturing*, 7(1), 1992, pp. 29–46.
4. Michael Porter, *The Competitive Advantage of Nations*, Free Press, New York, 1986.
5. Richard N. Foster, *Innovation: The Attacker's Advantage*, Summit Books, New York, 1986.

3

The Information Incubator

Jane Fedorowicz
Associate Professor of Management Information Systems, Boston University School of Management

Americans thrive on data—baseball scores, stock prices, movie trivia. Children in grade school trade baseball cards and memorize the statistics on the backs of the cards. Our grocery stores contain more brands of food than anywhere else in the world, and frequent shoppers are familiar with the contents and prices of most of them. *Jeopardy*, a top-rated game show, rewards contestants on their knowledge of trivia. Our interests are broadly based: over 11,000 different newspapers and over 11,000 different magazines are published in this country each year. We watch over 300 public television stations on two television sets per household. Over half the country subscribes to cable TV. Over 17,000,000 satellite earth stations were shipped by U.S. manufacturers from 1985 through 1989.[1]

As can be seen in Table 3-1, Americans, as a society of consumers, are inclined to quickly embrace new products and technologies. Television has replaced the newspaper as the most timely source of public information. The telephone and computer have joined to provide information on a more personal level. Witness the unparalleled

Table 3-1. Telephones, Newspapers, Televisions, and Radio, by Country
(Per 1000 Population, 1988 Data, Except Where Noted)

Country	Telephones*	Daily Newspapers	Televisions	Radios
United States	76.0 (1984)	256 (1986)	812	2120
France	60.8 (1985)	193 (1986)	399	895
Italy	48.8	105	419	790
West Germany	65.0	347 (1987)	379	956
Japan	55.5 (1985)	566 (1986)	589	863

*per 100 population, 1987 data.
SOURCE: U.S. Bureau of the Census, *Statistical Abstracts of the U.S.*, 11th edition, U.S. Department of Commerce, 1991.

success of CNN as a worldwide news provider, and the popularity of *Prodigy* on home computers.

The publishing and television industries are not the only ones to have profited from this insatiable demand for information. A dynamic information industry has evolved in this country in response to the high demand for information and information technology. Of the top 100 firms in the worldwide computer industry, 66 hail from the United States.[2]

On the hardware side American networking products and personal computers are world leaders. Novell and Banyan lead the local area network market, and IBM and Apple retain their control of the personal computer business.

Software to operate the technology, such as operating systems, database management, and network protocols, and software used directly by knowledge workers, such as decision support systems, executive information systems, expert system shells, and transaction processing systems, were all developed in the United States. The Top 100 U.S. software vendors totaled $13.9 billion in revenue in 1991, up 22 percent over 1990.[3] Microsoft Corporation and Computer Associates International had combined revenue exceeding $3 billion in software sales alone.

Other companies provide information services directly, selling access to thousands of databases covering many topics of economic and competitive interest to manufacturers. Worldwide, there are estimated to be over 7000 on-line databases covering a myriad of subjects. Many of the firms providing access to these databases reside in the United States, including Dow Jones News Retrieval, Compuserve, Dialog Information Service, and Mead Data Central. Business is booming. In the mid-1980s, U.S. businesses increased their spending on these services by 113 percent in only three years.[4]

By virtue of the country's size and the size of its information industry, there are more software engineers trained and working in the United States than anywhere else in the world. Children are exposed to computers throughout their educational experience, raising the comfort level and expectations of current and future generations of workers. There is currently one computer for every 20 students in U.S. classrooms, compared to one for every 80 students in Japan.[5]

The result is that an economic cycle has developed where the demand for information by individuals and businesses has led to the growth of an industry with a high information production capacity. This, in turn, has led to low-cost information technology, which translates into low-cost access to and processing of information. Thus, for a given budget, more information can be processed, leading back to a higher demand for information. The hunger for information and information processing capacity in the United States has begotten a burgeoning information industry.

To what can we attribute this hunger? In a sense, it is a product of the American culture. Americans have learned to expect immediate gratification of their information needs, making fast, easy access to facts and figures a highly profitable business domain. This is equally true of the market for business information, and the demand for internal and external data is increasing within all sectors of U.S. industry.

U.S. leadership in the information industry is indicative of a culture that promotes pioneering and innovation. Our proclivity to try new things is illustrated by the large number of start-up companies that literally begin in someone's garage. Our reputation is built upon "leaps" of invention in technological products, in sharp contrast to the Japanese orientation to continuous improvement and process innovations in manufactured products.

Innovation applied to existing informational processes meets with less resistance in the United States than in other parts of the world. "American workers are very fast at picking up new ideas. You can get them excited about a concept...in one or two meetings. In Germany you'd need presentations by three or four Ph.D.s and months of discussion afterwards."[6] Fast response to this type of change puts pressure on the information system needed to support the new process.

The inherent flexibility of an integrated *information infrastructure* is essential to permit quick reaction times required in today's competitive marketplace.

Both the development of the information environment and our capacity for innovation rest in our economic "genes," which influence us from cradle to grave. That we lead the rest of the world in information availability and technology is no secret. But that those who utilize this combination of information infrastructure and inherent innovative talent have much to gain may not be as clearly understood.

A *corporate information infrastructure* encompasses the information needed to run a business and the methods and policies employed to collect, process, and distribute it. It includes computer hardware, data networks, telecommunications capability, the installed software base, and the information professionals that support it.

Over time, the United States has built up a *national information infrastructure* that permits U.S. manufacturers to effectively integrate information into the culture and management of American business. I call this national infrastructure the *information incubator,* a term that captures the supportive or nurturing role that the United States and its culture have provided for the benefit of U.S. industry. The combined existence and reliance upon national and corporate information infrastructures enables the United States to compete successfully in the global marketplace.

The Role of Government

The U.S. government has played a key role in the establishment of the information incubator. Investments in research and development, supportive legislation, and provision of key infrastructure components are all a part of the underlying U.S. framework.[7]

On a percentage basis, U.S. investment in R&D is about the same as our Japanese and European counterparts. In actual dollar terms, though, the U.S. government invests more in R&D than all other countries of the world combined. Table 3-2 shows that the United States spends relatively more on defense-related research than do other countries, but, even so, the difference in nondefense investment is considerable. In fact, the 1990 Department of Defense budget included approximately $31 billion for software development and maintenance, which accounts for more than 10 percent of all defense-related spending, and equates to 20 percent of all U.S. spending on software for that

Table 3-2. National R&D Spending Comparisons, 1988
(Billion U.S. $ according to OECD Purchasing-Power Parities)

Country	R&D spending	Defense R&D	R&D/GDP (%)	Nondefense R&D/GDP(%)
United States	$133.7	$43.0	2.7	1.9
Japan	47.0	0.4	2.6	2.6
Germany	24.6	1.1	2.8	2.7
France	17.5	3.9	2.3	1.8
United Kingdom	17.0	3.3	2.2	1.8
Italy	9.1	0.6	1.2	1.1
Canada	6.4	0.3	1.4	1.3
Netherlands	4.3	0.1	2.3	2.2
Sweden	3.6	0.4	2.9	2.6
Switzerland	3.2	0.1	2.9	2.9
Non-U.S. Total	$132.9	$10.2	2.3	2.1

SOURCE: Alic et al., *Beyond Spinoff: Military and Commercial Technologies in a Changing World*, Harvard Business School Press, Boston, 1992, p. 89. Copyright © 1992 by the President and Fellows of Harvard College. Reprinted by permission.

year![8] When combined with nondefense spending, U.S. government investment in hardware and software development may well equal the total information technology spending of many other economies.

Government funding of R&D in the U.S. comprises less than half of all R&D funding, with the remaining portion coming from industry, academia, and consortia. The government has taken note of the strategy in Japan, and more recently in Europe, to fund and support intercompany alliances for conducting research. Microelectronics and Computer Technology Corporation (MCC) and Sematech are two recent U.S. consortia attempts in the area of information technology. The United States still has a way to go to match the efforts of Europe in this regard.

Our strength in R&D lies in our diversity of innovative sources of research. Beyond government agencies and consortia, we have a strong university research environment that is unequaled in the world. In addition, the concept of venture capital and our entrepreneurial spirit are unmatched.

The government is the country's leading consumer of information. Because of the elaborate set of databases that have been created in response to regulations and reporting requirements, the government is also a prime source of information. Research results, census and survey data, SEC filings, and many other types of information can be obtained at minimal expense through a number of government agencies, including the National Technical Information Service, the U.S. General Accounting Office, the Government Printing Office, the Securities and Exchange Commission, and the Library of Congress.

Government R&D involvement has also led to the development of an increasingly sophisticated series of communications and data networks. From the early days of DARPA's Arpanet, which connected defense researchers, to Bitnet, NSFnet, Usenet, and today's Internet, the government has provided a pathway for university and industry participants to communicate freely, and in many cases, without charge. Many companies such as Digital Equipment Corporation and Sun Microsystems have connected their own employee networks to the web of networks comprising the Internet. Other countries have also joined the Internet, making it a global de facto standard for communication. Bulletin boards, database access, and other capabilities have been added to the electronic mail facilities offered by Internet.

A new national computer network, proposed on the federal level, is showing signs of becoming a reality in the near future. The National Research and Education Network (NREN) is to be a high-speed network to support communication and shared-working environments. Such a network would permit faster communication and cooperation among dispersed research teams, including access to remote databases and computing facilities.

The United States is also a leader in satellite communications support. The government has pioneered the use of satellite technology, and the private sector has created an industry to lease bandwidth to individual companies. General Electric, Hughes Aircraft, and GTE are three companies that support this venture.

All of these activities promote the advancement of a national information infrastructure. The combination of an inquisitive citizenship, a supportive government, and an aggressive private section enables a distinctive U.S. approach to successful manufacturing management.

Productivity and Manufacturing Management

Despite claims to the contrary, manufacturing productivity continues to grow in the United States. In Figure 3-1 actual U.S. manufacturing productivity levels are compared with corresponding expenditures on computer hardware and software. In the early to mid-1980s, when larger and larger amounts of money were spent on information tech-

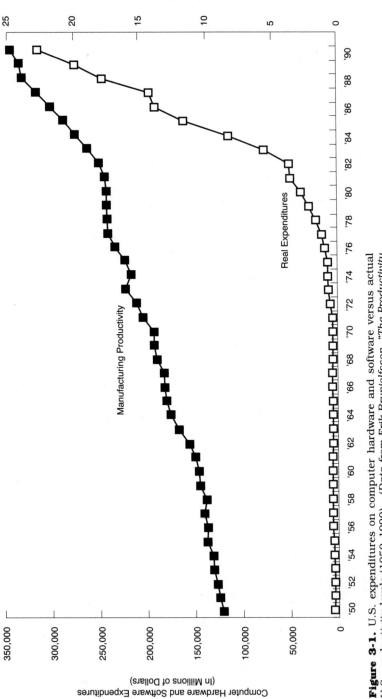

Figure 3-1. U.S. expenditures on computer hardware and software versus actual U.S. productivity levels (1950–1990). (*Data from Erik Brynjolfsson. "The Productivity of Information Technology: Review and Assessment," Center for Coordination Science Working Paper, Massachusetts Institute of Technology, December 1991.*)

nology, significant productivity improvements are observed. In fact, as seen in Figure 3-2, manufacturing productivity grew in this period at a much greater rate than that of the service sector, which appears to have reached a plateau during the same time.

The late 1980s saw a flattening of the manufacturing growth rate. Many of the information-technology improvements of the 1980s were intended to get rid of some of the fat in organizations, but the booming economy delayed this. The recent recession has reemphasized the need for widespread cutbacks. The existence of the information infrastructure has made these cutbacks easier for organizations to absorb, since the flow of information within a company can continue unaffected. Two takeover attempts at Phillips 66 some years ago left the company financially drained. Drastic downsizing, including the elimination of several layers of management, was made possible through the effective deployment of their executive information system.

The press has focused on the disparity between the productivity growth of Japan and Europe and that of the United States. Although it is true that U.S. productivity is growing at a slightly slower rate than in Japan or Europe, the fact remains that the actual level of productivity in the United States is 15 percent *higher*. We are, in effect, relying on our productivity buffer while we "retool" our information infrastructure. Our investment in an expensive information infrastructure has accounted for our inferior growth rate, but this investment should enable us to excel in the future, as long as we can maintain this advantage.

It is the productivity of the workers surrounding the core manufacturing process that continues to stymie efforts to improve productivity. Figure 3-3 depicts these knowledge and service workers. They include engineers who design the products and processes, product managers who coordinate marketing efforts, distribution workers who monitor inventory levels, and executives who plan and monitor the strategic direction of the company. Figure 3-4 shows that white-collar productivity has stayed relatively constant over the past 30 years, and remains below its peak level of the early 1970s. In a recent article on productivity, Peter Drucker concurs with this emphasis: "The single greatest challenge facing managers in the developed countries of the world is to raise the productivity of knowledge and service workers."[9]

Just as the Industrial Revolution automated the manufacturing process, the Information Age is transforming the management of manufacturing. Given our success in the Industrial Revolution, American society tends to view automation as a primary tool for improving productivity. The gains of the Industrial Revolution are attributed to automation, which becomes an obvious engine for the gains of the

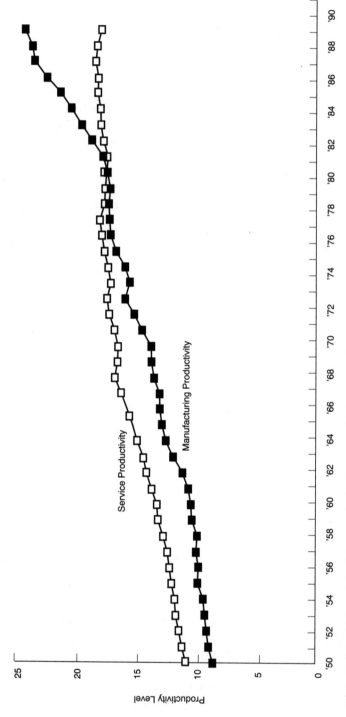

Figure 3-2. U.S. productivity levels in the manufacturing and service sectors. *(Data from Erik Brynjolfsson, "The Productivity of Information Technology: Review and Assessment," Center for Coordination Science Working Paper, Massachusetts Institute of Technology, December 1991.)*

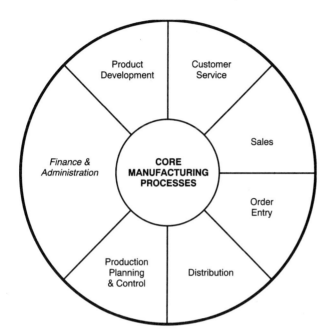

Figure 3-3 Knowledge and service workers supporting core manufacturing processes. (Note that all except finance and administration can contribute directly to manufacturing productivity.)

Information Age. Where, then, is the expected corresponding impact on performance?

Automation alone will not increase management productivity. Industrialization mandated major changes in manufacturing processes and worker culture before automation was deemed successful. The same must occur in the Information Age. Automation in support of information-dependent work must be embedded in a carefully planned and executed information infrastructure. Changes in business and decision processes and corporate culture must accompany the introduction of new technology.

The Corporate Information Infrastructure

Planning, policy-making, and management of American business takes place in an environment surrounded by data and technology. Information nurtures our growth; it is difficult to envision plant man-

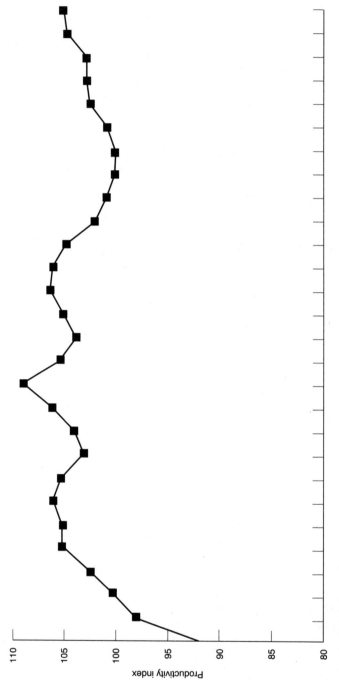

Figure 3-4 White-collar productivity index. *(Data from Erik Brynjolfsson, "The Productivity of Information Technology: Review and Assessment," Center for Coordination Science Working Paper, Massachusetts Institute of Technology, December 1991.)*

Table 3-3. PC Penetration Rates

Country	Number of PCs (millions)	Population (millions)	Penetration (%)
United States	48	250	19
Europe	24	330	7
Japan	7	123	6

SOURCE: *U.S. Industrial Outlook,* U.S. Department of Commerce, September 1990.

agement, marketing, R&D, or sales functioning without information systems. The information infrastructure in a U.S. firm relies heavily on information technology at its base. We have made a large investment in technology to be used by knowledge and service workers. Use of computer hardware is more pervasive in the United States than it is in Japan and Europe. Table 3-3 demonstrates this difference. Personal computers have a 19 percent penetration rate (per capita) in the United States as compared to 7 percent and 6 percent, respectively, in Europe and Japan.

What role does information and infrastructure play in improving organizational productivity and performance? Drucker asserts that knowledge and service workers must "work smarter" at their tasks, as this is the only way to enhance their productivity. Technology then becomes a "tool" of production in knowledge and service work. Productivity is not raised by the introduction of a tool but by employing the tool to perform work "smarter." Drucker recommends focusing on how work should be done by defining the task, concentrating work on the task, measuring performance, and continuously working to improve performance.[10]

The role of the information "tool" is then easy to ascertain. Information is the key input to many tasks, and quick, easy, and flexible access to information will increase efficiency and effectiveness of knowledge work. An engineer with CAD technology will outperform one with traditional drafting equipment. A product manager with a decision support system will be able to analyze more market information from both internal and external sources, and do it more quickly, than a manager working without this system. With the elimination of much of the tedious data gathering and manipulation, the task becomes one of analysis and planning. In effect, the technology can off-load many of the unnecessary and unproductive delays caused by inefficient distribution and communication of information.

Information for
Performance Measurement

Our preoccupation with bottom-line data in business is seen by many as a function of Wall Street's short-term focus, which is thought to be the underlying problem in American business. However, as a recent study by Ernst & Young points out, "Businesses that have gone sour on Wall Street have first gone sour on Main Street."[11] The problem is not that Wall Street has a short-term focus, but that management compensation based on short-term performance measures has led to improper motivation. Financial data has been easy to access and measure, making it an obvious choice for determining performance.

Firms that base rewards on both long- and short-term criteria convey the proper incentives. More and more firms have recognized this and have moved to change their mode of employee evaluation. In a recent survey, 54 percent of the responding firms reported that employee compensation is tied to quality measures such as customer satisfaction, prevention of defects, and reduction in cycle time. Of these companies, 91 percent plan to use customer satisfaction instead of traditional financial measures to determine compensation.[12]

A well-structured information infrastructure designed to change the focus and methods of performance measurement is endemic to continued success. In the words of Robert Eccles, "Information technology has played a critical role in making a performance measurement revolution possible."[13]

Performance measurement is enhanced by an information infrastructure properly designed to allow other priorities, like customer service, quality, and market share to be highlighted. The infrastructure permits all aspects of the organization to be monitored in an integrated fashion. Both cause and effect of observed conditions can then be disseminated in a timely manner. Executive information systems, for example, inform top-level managers of changes in internal and external conditions in "real time" so that immediate investigation and response can occur. The added benefit, access to a wide range of quantitative and qualitative information, may be as an old adage predicts, "That which is monitored improves."

American Competitiveness

The 1990 study of American competitiveness by Ernst & Young mentioned earlier showed that U.S. manufacturing firms have uniformly identified productivity and quality as key strategy components in the effort to regain advantage over foreign competitors. The study found that manufacturers who were relatively more profitable than their competition were distinctive in "the way they planned, the market strategies they pursued, the way they organized people, the performance measures they took on their businesses, and finally, the level of investment emphasis they gave to people versus technology. Overall, it was this softer side of the business that made the difference in financial performance, marketplace position and even the success of technology deployment itself."[14] (Note that here, technology encompasses manufacturing as well as managerial systems.)

In the section focusing on products and markets, the study concludes that six factors lead to improved profitability. All six have implications for knowledge and service workers in manufacturing companies. Each factor can be viewed as a task for which productivity must be raised. The six factors identified by Ernst & Young are outlined here. We illustrate each factor with an example of a company that has effectively used information technology to achieve success in its business practices.

Broad Product-Line Scope

Successful firms reported that their broader product lines enabled them to achieve a higher relative price position and a higher market share than their competitors. Broader, more customized product lines led to higher relative profitability for these firms. The challenge associated with a broader scope is greater management complexity. Complexity implies additional information needs, drawing on elaborate interlocking databases.

As an example, Frito-Lay installed a sophisticated decision support system to gather supermarket scanner data and analyze it for performance trends that provide executives with immediate access to market problems and opportunities. In addition to changing the locus of executive-level decision processes pertaining to product-market decisions, the system has also enabled Frito-Lay to reduce time to market, adopt micromarketing strategies for individual stores, and optimize its distribution network. Frito-Lay has expanded the number of products it offers and it can target specific regions as well as local competitors through its application of information technology.[15]

Product Innovation

The Ernst & Young study showed that more frequent innovations resulted in the need for producers to charge higher relative prices for their products, as innovation tends to increase the cost of doing business. Successful firms found that profitability is closely linked to capacity utilization and an advantageous relative cost position. A company that is able to change products frequently in response to market demands will support a higher pricing structure. If product changes also yield lower costs, higher margins will also result. Product changes must be strictly monitored to be worthwhile.

Unnecessary product changes can be forestalled with good design process management. The design team for the Kodak Fling camera used a common engineering database to tackle configuration management. Team members could suggest changes to assemblies using e-mail or voice-mail, but only the engineer in charge of the part could make the change, which was then distributed through the database. The product set two Kodak manufacturing records, time to market and fewest engineering changes needed during production.[16]

Reputation for Quality

Most companies have recognized the need for an emphasis on quality in both product and service offerings. Those companies that achieve superior quality must convince their customers of the relative advantage of their product. The Ernst & Young study also found that exceptional product and service quality must become a major component of a company's reputation in order to produce financial advantages. A quality reputation requires increased product promotion and service performance. Superior service frequently relies on the timeliness of the integrated data supplied by information technology.

Steelcase, Inc., is a case in point. It developed a comprehensive system to support its distributors and dealers. By offering a large variety of office furniture options in easy-to-access personal computer applications, Steelcase aids its distributors in placing orders, exchanging information, running their business, and advising clients on furniture selections. Customers are helped to envision office layout, prepare space plans, and specify their own configurations. Eventually, customers will be able to place their own orders with the manufacturer, freeing dealers to provide other services and handle larger numbers of clients. Customers will also be able to use the system for furniture inventory management to improve internal operations and save money. At the same time, Steelcase has improved its reputation for quality service.[17]

More Vertical Integration

Vertical integration reflects the degree to which a product is manufactured in-house versus being assembled from purchased materials. The more a company is vertically integrated or relies on a relatively small number of suppliers, the more likely it is to have better relative cost, price, and profit positions, as long as it can maintain higher-quality products. Vertical integration adds complexity to the production process. This added production complexity will require a greater scope of information flow, leading to the need for extensive integrated information systems.

Automobile production is a very complex process, combining manufactured and purchased subassemblies. The Ford Motor Company is introducing a new information system throughout its manufacturing process with the goal of cutting costs, speeding turnaround, and improving quality. The Corporate Manufacturing Management System (CMMS) governs everything related to manufacturing at all Ford plants worldwide. All aspects of material management, assembly, and supplier and order information are monitored in accordance with a common set of business practices. A number of plants are already successfully using the system.[18]

Larger International Scope of Operations

Although most companies do not compete globally, the Ernst & Young study found that those companies that do compete globally, are in a superior profit position. Global operations reflect higher profits, while enabling the company to maintain relatively higher prices. International operations will obviously add to a firm's interpersonal and data communications complexity. Technological solutions will mediate the impact of geographic and time differences within the organization by providing computer networks, common systems, and executive information support.

The 3M Company operates in 52 countries and has more than 194,000 products. The "technology bridge" it uses to link up its operations is a telecommunications network with some centralized information system services, including corporate databases, human resources, and manufacturing. Other systems, like marketing, are tailored by individual IS functions to meet the local goals of the dispersed company. Outstanding local systems are expanded upon by corporate IS for use by the rest of the company.[19]

Competitive Pressure Driven by Competitors

Most companies in the Ernst & Young study reported that their leading source of competitive pressure was existing competitors. For the smaller percentage of companies where customers exerted greater pressure than competitors, lower relative profitability margins were noted. In most firms, then, this would imply a greater need for competitive intelligence and the employment of sophisticated information retrieval and artificial intelligence techniques to analyze a wide variety of internal and external databases.

Digital Equipment Corporation employs a 50-person department to gather, interpret, and distribute information internally. They purchase access to external databases, administer three on-line market intelligence systems, and provide custom research on industry and market trends. The group spent $8.2 million in 1990.[20]

These competitiveness factors provide a foundation for moving decision-making authority down in the organization to the individual who is closest to the source of a problem or opportunity. In fact, the Ernst & Young study found that "more successful companies were more likely to have decentralized organization structures, focused factories, more decision-making authority residing at the operating level of the business, a management focus on establishing a proper culture versus tighter control, and finally, executive compensation systems based on a balance of short- and long-term performance measures."[21]

Successful firms were also more likely to consider their information systems valuable tools for running the business. Whether the source is the customer or the production process, an integrated information infrastructure will "empower" knowledge and service workers, enable the distribution of decision making, and maintain top management's ability to monitor performance.

Maintaining the Advantage

The technology on which to base an integrated information infrastructure is readily available. Although there is nothing inherently

"American" about information technology, especially now that it has become easier to produce German, Italian, or Kanji versions of commercial software packages, the widespread acceptance of English as the universal business language gives the United States an advantage in producing popular and cost-effective software for worldwide distribution. High demand and low production costs in this innovative industry gives the United States the leadership position.

Most countries have boards that set or recommend national standards in technology. But American industry more often relies on the marketplace to determine de facto standards for hardware and software. These unofficial standards govern the development and use of the major components of the corporate information infrastructure. De facto standards evolve faster than official standards adopted by national standards boards. They are also frequently based on products sold by large technology companies. A common consequence of this process is that these standards pervade worldwide, again reinforcing America's innovation leadership and market share.

Although the United States has a commanding lead in software development, there are indications that our competitors are moving on this front. The Japanese have set up software factories to better meet the demands of business, although there appears to be a shortage of available software engineers with which to staff these factories. The European community has adopted standards for software and communications to minimize the difficulties of sharing information across international borders. The question arises, then, about how long it will take for these countries to acquire the technological basis to build their own "information incubators."

If an information infrastructure consisted only of technology, it might not be long before the American advantage was diminished. Luckily, the "incubator" is not purely technology-based. There is a large cultural component that will allow the United States to maintain its distinctive position. First, in response to the demand for information, the United States has built up a very large, publicly accessible information base. Although the nature of competition calls for companies to preserve internal secrets, the information industry has collected independent sets of R&D, marketing, and financial data that are unequaled in the world. Internal historical data is also digested and shared cross-functionally. Many consumer products firms, for example, purchase links to the databases of Information Resources, Inc., to monitor market share, price, and advertising of their competitors.

Historically, the strict hierarchical reporting structure of U.S. companies has limited the sharing and integration of information. Japanese firms have long been praised for their interfunctional orientation and group decision-making techniques. Although U.S. firms are beginning to move toward a similar goal, our approach is very different. The Japanese culture promotes much interpersonal interaction, but very little formal integration of information systems. Kaizen II (a second movement to improve Japan's manufacturing process) recognizes that a lack of formal infrastructure hinders efforts at supporting continuous-improvement capabilities in light of environmental changes.[22] The main hindrances in achieving their integration objective are a lack of technical expertise and the entrenched culture.

Successful U.S. companies have used their information infrastructure to evolve into more flexible or responsive organizations. Team-based or cluster organizations rely upon work group technology and telecommunications to support superior worker arrangements. Cross-functional teams, and teams that span large geographic distances, are easily accommodated electronically. At Xerox's Palo Alto Research Center, for example, four aerospace engineers in different locations "discuss" an engineering design shown concurrently on whiteboards in their respective locations. Team members anywhere in the world can see what their colleagues are doing as if they were in the same room.[23]

Innovation remains a key link to the incubation concept. The information infrastructure allows people to "tinker" with information by exploring new relationships in a relational database, simulating new business process designs, or exploring new product possibilities with external market data. This drive to seek out new possibilities from observing patterns or opportunities in data is a cultural phenomena that will continue to compel the U.S. economy forward.

Addressing Cultural Dysfunctions

There are aspects of our culture that may inhibit our ability to surpass the competition on productivity and performance measures. The information infrastructure provides us with a means of overcoming these unfavorable cultural characteristics. The ability to construct individualized, qualitative performance measures will instill a sense of ownership and empowerment to all workers in the manufacturing organization. Long- and short-term measures will help in moving our cultural focus to long-term preservation of the company, the environment, and the country. Team-based relationships will support a doctrine of management by consensus. An emphasis on roles will replace the current emphasis on relationships. Communications among all workers in the organization will improve. From the supplier to the ultimate customer, relationships with other participants in the manufacturing value chain will also be enhanced.

The American worker is more likely to voluntarily change jobs and companies than his or her foreign counterparts. Although this inclination carries expensive training and orientation costs, valuable cross-fertilization and sharing of ideas also occurs. Job-hopping reinvigorates the employee, bringing him or her into contact with new challenges, products, and colleagues. Team-based organizations allow individuals to experience new opportunities without having to change employers, thus mitigating the costly component of bringing new ideas and energy to a project.

Concluding Remarks

American manufacturing has survived two major revolutions. The Industrial Revolution introduced new production processes to the factory, leading the way to massive improvements in labor productivity. The second revolution has been dubbed the Information Age and has led to vast increases in the amount of knowledge and service work to be performed. Middle management layers have been added, and consulting firms have emerged to meet the growing need to process more information faster, to support complex strategic positioning, and to address competitive pressures.

The Industrial Revolution produced measurable growth in productivity and profitability for American factories. In the past few years, U.S. manufacturing productivity has shown little or no growth. At the same time, Japanese and European manufacturers have not experienced the same slowdown. This lack of improvement in U.S. manufacturing productivity has paralleled the introduction of a great deal of information technology into these same organizations. Some observers contend that information technology has not delivered on its promise of productivity improvement.

One hasty conclusion that might be drawn at this point is that information technology somehow drains an organization's profitability by reducing productivity. This chapter has shown that the opposite, in fact, is true. Information and information technology, properly employed, actually enhance the competitiveness of U.S. organizations. American business is well positioned to take better advantage of the availability of information because of the investment we have made in establishing an intensive information infrastructure, both nationally and within individual firms.

This investment in infrastructure was made over a long period, and its effect on productivity has only recently begun to be documented. In addition, the American culture encourages widespread accessibility and use of information in all aspects of life. This is being done increasingly by technological means. The American worker has not only the desire to gather and analyze abundant sources of information, but also the means to do so because of the existence of this infrastructure.

The American proclivity to innovate coupled with a hunger for information has fueled the creation of a national information industry. The U.S. government supports the collection and distribution of information through direct and indirect measures. The combination of cultural factors, government intervention, and a successful information industry has spawned a unique information incubator.

These factors have also had an impact within manufacturing firms. The existence of a supply of and demand for information has promoted the development of the corporate information infrastructure. U.S. manufacturing has a head start in supporting the information needs of its employees, particularly knowledge and service workers. The existence of the national incubator will ensure that this leadership position can be maintained.

References

1. Data from the U.S. Bureau of the Census, *Statistical Abstracts of the U.S.,* 11th edition, U.S. Department of Commerce, 1991.

2. *Datamation,* June 15, 1992, p. 13.

3. Judith Hodges and Deborah Melewski, "Revenue Nears $14 Billion," *Software Magazine,* 12(9), June Special, 1992, pp. 17–21.

4. Avery Jenkins, "Firms Work to Control On-line Database Charges" and "On-line Databases," *PC Week,* March 11, 1986, pp.41—42 and pp. 83–84+, respectively.

5. *Business Week,* April 6, 1992, p. 89.

6. Thomas A. Stewart, "The New American Century: Where We Stand," *Fortune,* August 26–September 4, 1991, p. 22.

7. National Research Council, *The National Challenge in Computer Science and Technology,* National Academy Press, Washington, D.C., 1988.

8. John A. Alic, Lewis M. Branscomb, Harvey Brooks, Ashton B. Carter, and Gerald L. Epstein, *Beyond Spinoff: Military and Commercial Technologies in a Changing World,* Harvard Business School Press, Boston, 1992, p. 285.

9. Peter F. Drucker, "The New Productivity Challenge," *Harvard Business Review,* November–December 1991, pp. 69–79.

10. Ibid.

11. Ernst & Young, *American Competitiveness Study,* E&Y No. 58059, 1990, p. 12.

12. Study conducted by Handy HRM Corp. in conjunction with the American Society of Quality Control, undated.

13. Robert G. Eccles, "The Performance Measurement Manifesto," *Harvard Business Review,* January–February 1991, p. 133.

14. Ernst & Young, op. cit., Foreword.

15. Jane Fedorowicz and Benn Konsynski, "Bridging Business and Decision Processes: Organization Support Systems," *Journal of Management Information Systems,* March 1992.

16. Allan E. Alter, "Team Boosters," *CIO Magazine,* April 1, 1992, pp. 36–42.

17. Fedorowicz and Konsynski, op. cit.

18. David Freedman, "Gearing Up," *CIO,* June 1, 1992, pp. 48–50.

19. *Computerworld* Premier 100, September 30, 1991, pp. 50–52.

20. Digital Equipment Corporation: Leadership in Corporate Intelligence, Harvard Business School case 9-192-002, 1992.

21. Ernst & Young, op. cit., p. 6.

22. *Manufacturing 21 Report: The Future of Japanese Manufacturing,* Association for Manufacturing Excellence, Wheeling, Ill., 1991.

23. Alter, op. cit.

4
Teams

Janice A. Klein
Visiting Associate Professor, Massachusetts Institute of Technology Sloan School of Management

Integration, whether it is global, functional, or technical, necessitates bringing together pockets of knowledge and expertise. In an effort to cut across borders, hierarchies, and functional silos, teams have become a primary vehicle to get work accomplished. But teams come in many different shapes and forms. One key differentiating factor is how the work of the team and of its individual members is accomplished. Another factor is the breadth of responsibility given to the team.

Since the building of the pyramids (and before), managers have been searching for the "best" way to organize work. Over the years, a variety of different work group design models have been extolled. The craft guilds in Europe gave rise to the apprentice model, where highly skilled workers became experts in their particular craft. Then Frederick Taylor came along and proposed scientific management as the "ideal" for mass production. More recently, "lean production," epitomized by the Toyota Production System, has been praised as the most effective model.[1] But now it appears that Toyota is revamping its production system to humanize jobs.

A fourth model, which strives to optimize the fit between the technical system and the social needs of the work force, originated in Europe but has found a home in the United States. (This model has also found a home in Canada, but for purposes of this book, the discussion will focus on the United States.) Over the past few years, it has accumulated a number of labels, including high-commitment systems, high-performance teams, sociotechnical work systems, self-managed or self-directed teams, and new work systems. The label used in this chapter is *small business teams* (SBTs) because this term aptly describes one of the model's key objectives, that is, organize the work to encourage and enable workers to use their knowledge/skills to manage their daily activities as if they were owners of their own business.

Many describe work force involvement in both lean production and SBTs as empowerment. Indeed, both systems strive for improved competitiveness through better utilization of the production worker's knowledge, but the means by which they accomplish this are very different. Plants using the lean production system are noted for team-based production, where employees are cross-trained to perform all jobs assigned to the team; team members are also responsible for quality, minor maintenance, and continuous improvement. Production workers in plants using SBTs are also trained to do a wide range of team tasks and assume responsibility for the daily management of their team. But a closer look at the two team-based organizations reveals significant differences, particularly in the level of decision making delegated to the teams and in the types of tasks assigned to team members.

This chapter argues that SBTs provide a unique opportunity to fully utilize human resource potential, especially when team members are empowered with the responsibility and provided with the skills and information to manage their own activities. Furthermore, when optimally designed and managed, SBTs naturally fit the American culture, providing an outlet for the country's proclivity toward individualism and entrepreneurism. Although its application is still limited, the SBT model is not secret; in fact, the popular press regularly sings its praise.[2] The United States has a head start and, at least in the near term, a sustainable edge due to the breadth of skills and preferences in its diverse work force.

Job Design Dimensions

To produce a product or service, a number of skills and abilities must be brought together and a variety of tasks must be performed. Although there are an infinite number of ways this can be accomplished, four dominant models have emerged for designing jobs within manufacturing—the apprentice model, Taylorism, lean production, and SBTs. To compare and contrast the four models, it is first necessary to examine three key dimensions of jobs: (1) the number of functional tasks included, (2) the scope of managerial/administrative activities, and (3) the depth of knowledge related to each of those tasks or activities.

Number of Functional Tasks

In manufacturing, functional tasks are often associated with traditional blue-collar work. Functional tasks within a machine shop might include machine operation, inspection, material handling, and machine maintenance. Since conventional wisdom has held that specialization maximizes quality and efficiency, jobs have traditionally been designed with a minimum number of different functional tasks. This has led to narrow job classifications, to low morale due to monotony, and to poor quality resulting from lack of attentiveness. In addition, productivity has lagged because of the lack of work force flexibility. To alleviate such problems, there has been a move toward job rotation across multiple functional tasks, commonly referred to as *job enlargement*.

Scope of Managerial/Administrative Activities

Managerial/administrative activities cover a wide gamut of responsibilities, including work scheduling, job assignment, employee selection and training, work-methods design, problem diagnosis, and process improvement. These activities, traditionally the purview of supervisory or support (including technical) personnel, require the thinking associated with coordinating and managing a manufacturing operation. During the sixties and seventies there was a move toward *job enrichment*, that is, loading production jobs with multiple managerial/administrative tasks, in an effort to provide the work force with a sense of ownership or responsibility over their daily activities.

Depth of Knowledge

There are also various levels of expertise associated with either functional or managerial/administrative duties. For example, some operators learn only how to load parts into a machine, while others are able to diagnose and solve problems associated with keeping the machine operating. An individual's knowledge about any particular task typically falls within one of two areas—*operational expertise,* which includes how to best perform the task, or *analytic knowledge,* which encompasses an understanding of the scientific principles underlying the task. These two aspects of task expertise often reside in different individuals in different functions: production employees generally possess operational expertise, and analytic knowledge typically resides in the engineering organization.

Although basic skills and knowledge can be learned in a classroom, operational expertise develops over time through repeated performance on the job. As new situations or problems arise, trial-and-error methods are usually used to find solutions. Each solution expands the body of operational expertise.

Analytic knowledge, on the other hand, is primarily acquired through formal education and evolves through the application of scientific methods. Since this knowledge focuses on the theory of *why*, rather than *how*, a task is performed, an individual might possess analytic knowledge without ever performing the task.

In addition to task expertise concerning a specific functional or managerial/administrative task, there is also a level of knowledge required to integrate across multiple tasks—knowledge typically required of managers or supervisors. *Integration expertise* does not necessarily require in-depth operational expertise or analytic knowledge concerning the tasks to be integrated. What is required, though, is enough understanding of the basics to recognize when problems arise and whom to turn to solve them.

The sum of these three types of expertise—operational, analytic, and integration—comprise the knowledge required to produce a product or service. Furthermore, continuous improvement and learning require a combination of all three. How a work group is designed to develop and utilize knowledge will impact its ability to meet the new manufacturing requirements identified in Chapter 1.

Traditional Models— Apprentice and Taylorism

One of the oldest work group designs is the apprentice model. Although it can be found worldwide, particularly in the skilled trades, Germany has used it extensively and has probably developed it to the greatest extent. The aim of this model is to develop in-depth expertise in a particular function, whether it is machine operation or a craft such as carpentry. A machinist, for example, is expected to set up and operate several types of different machines within an equipment family and also to diagnose problems and do minor repairs. As a result, the worker becomes the task expert, possessing in-depth operational know-how and a high level of analytical knowledge for all the tasks within a particular craft. Advanced analytic knowledge, however, may still reside in a separate engineering function. And, although the craftsperson possesses an ability to innovate as needed within a specific area of expertise, integration across tasks is typically limited to those tasks within a particular craft.

Figure 4-1 plots the apprentice model along the three job design dimensions discussed earlier. The result is a long thin rectangle that stretches most of the depth of the knowledge axis, but is narrow on the horizontal axis, since the job is usually limited to one craft or function. The vertical dimension is also limited because, with the exception of process improvements, managerial/administrative activities remain the purview of managers and technical staff.

The benefit of the apprentice model is top-notch quality products, because the craftsperson possesses the ability to adjust to any process or material variability to ensure that each component part fits precisely. The downside is high labor costs, because achieving such depth requires extensive education and training.

Frederick Winslow Taylor, on the other hand, looked at the needs of mass production and proposed that the key to success was low-cost labor. In his scientific management system engineers determine the optimal procedure and then standardize the processes so that jobs can

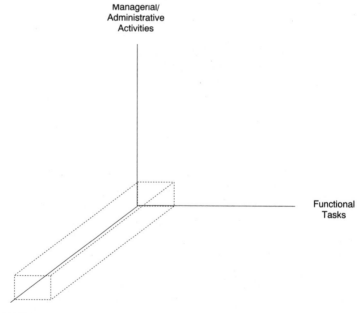

Figure 4-1. The apprentice model.

be broken down into minute tasks. These tasks can then be laid out with detailed instructions that require minimal training to be routinely performed. In comparison with jobs designed under the apprentice model, Taylorized jobs require minimal depth of knowledge on the part of the work force; workers merely follow procedures set forth by engineers.

As shown in Figure 4-2, Taylorized jobs are also narrow on both the horizontal and vertical dimensions. A machine operator in this model would be trained only to run the equipment. A higher-skilled operator would be responsible for the setup, and a maintenance person would perform minor repairs. With such narrow training, workers in Taylorized jobs have little ability or opportunity to be involved in process improvements or other managerial/administrative tasks, which are typically just as narrowly defined. Although scientific management was instrumental in fueling the growth of mass production, Taylorized jobs often led to low morale and lack of flexibility.

Both the apprentice model and Taylorism produced outstanding results under the competitive requirements of their eras. Today's environment, however, requires both low-cost operation and flexibility. As outlined in Chapter 1, there is a need for greater integration across

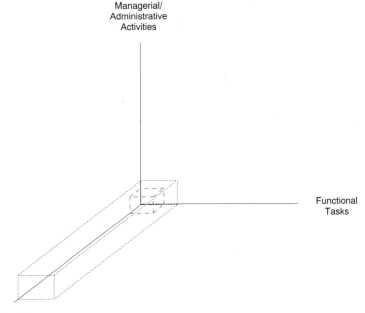

Figure 4-2. The Tayloristic model as compared to the apprentice model.

jobs, organizational functions, and layers of the hierarchy. Two more recent models—lean production and SBTs—have emerged to respond to this changing competitive environment.

Lean Production

In contrast to the apprentice model, lean production is a trade-off between depth of knowledge and breadth of tasks, as shown in Figure 4-3. Team members are expected to learn all functional tasks assigned to their team. In addition, lean production jobs move slightly up the vertical axis with the addition of process improvements as a primary work force responsibility. As a result, lean production team members can not attain the depth of expertise possible when employees focus on a narrower set of activities.

On the basis of an in-depth study of the automobile industry, the International Motor Vehicle Program at the Massachusetts Institute of Technology concluded:

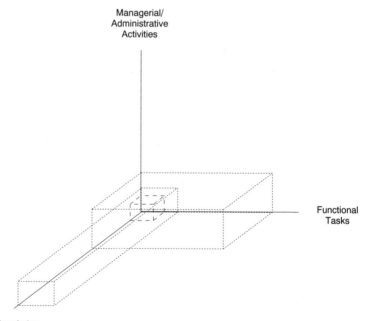

Figure 4-3. Lean production as compared to the apprentice and Tayloristic models.

Lean production is a superior way for humans to make things. It provides better products in wider variety at lower cost. Equally important, it provides more challenging and fulfilling work for employees at every level, from the factory to headquarters. It follows that the whole world should adopt lean production, and as quickly as possible.[3]

This conclusion is based, in part, on the outstanding levels of workplace productivity and flexibility lean producers have achieved through their use of multiskilling across functional tasks. For example, a machine operator might be required to operate multiple machines, as noted by Monden in his description of Toyota's Production System:

> In the gear manufacturing process, for example, each worker attends to 16 machines. Unlike many typical production situations where a worker would interface with only one type of machine, the Toyota set-up involves 16 machines which perform different types of operations: grinding, cutting, etc. The laborer as a multi-function worker first picks up one unit of a gear brought from the preceding process and sets it on the first machine. At the same time, he detaches another gear already processed by this machine and puts it on a chute to roll in front of the next machine. Then, while he is walking to the second machine, he pushes a switch between the first and second machine to start the first machine. He performs a similar operation on the second machine and finally returns to his initial process.[4]

In addition to lean production team members learning all the production-related jobs associated with the team, they are required to do inspection activities and perform tasks associated with autonomous maintenance (i.e., cleaning and inspecting equipment, bolting, and lubricating). Furthermore, lean production workers are given a significant amount of discretion in stopping the line if there is a production problem and in continuously improving the production process.

Employee discretion over work methods, however, must fall within the boundaries of standardized work methods. To the casual observer, standardized work appears to be a reincarnation of Taylor's "one best method" to perform a job, since lean production workers must strictly adhere to detailed job procedures. There are, however, two significant differences, which could be labeled "dynamic Taylorism" and "Taylorism without an ego."

■ *Dynamic Taylorism*   Taylor advocated that there was an optimal way to perform a task and that employees should perform that task specifically as designed until there was a change in equipment, product or process specifications, etc. In contrast, standardized work in lean production is based on stabilizing the procedure so it can then be improved upon, via the Plan-Do-Check-Action improvement cycle. Hence, the "one best method" is a moving target.

- *Taylorism without an Ego.* Under traditional Taylorism, industrial engineers were assumed to be the sole experts in setting work methods. In lean production, team members are taught the mechanics of setting standards. It is the team members, themselves (at times, in conjunction with engineers), who establish the methods. This recognizes that the major source of operational expertise resides in the people doing the job.

  However, because of a strong belief in clear lines of accountability, lean production managers typically do the managing and workers are responsible for the production process. There is no question that employee suggestions are encouraged as part of the continuous-improvement effort, but human resource brain power is more narrowly channeled toward improving the process rather than toward the management of the business or the daily team activities. Hence, team members in lean production seldom get involved in activities that have traditionally been considered the purview of first-line supervisors, for example, selecting new team members or team member (peer) evaluation.

Lean producers place a premium on skill formation, which results in a high degree of operational expertise. Rotation within and between teams is an integral part of career development. In addition, job rotation is viewed as necessary to develop the knowledge base needed to fully contribute to continuous-improvement activities, such as Quality Control circles or Kaizen teams. These improvement activities, however, typically occur at the end of the work day (on a "voluntary" basis, that is, no overtime pay) so that they do not take away from production time.

Lean producers engender incredible levels of employee commitment to productivity and process improvement through a system of reciprocal obligation between workers and their employers.[5] This system revolves around a belief that management is looking out for the best interests of employees and that employees will be rewarded for their dedication to the company through financial bonuses, employment security, and career development. Employee commitment is, therefore, based on loyalty to the firm; employees work hard and contribute ideas for improvement because it is their duty as a member of their corporate family. Although this expectation is clearly more prevalent in Japan, there are American companies (e.g., Procter & Gamble, Motorola, Polaroid, and Lincoln Electric) who have developed similar corporate cultures, which tends to mitigate the perceived Japanese advantage in work ethic.

There is growing evidence, however, that lean production might not be providing as challenging and fulfilling work for all employees as it did in the past. The Toyota Production System works well with a select group of employees (traditional Japanese workers and very carefully screened and selected American or European workers at Japanese transplants). As the Japanese work force loses its homogeneity, future employees may not identify as closely with the goals of the enterprise. As such, "belonging to the family" may not be as important and the reciprocal link may be broken. Furthermore, many young Japanese workers are less willing to work in physically demanding factory jobs. As a result, even Toyota is revamping its lean production system in its new Tahara plant in Japan to make working conditions more attractive to workers. As one journalist noted, "Ironically, many of the changes were inspired by Toyota's experience assembling cars in the United States."[6] Other Japanese firms are facing similar problems and several are beginning to experiment with the SBT model.

Small Business Teams

The United States began experimenting with the idea of small business teams in the late 1960s. While the best documented case is probably General Food's Topeka pet food plant, several other companies, including Procter & Gamble and Cummins Engine, began designing new work systems during that same time.[7] Over the past 25 years, numerous companies have begun redesigning their workplaces. Although each work system is designed around its operations' unique mix of process technology and work force characteristics, a U.S. model is beginning to emerge.

The "blue collar blues" of the 1960s raised the issue of boredom on the job. The initial response was to rotate workers across different jobs. Soon it became apparent that moving people from one boring job to another did not really solve the problem. As a result, jobs were redesigned to include a variety of different functional tasks, such as material handling, inspection, and, more recently, routine preventive maintenance activities. This horizontal loading of jobs, that is, job enlargement, provided task variety, plus an opportunity to identify with and be responsible for a larger portion of the operation and, thereby, better understand how the pieces fit together. The inclusion of quality checks also provided immediate feedback on job performance.

But job enlargement was, in many cases, insufficient to alleviate the root cause of worker disenchantment—American workers wanted more influence over their daily activities and wanted to have their skills and talents acknowledged. The result has been an ever increasing emphasis in the area of job enrichment, or empowerment, which began with the quality of work life and employee-involvement movements of the 1970s.

SBTs strive to provide *both* job enlargement and enrichment based on the assumption that if employees are organized into teams and each team is assigned all activities associated with a unit of production (or a portion of the process that has a logical beginning and end), they will feel more responsible for the cost and quality of their labor, because they have greater control over the entire process. Furthermore, by giving team members the necessary skills and information to competently perform their tasks, and then delegating to them the decision-making authority associated with the daily operation of the team, it is assumed that team members will be more committed to their jobs and ultimately more committed to accomplishing their team's production objectives.

Vertical job loading is, thus, a cornerstone of SBTs; team members assume many of the responsibilities typically assigned to line supervision or staff support. Often, this vertical loading is extensive, with as much as 25 percent of team members' time being devoted to administrative or business-related activities. For example, in addition to team members, trained as machinists, being responsible for setting up, operating, and performing minor maintenance on several types of machines within their team, they might also be trained to either monitor their team's cost and quality performance, assign work to fellow team members, or interview new team members. They would also be involved in team, or plantwide, improvement activities. Through the use of computer technology, team members, in facilities such as Timken's Faircrest, Ohio, steel plant, have been provided sufficient production, quality, and cost information to modify and improve the process within set parameters.[8]

A direct comparison of SBTs and lean production reveals important differences along the vertical and horizontal design dimensions. For example, a manager at a lean production Japanese automobile transplant operation in the United States, who had previously worked at a plant designed on SBT principles, observed that there was an equal amount of communication in both plants relative to sales and quality, but that lean production team members had a narrower focus in that they did not worry about suppliers or production control. He also noted that while lean production team members focused more on enhancing their process ability to modify the job, the SBT members had a broader understanding of the plant. In other words, lean production team tasks are generally traditional line responsibilities and do not tend to cross functional lines to the same extent as in the SBT model, where team members are typically responsible for their own material handling, etc. In addition, the lean production model focuses solely on the vertical task of process improvement and does not include such tasks as production scheduling or budget monitoring. The further broadening of horizontal and vertical job responsibilities within the SBT model provides the opportunity for greater depth of knowledge relative to integration across tasks.

With the added breadth and height of jobs prescribed in the SBT model, there is constant tension between maintaining the flexibility associated with being a generalist and retaining the necessary depth of expertise for each task. Many operations have addressed this by taking advantage of individual employee differences as to skills and job preferences—some people prefer being generalists, while others prefer knowing a specific task in detail. Initially, it was thought that every team member should rotate through all team tasks, both functional and managerial/administrative. Experience has shown, however, that rotation has costs (training, learning curve, etc.) which must be balanced with business needs and individual preferences and abilities. Differences in job requirements are often compensated by pay-for-knowledge-type pay plans.

The breadth, depth, and height of a typical SBT's skill needs typically far exceed the average employee and transcend even the best team members. Hence, in contrast to the three previous job design models, where *all* individuals are expected to learn and perform all the assigned tasks within their job scope or team, SBTs are comprised of a *group* of individuals who, in total, cover all the dimensions of the box, as shown in Figure 4-4.

The SBT model recognizes that it is, in most cases, humanly impossible and generally uneconomical to expect any one individual to possess in-depth knowledge of all the functional and managerial/administrative tasks assigned to that individual's team and to perform them. The success of the SBT rests on the combined skills of individual team members who, as a group, cover all the breadth, height, and depth job dimensions needed to manage and effectively perform their assigned duties.

There are often work situations that do not require the same level of in-depth task expertise associated with the apprentice model. In cases where in-depth skills are not needed on a regular basis, experts, such as electronic technicians, typically remain in a centralized support function to be shared across multiple teams. The SBT concept is being

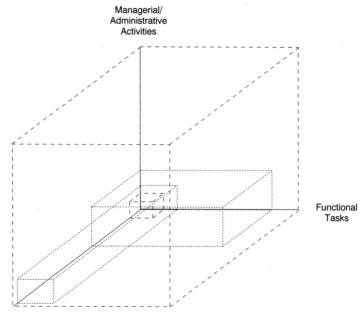

Depth of Knowledge

Figure 4-4. Small business teams as compared to the other three models.

applied in many of these support areas, as well. While skilled trades, a traditional stronghold of the apprentice model, generally retain and refine expertise in their primary craft, they are now becoming multi-crafted on basic equipment and facility upkeep and repairs. As a result, their operations reap the benefits of having flexible all-around generalists who retain state-of-the art expertise in specialized fields. Tradeworkers are also being given the opportunity to broaden their skills and take on greater areas of responsibility in the area of managerial/administrative activities.

The Competitive Advantage of Small Business Teams

What makes the SBT job design model superior? Although the apprentice model may have an edge in task expertise and lean production may excel in functional job rotation, SBT-based operations have found a way to maintain expertise while broadening jobs both horizontally and vertically to fully utilize diverse human brainpower. Furthermore, even the level of total job knowledge has been enhanced: While the apprentice model is skewed toward task expertise and lean production emphasizes operational knowledge and continuous improvement of production tasks, SBTs provide a greater opportunity to develop integration knowledge across the entire business.

SBT jobs have been designed to balance the development needs of individual team members with business and customer needs. In so doing, manufacturers have been able to capitalize on the American culture, which breeds individualism and diversity. This has led to significant competitive advantages in decision making, flexibility, costs and cycle time, and innovation.

Better, Faster Decisions

SBT managers who have delegated decision making cite speedier and better decisions. This is a result of letting the people who have the most knowledge about the workplace, that is, production workers, use that knowledge to make daily decisions. Eliminating the need to pass information up and down the hierarchy, minimizes time delays and data distortion, which occurs whenever information transfers hands. In addition, a broader business understanding gained through performing managerial/administrative activities leads to decisions that take into account the total organization, not only production. In other words, there is less risk of optimizing a specific activity to the detriment of the entire business.

Flexibility

By using nontraditional staffing (i.e., allocating a portion of team members' time to training or managerial/administrative tasks), employees can vary their daily tasks to match production load fluctuations. Furthermore, since employees are cross-trained in a variety of tasks, they can be reassigned to fill in for absences.

Reduced Costs and Cycle Times

Putting decisions in the hands of the knowledge holders also reduces the need for non-value-added information brokering and top-heavy organizations, which merely add costly overhead and increase the time for information exchange. By setting the team boundaries to include all tasks or functions required to perform the team's daily requirements, redundant or unneeded tasks and functions which occur within or across functional silos can be eliminated. This reduces both cost and time. In addition, increased team-member flexibility eliminates the need for calling in employees on an overtime basis to fill in for absent team members.

Innovation

The diversity of breadth, depth, and height of team members' skills also aids in problem solving and in the introduction of new products and processes. Organizations find that there is a competitive advantage in the multiple perspectives, which lead to both continuous incremental improvement and breakthrough thinking.

The American Edge

American manufacturing has come under attack for its general inability to motivate its work force. The criticism may have been valid in the past and may still be warranted in "traditional" work settings, but the country now has numerous examples of companies experimenting with and reaping the benefits of SBT work systems—and the number continues to increase daily. This, however, is not a uniquely American trend; companies in Europe and Japan are also experimenting with work systems based on the SBT model. But culture plays a major role in how well any particular work system performs. Here, the American culture provides a head start and, at least in the near term, a sustainable lead in the introduction of SBTs.

For example, sharing supervisory decision-making authority with production workers does not fit traditional Japanese ideology. As Ezra Vogel noted in describing Japanese ideology:

> Workers do not share in management. Management is often frank in sharing basic information about a company, but in the end the decisions are in the hands of management. This is considered necessary for timely and effective responses, and it is generally accepted that management is looking out for the interests of workers.[9]

An analogous cultural misfit exists in Germany. With a tradition of extensive apprenticeship programs, Germans have traditionally focused on the depth of knowledge dimension in designing jobs. Although this has led to a level of craftsmanship unequaled by any other industrial nation, it has also limited workplace flexibility and fostered professional elitism (not to mention, high labor costs). For example, in BMW's new plant in South Carolina, engineers will work alongside production workers on the factory floor, "something unthinkable in Germany."[10]

The United States also has a long tradition of people holding multiple jobs, often to increase their income, but sometimes just because they enjoy doing a number of different activities. For example, many hobbies turn into part-time business. It is also commonplace to find workers in the skilled trade (i.e., electricians, masons, or carpenters) who have set up independent contracting businesses at night or on weekends. Many of these moonlighting activities provide employees with valuable experience in running their own small business, which increases their ability and willingness to take on vertical tasks.

A final American advantage is the diversity of skills and individual job preferences within our work force. As described earlier, the SBT model depends on combining multiple individual skills and job preferences. Americans pride themselves on their individuality, and SBTs provide an avenue to more fully utilize their skills and knowledge. But exploiting the benefits of SBTs requires a new set of managerial skills and practices.

Making SBTs Work

Although the concept of SBTs is well known, such systems are far from widespread. The early experimentation with innovative work practices occurred predominantly in new plant start-ups. Increasingly, companies are beginning the conversion of traditional unionized factories. Those companies which have succeeded have had to transform entrenched traditional adversarial cultures and overcome significant organizational barriers.

Paradigm Shift

Scientific management, as applied in the United States, has led to an attitude that only managers and engineers possess the know-how to best design and manage the workplace. This assumption runs counter to the premise underlying SBT work systems, that is, production workers possess the ability to develop the necessary competencies to make intelligent decisions concerning their workplace. Furthermore, team-based operations require a long-term training investment to develop needed competencies along all three job dimensions.

Functional Silos

Another offshoot of scientific management has been the growth of narrow functional departments. As a result, critical knowledge about the production process has been dispersed throughout the organization. If decisions are to be made at the workplace, this knowledge must be transferred to the work teams. This requires redesigning the entire organization, not only production workers' jobs. The SBT model can also be applied to professional work as companies attempt to merge functions and reduce organizational layers.

Employment Security

The view that labor can be treated as a variable cost to be hired or laid off as production loads vary blocks any hope of developing employee commitment to business goals. Multiskilling, particularly along the horizontal axis, typically translates into fewer jobs (and less overtime pay). Operations that have been successful in transforming their work systems tend to offer some form of employment security, such as reductions only through attrition (often including early retirement).

Labor Concerns

Most of the early experimentation with SBT work systems occurred in nonunion operations. This has led many managers to assume that such systems work only in nonrepresented workplaces. Unions, on the other hand, are leery to endorse such practices on several fronts. First, new work systems are often viewed as a union avoidance tool or a vehicle to weaken the union's role. Designed properly, however, SBTs provide an opportunity for unions to increase their influence through the broadening of jurisdictional lines.

The union's institutional role also comes into question when rank-and-file members become involved in workplace decision making. It is unclear as to whether the National Labor Relations Act supports labor-management cooperation to the extent found in SBT operations (i.e., team members making daily decisions concerning the workplace). Hence, unions who do embrace new work systems are paving new ground; the American Federation of Grain Millers was one of the first unions to officially promote union partnerships in the establishment of "new work systems," their label for SBTs.[11]

Measurement/Reward Systems

Organizations which move toward SBT work systems find that many of their measurement and compensation systems reward "old" behaviors. Successful transformations require a complete overhaul of the management systems. This often includes a sharing of monetary gains.

Team Leadership

Achieving consensus in a team comprising diverse skills and personalities requires strong and adept leadership. Managers and supervisors must become better trainers, coaches, and leaders. In addition, they must also become knowledgeable in the multiple disciplines they are expected to manage. Although they do not need to possess in-depth task expertise, they need to have sufficient integration expertise to know whom to turn to for support.

Conclusion

SBTs are really not a new, revolutionary way of managing the workplace. But rather an old idea whose time has come. The idea of organizing around small entrepreneurial business units has roots back to family-owned business establishments. SBTs are also a logical extension of innovations aimed at humanizing the workplace, which date back to the Human Relations School and Western Electric's Hawthorne Plant experiments in the late 1920s. It is not surprising that SBTs have taken hold in the United States; they are fueled by the country's entrepreneurial spirit and the desire to have control over one's daily work environment.

As with other dimensions of manufacturing management, organizations are continually searching for a better way to organize the workplace to address the new requirements for manufacturing outlined in Chapter 1 of this book. By capitalizing on all three dimensions of the SBT model—functional tasks, managerial/administrative activities, and depth of knowledge, American factories can gain a head start on their foreign competition in creating commitment-based work, which generates continuous improvement and learning. The SBT model is evolutionary; it will continue to be molded to the needs of specific workplaces and their work forces. The beauty of the model is its flexibility to do just that.

References

1. James P. Womack, Daniel T. Jones, and Daniel Roos, *The Machine That Changed the World*, Rawson Associates, New York, 1990, p. 225.

2. For example, see Thomas A. Stewart, "The Search for the Organization of Tomorrow," *Fortune*, May 18, 1992.

3. Womack et al., op. cit., p. 225.

4. Y. Monden, *Toyota Production System: Practical Approach to Production Management*, Industrial Engineering and Management Press, 1993, pp. 69–70.

5. Womack et al., op. cit., p. 225.

6. David Thurber, "Toyota Plant Lures Workers with Amenities," *The Toronto Star*, February 22, 1992, p. H18.

7. Richard E. Walton, "How to Counter Alienation in the Plant," *Harvard Business Review*, November–December 1972.

8. Albert B. Bishop, Robert T. Lund, Anne E. Newman, and Harold Salzman, *Designed to Work: Production Systems and People*, Prentice-Hall, Englewood Cliffs, N.J., 1993.

9. Ezra F. Vogel, "Japan: Adaptive Communitarianism," George C. Lodge and Ezra F. Vogel (eds.), *Ideology and National Competitiveness: An analysis of Nine Countries*, Harvard Business School Press, Boston, 1987, p. 157.

10. Timothy Aeppel, "BMW Runs Risk With U.S. Factory Plan," *The Wall Street Journal*, June 26, 1992, p. A7B.

11. "The Grain Millers' Role in Creating Labor/Management Partnerships for New Work Systems: A Statement of Policy and Guidelines for Local Unions," American Federation of Grain Millers, Minneapolis, 1992.

5
Production Managers

Wickham Skinner
*James E. Robison Professor of Business
Administration, Emeritus, Harvard
University*

This chapter seeks to answer the question: Will production managers be an asset to American industry as the nation's manufacturing sector attempts to survive and regain lost ground in global competition? Since the production manager is a critical element in the success of every manufacturing operation, and our manufacturing sector appears to have let us down for several decades, questions about the competence of these managers cannot be avoided. Although generalizations about a large group of managers must be treated with caution, any appraisal of America's industrial potential must certainly include an evaluation of production managers as a critical element in our manufacturing capability, past, present, and future.

The focus of this chapter is on top-level production managers: manufacturing vice presidents, plant managers, and the top four or five managers in the hierarchy of line and staff of a facility. Our interest is in those who plan, establish manufacturing policies and structure, make major system design decisions, and bear the final responsibility for the production unit's performance. Today there are many questions being asked about these key managers.

First off, the major questions that loom before us are these: Have our top-level production managers really let us down? Is our 25-year industrial slide their fault? Is it partly their fault? Just how "bad" or "good" does history suggest that they have been, anyway? We look first at these questions and then examine what is going on now in production management and how it may change future competence levels.

This chapter concludes that ineffective production managers have indeed contributed substantially to our problems in being competitive in manufacturing. In their defense, it is also shown that these managers have been badly constrained and their effectiveness has been reduced by a hostile management environment and a limited set of inherited ideas.

When we look at the present and the future, the situation looks better. The reason for this positive outlook is that there is now going on worldwide an unprecedented revolution in concepts, managerial techniques, and production management innovations to which considerable evidence suggests that American production managers are reacting more energetically, imaginatively, and massively than managers elsewhere. Exchanges of information, visits, conferences, and professional literature lead to the conclusion that the sheer scale of experimentation, networking, shared learning, and relentless, determined application of new ideas is at its greatest extent in the United States and is not being matched anywhere else in the world. This evidence begins to support the conclusion that American production managers may now be on their way to developing into a genuine asset to the nation as it seeks to regain its lost competitive edge.

Historical Role of the Production Manager

With certain exceptions the last three decades have produced a generally dismal U.S. performance against foreign competitors in dozens of manufacturing areas of the economy. To what extent can the top-level production managers of this country be held responsible?

The case against these managers rests on poor quality and high costs, on being slow to market, and on being shamed by a variety of new managerial concepts and techniques developed and effectively used elsewhere, especially in Japan. This looks like a strong case and indeed it is, but it is only circumstantial. The truth is that industrial performance is determined by a great deal more than just the design and operation of factories. Let's take a look at the defense.

In The Defense of Production Managers

Great managers cannot manufacture competitively if factors out of their control are too negative. These external factors can be economic and/or political; they may be socially based; or they may be within the managers' companies but beyond their influence.

Such external factors include exchange rates and trade agreements between nations, credit availability for customers, and costs and availability of capital. And then there are, of course, those elements involved in determining the "levelness of the playing field": comparative costs of health care, subsidies of direct or hidden varieties, costs of insurance, such as product liability insurance, social security and other taxes, and trade policy.

A nation's traditional arrangements and relationships between industry, government, unions, and political parties can also create advantages or disadvantages for manufacturing firms. For example, Germany is felt to have an advantage because the various stakeholders tend to work together in a relatively nonadversarial and cooperative manner for their mutual benefit. Similarly, the Japanese record of close cooperation between banks and their related manufacturing companies and the government through the Ministry of International Trade and Industry (MITI) have clearly created competitive advantages that place many U.S. industries at a disadvantage. Cooperation between companies within an industry is prevented in the United States by government antitrust laws. With regard to companies and unions, the record in America is one of generally adversarial conflict. All these factors (and many others well covered in the current literature of international competition) tend to create conditions that are beyond the influence of production managers.

A second set of "noncontrollable" factors external to the company is social or cultural in nature. For example, the educational level and skills of employees certainly influence their value as workers. Language skills and attitudes towards work and employers vary greatly from country to country. Over a period of years such resources may be improved by investments in training and effective human resource management, but in the short run they create problems not quickly overcome. The negative attitudes of millions of Americans toward factory work due to generations of wretched working conditions, brainless job content, and autocratic organizational climates, come home to haunt today's production managers, who wish they could attract the best of our men and women into the factory but often see far from the best at the door to the personnel office.

With much justification, production managers contend that within their own companies there always have been and generally still are many negative factors beyond their control that prevent them from becoming competitive. For instance, my own research and case writing experiences document the inescapable evidence that top managements, beginning in the early 1960s in many industries, became enamored first with marketing, and subsequently with financial strategies and manipulations, which led to the development of conglomerates, a great spate of mergers and acquisitions, and a declining interest and competence in manufacturing as a competitive resource. Beginning in those years and continuing until about five years ago, production managers were increasingly cut off from the top managements of their companies, banished from top councils of the firm. The manufacturing function was considered to be a necessary evil, a voracious consumer of capital to be judged primarily on costs and efficiency. During those years morale plunged, capital equipment deteriorated and became outdated, and the more promising young managers avoided assignments to the production function.

There are other and continuing company-based shackles on production managers that exonerate production managers from a significant share of responsibility for lack of competitive results. Clearly, losses in market share can come from mediocre marketing competence, poor product designs, inadequate product line span, and bad engineering. And equally clearly, production can and often does have its hands tied by (1) outdated accounting procedures and reports, (2) capital budgeting that prevents the acquisition of equipment which might have created strategic advantage but did not promise to "pay for itself," (3) personnel department policies that cautiously but thoroughly discourage innovation and experimentation in human resource policy changes, (4) engineering department practices that keep production engineers out of product design, (5) products designed for strength or durability rather than manufacturability, and (6) engineering design procedures that add to lead times for new products by doing product design in sequence with process design rather than concurrently. These are but a sampling of problems at the "interfaces" that drive production managers to say "don't blame us!"

Production managers can easily be defended; they are certainly not the major villains in the decline of the U.S. manufacturing sector. But just how strong and capable have they been? They may not be the only villains, but they have been a weak link in a chain. Further, would more capable, more energized, confident, and persuasive production managers have been less victimized, shackled, and demoralized? Should production managers have provided more leadership within the corporation?

We shift now to a critical look at the performance of production managers in these three decades.

The Failure of a Profession

The profession of production management failed the nation during those decades. This may seem unduly harsh, but our top-level production managers did let us down. It appears now that their failures were threefold: (1) their ideas and techniques slipped out of date; (2) they failed to provide leadership within their companies and indeed to business management as a profession; and (3) they suffered a failure of spirit.

It is well known that these past three decades saw an explosion take place in the number of countries capable of competitive industrial production, starting in Europe and spreading to Japan and Asia. There were explosions as well in information technology, equipment and process technologies, and in professional management concepts and techniques. It was a wild set of times, steadily more competitive, and exciting with intellectual breakthroughs in the profession.

But it was not so for American production managers. For them these were discouraging and disappointing times, and in strange contrast to members of the same profession in many foreign countries, these turned out to be times of low intellectual growth. Instead of rising to the challenge, they went dead in the water, like a sailboat when the wind gives out.

In the early sixties the basic concepts of the profession were essentially derived from industrial engineering, focused around the objectives of efficiency and productivity, and conceptually tied to the "rationalizing" of production. These ideas had apparently carried U.S. industry to global dominance, but that dominance had not in fact come from those ideas nearly as much as from an absence of competition and the resulting large economies of scale. The illusion was dominant, however, and the profession's intellectual base changed little until, with alarmed desperation, it began to massively and indeed wildly import ideas from Japan in the eighties.

In the meantime, aside from beginning to use some mathematics in "operations research" especially in production planning and control, production managers were cloned by their seniors and taught time-and-motion study and Gantt charts in school. They continued to try to maximize output and minimize costs. These old cardinal tenets of productivity, and the steadfast devotion to "basics," came close to being a mind-numbing religion.

Meanwhile, quality was frequently abysmal. Customer service was a low priority, inventory turnover was slow, new products took forever to get in production and generally had all sorts of "bugs" when they finally came out. Mass production and economies of scale were being eroded by marketing-driven customer specials, customer delivery promises were often broken, and processes and equipment were increasingly out of date compared to new plants in Germany, Japan, and Asia. Employees were uncooperative, unions ran rampant, and the companies were dominated by new concepts in finance and marketing. It was a bad scene, yet somehow production managers plodded along in their old tracks, with limited ideas and managerial techniques, little experimentation, and declining results on their major performance measure, productivity.

It was most of all a failure of ideas, both as to their development and to their use. The new ideas either came from Japan or were old ideas such as total quality management, which the Japanese imported and then applied with furious intensity. We employed few of the new ideas offered, even from the outpouring of those concerning employee morale and participation. There continued an operational point of view with a short-term time horizon and virtually no realization of the potential of manufacturing as a competitive weapon. Here, too, good ideas were available but were not assimilated, due apparently to the continued dominance of the notion of productivity, a limiting success criteria isolated from the notion of customer satisfaction and competitive strategy.

The idea of time as a performance criteria also failed to catch on, and even financial measures such as sales per asset dollar paled in comparison to the obsession with cost and worker efficiency. It amounted to a limited view of manufacturing as a competitive weapon, and for most of those decades that was the nature and practice of the profession. Few production managers fully knew and understood marketing or corporate finance or corporate strategy. The lack of finance skills and understandings of such concepts as "present value" rendered them powerless in fighting for much-needed capital appropriations. And being unskilled and unsure in marketing and strategy allowed them to be cut off from the customer and top-management councils. They could not contribute at those levels of abstraction.

It was still men, machines, and materials for them, their traditional, well-worn "bag," when the world of professional management had expanded its horizons tenfold. It should be added that academics in the field of production management also had a bad three decades and, with some exceptions, contributed little, hanging tenaciously to the heritage of industrial engineering and its intellectual base of measurement and mathematics.

There was a failure of spirit in those times. It was discouraging. Results were bad, criticism was rampant, and the profession was proving no route to the top. Self-confidence suffered from poor results to be sure, but also from feelings of inadequacy in handling discussions involving modern finance, marketing, and strategy. The production managers often felt like "clods" at meetings with vice-presidents of finance and marketing. As one manager explained, "There was nothing I could say or contribute. It was all too fast. They jumped all over the place. I couldn't keep up." And he added with real despair, "This happens all the time."

As I followed this developing scene in the 1960s and 1970s, I saw rising discouragement among production managers and the resulting mixture of anger and despair. They could see that they would never make it to the top and felt inadequate in management outside the factory. Even in the factory, life was rough, dominated by finance and engineering and encumbered with inadequate, ancient accounting systems. Restricted by top management and by personnel rules regarding what they could and could not do with employees, many just gave up. The plants got older and dirtier, competition got stronger; these managers were always fighting fires and on the defensive. Spirits failed.

Recent Changes in Industrial Management

When, somehow, our production managers finally began to regain their traditional attitudes of "we can fix anything" and confidence in late-in-the-game comebacks, their responses to uphill playing fields, adversity, pressure from top managements, and competitive decline add up to nothing short of a genuine renaissance in industrial management. After two decades of lack of support from the top and banishment from top-management councils, reinstated and pressed to restore a competitive edge, American production managers have rebounded with an astounding display of energy and revitalized enthusiasm. During the past few years there has been more experimentation, more innovation, more change, and more sustained determination to improve U.S. performance than in any decade in industrial history. Those are strong statements, but the evidence supporting these contentions is massive. This vast outpouring of effort and subsequent accomplishments can be described under the headings: (1) concepts and techniques, (2) experiments and results, (3) changes in academia, and (4) outside resources.

Concepts and Techniques

Figure 5-1 lists 33 concepts or techniques widely employed in U.S. industry in the past 10 years at an ever-increasing rate. Some of these

Production Management Concepts and Techniques

Just-in-Time (JIT) Kanban Inventory Management
Materials Requirements Planning (MRP, MRPII)
Flexible Machining Systems (FMS)
Flexible Machine Centers
Computer-Aided Design (CAD)
Computer-Aided Manufacturing (CAM)
Computer-Integrated Manufacturing (CIM)
Total Quality Management (TQM)
Zero Defects Program
Statistical Process Control (SPC)
Quality Circles
The Doctrine of Continuous Improvement
Benchmarking
Group Technology
Cellular Manufacturing
Manufacturing Strategy
Concurrent Engineering
Design for Manufacturability
Supply Chain Management
Technology Management
Management of Technological Innovation
Simulation
Value Analysis
Flexible Manufacturing
Agile Manufacturing
Lean Manufacturing
Manufacturing Information Systems
Product Realization Management
Time-Based Management (TBM)
Employee Participation
Nonsupervised Work Groups
Employee Empowerment
Activity-Based Accounting

Figure 5-1. New or rediscovered concepts and techniques widely used in production management today.

techniques or ideas are old, some are new, some overlap with others, some are Japanese or foreign in their origin, some are American, some are narrow, others are broad. The significant fact is that with few exceptions most of these management concepts and practices were rarely employed in American factories before the eighties. Now to one degree or another they are in wide use. Moreover, the proliferation of approaches is an extraordinary phenomenon in the history of management. In the last hundred years there have been only two periods anything like what is happening now, and each is modest in comparison. The first such period was at the end of the last century and is known as the birth of scientific management. Led by Frederick Taylor, managers were taught to measure, standardize, improve every detail, and plan. The idea was to rationalize production, and this had an enormous impact on industrial practices and subsequent economic history. The whole notion of management as a profession was spawned from these notions of measuring, planning, and rationalizing production.

The second period of major industrial change occurred in the decade of 1935 to 1945 when industrial engineering produced a spate of refined techniques, such as advanced time-and-motion study and the use of standards for planning and control of factories. The focus was on Taylor's rationalization and the tight control of workers.

While extremely important in industrial management history, neither of these periods compares in the slightest with what has been going on in U.S. industry in the eighties and nineties. The number of new ideas and practices and their sheer breadth and variety are on a scale of magnitude far greater than before.

The new era goes far beyond the focus of Taylor and industrial engineering. The new ideas and practices range from those affecting costs and productivity of workers to information management, scheduling and inventory management, quality, automation and mechanization, organization structure, employee participation and empowerment, computer integration of all functions, integration of engineering and purchasing with manufacturing, and indeed to concepts which call for the end of many of the old formal functional departments and barriers!

This sweeping renaissance is driven by thousands of managers, professors, and professional consultants; its motivating power is the sheer excellence of global manufacturing competition which is devastating the world's largest industrial nation. This renaissance is transforming an industrial age by an explosion in ideas and experiments utterly beyond and unlike any in the history of industrial management.

The list in Figure 5-1 is extraordinary not only because of its length (and surely many readers will find their favorite new idea missing and, thus, would like the list to be longer) but also because of its rich variety. These activities and experiments range from extending and revitalizing old industrial engineering techniques, such as the doctrine of continuous improvement, to big and way out, yet probably ultimately essential, ideas of totally reorganizing and reconceptualizing the factory and the whole industrial organization, such as product realization, which essentially eliminates the practice of organizing by functional departments.

New ways of planning and controlling production—including revolutionary ideas about inventory as an evil instead of an essential buffer between operations—make up one large and influential category of concepts. This would include, for example, JIT and MRPII. When successfully applied, these techniques drastically change not only inventory levels but lead times, cycle times, and job contents.

An entirely different concept reenergizes the old industrial engineering ideas of rationalizing every micromovement of worker and material. Under the new paradigm, the planning and improvement of setup time is modernized and updated into a major effort called *shideo shingo*. Its proponents consider it most fundamental and the key to successfully reducing lot sizes essential to just-in-time inventory management.

There are a raft of approaches to improving quality. Of all the newly applied techniques, those in the quality category are certainly the most widespread in their actual penetration. They include the cost of quality approach, quality is free, total quality management, zero defects, process control, and statistical quality management techniques. The impacts of these managerial programs on entire organizations are profound. For example, zero defects in products produced requires excellence in worker skills and training, which requires changes in recruiting and selection, supervision, and compensation. It requires excellence in product design, equipment, and process technology; excellence in production planning and control; superior communications inside the organization and outside with customers; and so it goes. The entire organization—its procedures, premises, performance measures—all have to be retooled to move from producing merely fair product quality to becoming competitive in global markets by allowing zero defects.

The application of electronics to control and precision, advanced automation and mechanization, computer controls, and system integration are rapidly changing manufacturing technologies. Moreover, the objectives of automation have shifted from merely saving labor to increased flexibility for short runs with more customer specials, repeatable processes with total control of quality, and rapid new-product development and introduction.

The people side of the manufacturing operation is receiving much attention on the solid premise that in most manufacturing firms the large proportion of workers are fully using neither their minds nor their efforts toward making their firms more competitive. There are thousands of innovations and experiments going on ranging from nonsupervised work groups to group technology and totally reinvented human resource management systems. Jobs are being redesigned, generally increasing the span or content of each worker's performance. Workers are being given more voice; they are being empowered to make more decisions and use their own judgment. Daily and weekly meetings among employees are encouraged for self-managed performance progress and problem solving. Unions and informal employee councils are being given information previously considered proprietary, including management reports to employees on financial and competitive positions.

Perhaps some of the most revolutionary changes have to do with the relationships between the manufacturing and those functions at its interfaces—engineering, personnel, accounting, marketing, and finance. Efforts are being made to make products more manufacturable and to reduce the length of the new-product development cycles. These efforts drive the organization toward more concurrent engineering techniques, which allow for manufacturing and engineering to be working on design and process planning of new products simultaneously and which involve constant teamwork, communication, and indeed exchanges of personnel for often lengthy periods.

In the area of accounting, the manufacturing function is developing nontraditional techniques, such as activity-based accounting, which relates costs to products and functional activities much more accurately than has ever been possible before. In the area of finance, manufacturing is developing new procedures for capital budgeting that surmount the limitations of "hurdle rates," which tend to knock out many strategic investments that are only marginal in projected paybacks.

In the areas of marketing, sales, and customer service, the emphasis has tended to be more on much better communications, closer relationships with customers, and an attitude of service throughout the whole "product realization" cycle. Old adversarial performance measurements are being replaced with organization structures that integrate the functions, eliminate functional barriers, and place a strong and vibrant emphasis on the customer. In some companies the old functions are actually being eliminated and replaced with flexible and frequently shifting teams organized around products, programs, or strategic objectives.

Manufacturing responsibility has often been delegated by top management who considered it too technical and detailed for them to handle themselves. Some top managements have now learned that they can understand, and indeed manage, the manufacturing function by using the concepts and techniques of manufacturing strategy, in which the whole manufacturing structure is designed to meet limited, focused but absolutely vital strategic objectives derived from the organization's competitive strategy. Top management's emphasis is on structural decisions—basic, expensive, and long lead-time decisions, such as the number, size, and location of facilities; make versus buy capacity; equipment and processes; and control systems. Hundreds of firms are discovering that using the manufacturing strategy approach, tends to focus the attention of the whole manufacturing organization on getting the fundamentals right and on the competitive realities.

The sense of vitality, experimentation, and urgency in the present manufacturing environment is wholly extraordinary. Nothing is sacred. The engines of change are fueled by the economics of historically unprecedented rapid changes in competition and by the technology of the computer, information science, and the plummeting of costs of solid-state devices, causing faster and deeper technological changes than ever before. These forces, adding impulse and power to each other, are driving industry in a whirlwind of ferment and change. Of substantial significance to this chapter is the growing weight of evidence that more of this activity is taking place in America than anywhere else in the world.

Experiments and Results

These new concepts and techniques are not at all limited to seminars, articles, and books; quite the contrary, they are being steadily and widely introduced into actual industrial practice. With so much going on, there are very few measures of the penetration of these concepts. It is clear, however, that the economic and technological forces cited above are driving managers to make changes and experiment, not just think about it. At industry seminars and professional management meetings, the agendas are full of success stories. Granted we more often hear of successes than failures, but the sheer magnitude of well-documented "how we did it" testimonials is impressive evidence that many companies have been investing in actually trying to change how they manage their factories.

It is beyond the scope of this chapter to describe case histories of the efforts and results of companies making these changes, but suffice it to say that there are hundreds of such examples. Probably the top three techniques in actual practice are TQM (total quality management), JIT (just-in-time) inventory and scheduling techniques, and DFM/CE (design for manufacturability and concurrent engineering).

Company executives eagerly appear at university seminars and consultants' presentations to present their success stories, with dozens of slides and well-prepared lectures. The mail received by managers and professionals in the field is crammed with dozens of such opportunities every week. The University of Dayton, for example, puts on several such extravaganzas every year, in which about three dozen speakers from generally prominent firms give enthusiastic talks about their great success with the various concepts and techniques listed in Figure 5-1. The show goes on, but it is not just for show. On about three dozen overheads per speaker, the facts and results are there; the data is spread out for all to see—lower costs or higher inventory turns or a shortened new-product development cycle have been achieved.

Changes in Academia

In the academic world, that intellectual territory called "production and operations management" (POM) went flat in the late 1940s after World War II and offered little or no leadership to the practitioners for the next 30 years. The single clear exception to this was the development of manufacturing policy theory by McClean, Miller, and Rogers at the Harvard Business School in the fifties. These ideas on manufacturing strategy were subsequently expanded and codified by others, including me (and hence a probable bias for readers to discount). These ideas spawned a great number of books and articles and an enthusiastic and successful practice in industry; but the penetration of these practices was small.

Overall it was a dry and barren period with reliance on squeezing the last refinements out of time-and-motion study, the development and application of standards, and controls and reports focused on worker efficiency. These ideas plus "economic order quantity," a limited mathematical approach to one small element of production control, were of little use to practicing managers in the sixties and seventies in stemming the tide of declining market shares of many U.S. industries.

In the classrooms, interest in POM courses also shrank. Many prominent MBA schools even gave up requiring unhappy students to take POM as a required course. Second-year electives were frequently dropped due to declining interest by students, who naturally wanted courses with more intellectual challenge and courses related more clearly to their probable career paths in marketing and finance. Faculties seriously questioned whether POM really belonged in an intellectually challenging and relevant MBA curriculum.

All this has totally changed in the last seven years. The extraordinary revitalization in this dormant field of production and operations management can be ascribed to five factors:

1. Japanese success with both new and old ideas—concerning inventories and shop floor control (such as JIT), rigorous and totally invested quality management, and the notion of controlling every element of every process—clearly reenergized a lot of bored academics.

2. The sheer desperation condition of many U.S. industries made POM important to companies and, therefore, important to deans and professors and students.

3. The enormous growth of knowledge and useful practices in information technology had a stimulating impact in POM and the factory, with applications as simple as real-time job order control to the complexities of CIM (computer integrated manufacturing).

4. The profuse generation of dozens of new production technologies, ranging from lasers to flexible machining centers, robotics, new approaches in metal cutting, and automatic on-line testing.

5. The increasing interest by the faculties of MBA schools in the concept of manufacturing strategy. (Again Skinner's bias slips in, but in 1991 there took place two major conferences in which a total of about 110 papers on manufacturing strategy were presented, which is impressive evidence that a broadened, strategic, competition-focused approach to the subject is needed and useful.)

POM is booming in many U.S. academic centers. At Harvard, POM recently attracted more students to second-year electives than any other area, including finance and marketing. The first-year course had the highest student ratings for educational benefit of any course during the past several years. There is a new professional society, the POM Society, recently organized and now flourishing. In many schools there are more doctoral students in POM than in many decades.

The growth of important academic literature in the field is equally impressive. Scores of new books on production management are being published and the professional journals and business magazines, such as *Fortune, Business Week,* and the *Harvard Business Review,* regularly and increasingly are printing a wide variety of POM articles.

Manufacturing roundtables, where academics and practitioners get together to exchange experiences and ideas, are springing up all over the country. The Boston University Roundtable, which was the first of these exchanges, has been particularly useful in its publications, which compare managers' plans and objectives from the United

States, Europe, and Japan. Gone are the days of academic isolation as the POM sector of academia has found itself in the heart of reeducating first itself and now thousands of practitioners. Executive seminars are generally flourishing, especially where academics have learned to make their ideas relevant.

It is a new day and a hotbed of excitement; activity flourishes in the formerly sleepy, worn-out world of academic POM. As the necessity of excellence in manufacturing for survival in global competition became obvious, the revitalization of the POM area of academia in the United States followed. It has been a belated phenomenon to be sure; although academics in professional schools usually lag events in the real world, the energy and vitality in POM academia finally reawakened has become a positive resource for American industry.

Outside Resources

Another American phenomena has been the entry into the POM field, of the major consulting firms, such as McKinsey, Bain, Boston Consulting Group, Management Analysis Center, and Booz Allen, and the subsequent amazing growth of POM activity they have generated. These firms have been better known for work in corporate strategy, organization, finance, and marketing than in POM. But every one of these "boutique" firms, staffed with men and women of extraordinary abilities, has developed excellent POM skills and abilities. They have each in their own way formed useful approaches to manufacturing problems; Management Analysis Center (now Gemini) focuses strongly on manufacturing strategy, Boston Consulting Group on time-based management, and McKinsey on reducing functional barriers around manufacturing. Added to these elite general management consulting firms, who in effect have added manufacturing competencies to their product line, are such outfits as Arthur D. Little and A.T. Kearney and United Research, who have always been known for their POM focus and experience. These firms, as well as many others, now add to their useful bag of skills, concepts, and techniques in total quality management, concurrent engineering, technology management, and equipment and process technology. A spate of new or revived firms such as Rath and Strong, Pittiglio, Rabin, Todd and McGrath, and Ingersoll Engineers add a large second tier of smaller, more specialized POM consulting firms.

One further element, and one of great importance, is the aggressive and successful presence of the big accounting firms, such as Coopers Lybrand, Peat Marwick, Arthur Andersen, and the others. They have all added large consulting divisions, and without exception they have developed extremely large POM consulting staffs. Coopers, for example has more than 750 consultants in their international manufacturing practice, and much of this work is done for American companies. The derivation of these skills and client applications began naturally enough in internal control systems and inventory management. This led to production planning and control, cost and product cost controls, computer integrated systems, TQM, and so forth.

The work of these consulting firms spread like a grass fire to cover all of manufacturing, then back into engineering management and forward into distribution systems and customer service. The focus of these firms was on "systems," and while in the beginning this was somewhat limited in practicality, it was just what was needed once it was realized that close to 90 percent of all people costs are related to and derived from information demands and information handling. This is their "bag," and their contributions to POM in this country—especially because of the large scale of manufacturing and markets here and our preponderance of overhead rather than direct labor costs—have been substantial and growing.

Thus the POM consulting industry in this country has become astonishing in its size and energy and in the wide variety of firms. They are all generally flourishing, with plenty of business in manufacturing strategy, TQM, JIT, MRP, FMS, CE, and other special concepts and techniques. All these goodies are being gobbled up by thousands of worried companies and near desperate managers of production.

Often not thoroughly considered, and frequently driven by smooth and sophisticated salesmen for consulting firms, nearly everybody is "doing something." This is of course not all good, but it is energetic and optimistic. Cures are being undertaken, experiments are being underwritten, and lots of learning is taking place. Expensive education? Yes, often, to be sure. But it is learning and it is producing intellectual and street-smart growth.

A new generation of POM managers is being formed, right now, and these hungry, well-fed consultants are doing much of the teaching—and learning! In my opinion, there has never been anything like what is happening now in mass problem solving, application of concepts and techniques, and development of a new wave of professional managers.

A New Environment for Production Management

For 30 years production managers lived and worked in a steadily deteriorating environment. At work they played second fiddle to the heads of marketing, finance, and engineering. They were not considered to have (or to need) much knowledge of finance, accounting, marketing, the competitive situation, or even product engineering. In the realm of corporate literature, production was considered routine: Any company can produce the stuff. Producing it is straightforward. The important and exciting management challenges were assumed to be elsewhere. As mentioned earlier, top management gradually lost interest in production operations and several generations of top managers came into power with generally little background, experience, or interest in POM.

During the past five or six years, some of this environment has changed. There is still usually a dearth of personal experience in POM at the top, so it takes persistent education and explanation to get across needs and problems, but the mood is typically much more one of interest, support, and concern. There is widespread recognition that excellence in manufacturing is essential, and as a result, production managers are finding it easier to get investment money and support in their normal, everyday tugs with marketing, sales, accounting, personnel, and finance. They now have a more or less equal chance of getting the resources, systems, time, and information that they need.

In many companies TQM programs have vaulted POM managers into importance as leaders for quality performance throughout the company. In companies such as Copeland (a subsidiary of Emerson), Appleton Paper, Nucor Steel, Harley-Davidson, and in Chapparral Steel where manufacturing strategies have vaulted the firm into international market leadership, the role of production is unchallenged as the key to winning in competition. While there is a great range in the power and influence of production managers in manufacturing firms, it is clear that the environment, which is far better than in many decades and is steadily improving, gives the production manager a fair chance to do a good job.

Key success factors in manufacturing are in rapid change in most industries, and these factors are themselves changing what it takes to be a successful top-level manager of production. Recapping what is generally well known, the game is changing in the following ways:

- The levels of acceptable productivity, quality, lead times, inventory turns, new-product development cycle times, product offerings and customer specials, return on assets, sales to assets ratios, delivery reliability, and customer/warranty service have all risen dramatically in the last decade as a result of the pressures of global competition and new management and process technologies, which make new minimum levels both necessary and possible.

- Successful managers of production have learned that their jobs are no longer confined to designing and managing a production facility.

Those production managers who are playing the new game are managing—or playing a major part in managing—the whole product realization cycle. They must influence product design so that products are designed to be manufacturable at low cost. They must require that the product and the process are designed concurrently instead of sequentially. They help accountants to develop new activity-based costing systems. They help information systems experts to integrate scheduling and shop floor controls. They help sales and marketing to plan and coordinate customer needs with production imperatives, thereby effecting customer-winning manufacturing strategies. They help top management with manufacturing strategy. They help design, delivery, and logistics managers to extend factory service right to the customer and use of the product. And they help finance-based capital budgeters to pave the way for strategic investments in equipment and process technologies. The job of POM is broad, covering the whole firm, and it is long in time scale, moving four or five years ahead in scope while still focusing on costs and customer satisfaction today. The job is no longer just specific and literal; it is conceptual and it demands an ability to design. The job of the production manager has changed from housekeeper to architect, and from nursemaid to statesman. The game is a new one, and everywhere in the world, the winning players must be a whole new breed. The question for American manufacturing is whether, and how fast, we can develop new players for the new game.

The New Wave of Production Managers

For the three decades of decline in U.S. manufacturing, our production managers were a serious part of the problem. Now new ideas, a new supportive environment in top management and in academia, and the resources of consultants are creating an entirely new American wave of leadership for the production function. Success demands more organizational, political, technological, and architectural skills than ever before. This still leaves a number of questions to be answered or, at least, framed for analysis:

- Can it be expected that the underlying, long-entrenched weaknesses in the profession, which contributed to the decline, will be truly and fully overcome? Will there be a new generation of production managers sufficiently different from those of the past?

- If the production manager, this vital and important factor of manufacturing, does become an asset, rather than the liability it has been until recently, is this to be an American edge? Won't there be a new breed of production managers in all industrialized countries?

There is, admittedly, a great deal to be changed. There have been about seven generations of production managers who have been crippled by the obsession with costs and efficiency on which the profession was conceptually founded. About five of those generations focused solely on productivity; quality, production control, flexibility, time and asset management, and new-product introduction have been included in the must-do skills of the profession for only one or two generations. The concept of manufacturing strategy, linking manufacturing with corporate strategy, is only one generation old.

There is more to replace than worn-out ideas. As new concepts and techniques are being adopted more widely and broadly than at any time in industrial history, that need is being rather well satisfied. A set of debilitating characteristics of thinking, acting, and decision making remain to be changed or replaced.

Research and recent case studies demonstrate common traits and tendencies that disqualify many top-level production managers from playing well in the new game. These disqualifying traits include a rubberbandlike tendency to snap back from any training for longer-range thinking to focus on operational rather than structural issues and a short-term preoccupation with budgets, deliveries, and annual plans. Current case studies reveal a lack of consistency in the infrastructure decisions made by these managers because of these traits. As a result, the single most common problem in American plants is that of noncongruent and inconsistent structures and infrastructures. This results in an absence of focus and in plants not very good at anything, be it costs, quality, flexibility, return on investment, or rapid product change.

There is still a long way to go and optimism for the future has to be guarded because, as we all know, old habits and mind-sets usually die slowly. The cloning process is a dominating force by which the mind-sets and skills that succeeded in one generation are forced upon those of the following wave, who must conform and meet the expectations of their elders in order to be promoted. But there is a countervailing force at work as well, and that is the opposing biological Darwinian process of the survival and subsequent dominance of the fittest. Which process will predominate in America, Darwin or cloning?

The American Edge in Production Management

Study of the present scene leads to no other conclusion but that Darwin is winning and will continue to win. The biological metaphor is not synthetic; it is real. But what is happening is less the survival of the fittest and more the elimination of the unfit. The whole nature of producing goods in the world has changed so fast that noncompetitive manufactures get wiped out quickly. With new technologies of communication and transportation and with the expansion of free trade, there are few places in which to hide. Protected sectors of the market and unexposed niches are increasingly rare.

The result of alert, aggressive competition is a more rapid movement of production geographically to where it can survive. Where cost is critical production moves to low-cost areas. But those areas are becoming more scarce and their cost edge less clear, as developing countries all over the world increase wages and add social benefits so that their cost advantages shrink accordingly. The trend is for successful manufacturing in the advanced industrial nations to produce higher value-added products, using advanced and sophisticated process, information, and management technologies. Very high volume products, such as consumer electronics and standard textiles, migrate abroad. The survival of the manufacturer in the United States, Western Europe, and Japan depends on its ability to be a fast, agile, lean producer of very high-quality products.

The biological parallel is that when environmental change happens too fast for the organism to adapt, it dies, like the dinosaur, which was apparently wiped out by rapid climatological change. Production managers with old, limited ideas and mind-sets are being steadily wiped out today. Their firms are either downsizing and eliminating thousands of management jobs, cutting out organizational layers, going offshore, or going out of business. It is happening every day. The survivors are running their operations in an entirely different manner than before; those men and women are the brand-new breed. They have the long-range thinking, cross-functional skills, and strategic point of view now necessary.

This new breed of manager is essential in the high-value-added kinds of industries and products that are gradually commanding world markets. The big question is whether America will move faster than its competitors in developing this critical resource. There are encouraging positive factors and signs that this can happen. The very size of the country, its markets, the manufacturing sector, and the corps of production professionals all add up to a critical mass that supports rapid professional change and a condition of "everybody's doing it." It is this sheer size that creates opportunities for the thousands of consultants eager to train and convert managers to new, more effective ways. We have the academics, also awakened at last, writing papers, educating, giving conferences, all aimed toward increasing the skills and sophistication of this key group of production managers.

Another factor in the American edge is that as a result of the short-range focus of a stock market-driven top management the momentum for change started 10 years ago.

Another edge is certain attitudes in American factories. American production managers have some positive and healthy traditional attitudes toward their work. These tendencies and mind-sets are powerful and do not seem to change much. The first is that of being very responsive to what is asked of them. When top management and corporate America was coasting and looking elsewhere than manufacturing for competitive advantage, production managers responded appropriately enough by relaxing. They are also good soldiers, a bit simplistic as soldiers may be, but as soldiers they go full out in near-heroic style when the need is made clear. They are people of action as well. They do not believe in drifting when there are problems at hand. "Do something" is the value they share. They always want a program, a plan, a solution, or an experiment. Try anything. They will, as our soldiers always do in war when left on their own, innovate and grab for anything that seems to offer some sort of improvement. There is a strong belief among production managers at top levels that there are always answers and that anything can be improved. The ethic is that adversity can be overcome by hard work.

The American edge in bringing about sweeping changes faster in the development of the production manager also derives from the massiveness of our efforts, our markets, our manufacturing sector, our academic and consulting resources, and our knowledge base. The sheer weight and power of the production management revolution going on in the United States is not and cannot be matched for decades by any of our competitors. Many of our competitors are very good; many are ahead of us in many ways. However, there is no competitive area where development is happening on anywhere near the same scale, intensity, and rate of change as that happening in the growth of top-level production managers in America.

PART 3
Outsiders

6

Work Force Diversity

Sheila H. Akabas

*Professor and Director of the Center for
Social Policy and Practice in the Workplace,
Columbia University School of Social Work*

Lauren B. Gates

*Research Director, The Center for Social
Policy and Practice in the Workplace,
Columbia University School of Social Work*

The level of internal strife among contending groups within many major countries of the world is a phenomenon causing deep concern to most observers. For some, the end of the cold war appears to have provided license to renew age-old antagonisms, leading to armed aggression. The situations in the former Yugoslavia, and in and among the various republics of the old Soviet Union, involving the different ethnic groups, stand as prime examples. For others, technology has thrust together those who have always been sufficiently distanced to avoid conflict. In the mines of South Africa, members of different tribes must be housed separately and given different work assignments if open hostility is to be avoided.

For still others, political reconciliation necessary for long-term national development has eluded opposing groups. Tribal groups brought together to develop a new government for Afghanistan, or disparate religious groups in Ireland, have struggled, unsuccessfully, to fashion a national agenda. Elsewhere, most particularly in highly industrialized countries such as Germany and Japan, the pleas for equality and humane treatment are equally poignant and pervasive and have even become physically threatening. It would be difficult to imagine more internal strife among different ethnic, religious, gender, or racial groups than can be identified in even a cursory reading of the daily press.

What, the reader may ask, is the significance of this for a discussion of America's hidden assets in the manufacturing sector? These conflicts, which play themselves out at all levels—political, social, economic—have great impact on the workplace and the economic health of a country. An often repeated truism is "the world is getting smaller." Said another way, it is a widely recognized fact that diversity is everywhere and unavoidable.

International migration, the analogue for this last decade of the twentieth century, and beyond, and the search for empowerment by racial, gender, ethnic, aging, and other differentiated groups in society, make it essential, we believe, that a nation and its contributing parts be able to manage diversity effectively if the whole is to achieve success in the global competition for economic advantage. Diversity can be treated as a resource or a barrier to productivity. The competitive test for a particular workplace or economy is, or will be, the management of that diversity. We believe that the United States, and particularly its manufacturing sector, has a leg-up advantage in the management of diversity that will accrue significant economic benefit to it in the short run.

In important ways, managing diversity represents a reconfirmation of basic American values. As a nation we believe in fair play, in a level starting field, in equal opportunity for all, in the right, and possibility, that every American-born person can be a future candidate for the presidency. Although the interpretation of these values, when spelled out in individual situations involving specific governmental units or firms has made us uncomfortable, unsure of our direction, and often has been the subject of litigation, we have not abandoned our verbal commitment to those values. Most Americans are embarrassed by anyone who expresses an alternative view. The 1992 Presidential campaign included calls from all candidates for recognizing and promoting "us" and unity. In short, we are as decent a society as human beings have yet been able to advance, and that decency has been evident in the struggle to manage diversity.

The reader should not interpret the identification of this advantage, however, as suggesting that we have accomplished the acceptance of diversity needed to maintain an advantage or the level required to maximize the gains which well-managed diversity can offer. Over the long haul the favorable position will be assured only if our diversity continues to receive attention and positive reinforcement. We make a claim, however, that diversity is here to stay. Neither we, nor our competitors, can avoid its impact. The question we all face is whether it will constitute a drag on the economy or a resource. As a nation, we want to employ everyone, and to do so at a level that will maximize each person's productivity. We are challenged by how to do this, but we are paying more attention to it than any other nation is. We assume that the investment will pay off.

Throughout our history in the United States, the acceptance of racial differences has been the most elusive of the challenges, but there are a significant number of casualties among women, persons with disabilities, and the aging as well. The workplace, as compared with the housing market, educational opportunity, and more general social integration, has struggled with issues of difference most effectively, guided by legislation and, often, by trade union and corporate intent. As one looks around at achievements, the picture is surely mixed. But even in the worst-case scenario, American management meets the requirements of law—laws that are more demanding in their acceptance of diversity than those of any other country in the world. In the middle range, progress has moved beyond that, and in the truly successful efforts, the white male "cultural lock" has given way, allowing for the achievement of a competitive edge by the efficient management of diversity. A few companies, like Xerox, Avon, Digital, and Corning have led the way in this process.

Candidates for promotion at Xerox, for example, are appraised on their past effectiveness in managing diversity. Among companies other than those mentioned, local operations have achieved effective outcomes, such as neighborhood banks or a plant in a particular geographic area. The key fact is that American industry has joined the struggle. It has made an out-of-pocket investment in the training and evaluation of outcome. In this we are clearly a step ahead of the rest of the world. However, other nations, especially Japan, are likely to more quickly experience the labor shortages which will place a premium on their ability to manage diversity.[1]

The process is not an easy one. America has been managed by white males since its inception. It has been these males, in the first instance, who have had to develop the facility to value, respect, and include those who will eventually be their replacements. It is not surprising that many believe that diversity hinders productivity. At the beginning certainly, coordination may be tougher than for a more homogeneous work group, especially in tightly controlled environments. But the rewards of success are high.

This chapter will define diversity and review the concepts that support the idea that managing diversity effectively is an opportunity for competitive advantage. The diversity we are concerned about is inclusive—the varying racial, gender, age, and national origin groupings in the population. The discussion includes an analysis of the experiences of Germany and Japan and their responses to issues of diversity. We compare that experience with the situation and accomplishments in the United States. The chapter continues with an examination of the extent of diversity in the American labor force and the supports that exist at this time to promote the gains that diversity can offer. It concludes with a few case examples of American experience and suggestions concerning the next steps in managing diversity both in the individual firm and in the national arena.

Significance of Diversity and Its Management

Although only a few dimensions of diversity will receive specific attention here, the concept of diversity suggests that each and every labor force participant is *different* from all others in some dimension. Managing diversity represents an effort to celebrate and release the full creativity of those differences, be they of religion, gender, sexual orientation, physical or mental ability, ethnic affiliation, national origin, racial characteristic, cultural background, or life experience. It is obviously distinct from the concept of the melting pot, which seeks to co-opt new entrants to the workplace into the assimilated master model that existed there at the time of their entry. Managing diversity can also be distinguished from affirmative action, which is designed by a majority group (in the United States, white males) to *include* a "fair" representation of employees with other racial and gender characteristics but which does not guarantee fundamental change in the practices and procedures of the workplace to assure a maximum contribution from those new members of the work force.[2]

Consider the determinants of a firm's or a nation's economic position. They are the aggregate of the marginal productivity of each worker. The level of education, knowledge, and skill that individuals bring to the workplace is a vital ingredient of their potential to be productive. But so, too, is their *motivation* to work and their *commitment* to the work to be done. It is worthwhile to pause and review what we know about people's willingness to perform.

Three elements have been identified as contributory to effective outcome within organizations: namely, individual motivation, work group cohesiveness, and the commitment of both to organizational goals. There are many theories of individual motivation, but all have in common the understanding that behavior responds to the fulfillment of needs. Those needs have been variously identified as follows:

- Maslow established a hierarchy of needs from physiological, to security, affiliation, esteem, and finally self-actualization.[3]
- McClelland described a more specific formulation of the needs for power or affiliation or achievement.[4]
- Herzberg established a classification system that separates needs into hygiene factors (e.g., salary, security, working conditions) to eliminate dissatisfaction and content factors (e.g., challenge, responsibility, growth) to act as motivators.[5]

The significant differences among employees are reflected in their different needs. It follows that maximizing the contribution of each will require tapping into the needs of each, not unlike the importance of selecting the fertilizer that is specific to the particular plant that one is seeking to grow. A student can hardly complete a college sociology or psychology course without being exposed to these concepts. As a result, American management is well steeped in motivational theory, all developed by American sociologists.

Another well-known research-derived idea is the halo effect resulting from paying attention to workers and their needs. Ever since the experiments of the 1920s at the Hawthorne Western Electric plant, in which a group of workers was treated differently (though not necessarily better) than the remainder of the work force, and responded positively in relation to its productivity, we have known that group cohesion makes an important contribution to goal achievement.[6] Research has also confirmed that employees tend to be more satisfied with their work, and are also more likely to reflect a high commitment to achievement of group goals, when they are a part of a cohesive work group. Conflict among workers can divert them from developing cohesion. Recent experience has confirmed that an assimilationist model that denies difference has, as its by-product, individual rage and inability to cooperate.

For a significant period of our manufacturing history, we dealt with diversity by engineering the workplace. Known as Taylorism, the process of "de-skilling" jobs was undertaken so that workers became interchangeable.[7] During the period of industrialization when machine-paced work was paramount, this proved an effective means of utilizing an unskilled, often uneducated, multilingual immigrant labor force that willingly undertook any work in order to subsist. It was widely copied around the world. But the high technology of today's workplace, with "up-skilling" and job enlargement as the ingredients of a newly sophisticated production process, has meant the replacement of rote performance with a demand for problem-solving ability. Such workers, as Eli Ginzberg has pointed out, will accept only "good jobs."[8] Without new vistas in work force management the secret to success may elude a business.

Given the major distinctions among diverse groups in the workplace, the challenge to developing group cohesion is as obvious as is the well-documented need for it. Managing diversity has been the response to that challenge. Its goal is to help the workplace organize to accomplish group work, not stand in its way. Managing diversity hinges on the need for all members to appreciate each other's contributions; it fosters the desire to develop a cooperative work climate in which group members feel that their individual needs are met and that, therefore, each member can feel loyal to the group and to each other. Such a development allows the formal and the informal culture to be mutually reinforcing. Everyone can join together to promote group cohesion and productivity goals.[9] American workplaces have been promoting these ideas for a long time.

It is our contention that this past experience in managing diversity has fostered sufficient knowledge and skill development among American managers and workers that it gives the United States manufacturing sector just the competitive edge that the potential suggests. Further, we claim that there are a number of ways diversity contributes to that competitive edge. Consider the potential benefits of managed diversity:

- The improved quality of employees available when a manufacturer is attractive to all labor force participants because the firm is known as a congenial place for a diverse population of employees to work.

Job satisfaction surveys have confirmed that pay alone does not make a happy worker. Workers seek a sense of participation and personal accomplishment from their work, that is, they want good jobs. Any college placement office will confirm the interest in Digital that existed until its recent downsizing. Interview slots on Digital's recruitment calendar had to be allocated by a lottery system at most schools. The company's reputation preceded it. Students had not only read about the firm's efforts at creative inclusion and participative teamwork, but had reports from their diverse friends who succeeded in gaining employment there. It was the kind of place in which they *all* wanted to work.

- The availability of a labor supply that will perform the dull work inherent in certain manufacturing operations because their horizon is future- and family-oriented.

Loden comments, "The phrases...such as 'stronger work ethic' and 'getting one's hands dirty,' call to mind the image of the hardworking, first-generation immigrant. For the vast majority, hard work became the key to satisfaction and success. Because they are less politically aware, they are more likely to ignore politics in performing their work, and to use one set of standards to measure performance, regardless of whether it is their own or someone else's."[10] Immigrants continue to come in great numbers. The United States is alone in offering all such persons citizenship for them, their spouses, and children.

- The maximization of productivity because of a committed, cohesive work force that comes from valuing difference within the employee population.

Recent advice to managers is to pursue "management by walking around."[11] In this scenario "walking around" makes a manager effective because he or she becomes aware of how each employee feels about different situations. Management is able to be responsive to diversity. The concept recognizes that rational planning alone will not achieve productivity and, therefore, profit in the present era.

- The release of creativity and consequent development of innovative product ideas that reflect different consumer needs and desires, as understood by a diverse, committed, cohesive work force.

Marketing specialists have used mixed consumer focus groups for many years to test the viability of new products. Internal diversity allows the product to be *developed* by such a group, avoiding the shock that sometimes occurs when rationally planned product development fails to capture consumer interest. Diverse workers can also identify new consumers for a firm's product.

- The improved and more efficient problem solving that occurs when everyone's input is valued.

Experiments with problem solving that have compared outcomes with single-gender and mixed-gender groups, for example, have invariably confirmed that mixed-gender groups develop superior solutions, although those solutions may take slightly longer to be achieved. When people feel valued, they participate and the process is superior to the old militaristic methodology of a small group of commanders deciding on the battle plan and then ordering the troops to field it.

- The ability to sell in different markets internally and around the world that results from both the language facility and cultural understanding characteristic of a diverse work force.

It is noteworthy that the United States has become the largest exporter to Africa and that that continent constitutes our largest market. It seems logical that having the largest population of African descendants among our citizenry explains a major part of that success. The authors are aware that, as Eastern European markets are developing, companies are combing the ranks of their employees for those who speak the languages, and are aware of the cultures, within those countries. On the other hand, the popular press carries consistent complaints about the difficulty of entering the Japanese market, attributed in part to the complexity of understanding the Japanese culture.

- The increased organizational ability to handle change once the organization has struggled with, and introduced, the changes—structural, attitudinal and behavioral—needed to respond effectively to managing diversity.

Everyone is aware that the pace of change has accelerated geometrically in the recent past, and there is equally universal agreement that, "we ain't seen nothing yet!" There is also agreement that change is difficult for organizations and especially for large-scale bureaucracies that typify our manufacturing sector. As indicated throughout, managing diversity represents a *significant change* when compared to the usual human resource policy of "enter, then sink or swim, but please don't expect us to accommodate to you." Managing diversity can be a model for change. Once mastered, it can carry a momentum to help make other necessary change occur. It is, in short, an efficient strategy and a reusable achievement.

We started this section with the claim that the American Experience with managing diversity provides a competitive advantage. To understand the full impact of how the American approach offers an edge in world markets, we can juxtapose American values, as expressed through civil rights, immigration and employment policies, and legislation, against those of other major industrialized countries. The German and Japanese response (or, more correctly, lack of it) to diversity, sets the American advantage into sharp relief.

Work Force Diversity in Germany and Japan

Current immigration policies in Japan and Germany have, to varying degrees, intentionally limited the participation of foreigners in their societies. Japan refuses to provide legal recognition to the presence of most foreigners, that is, unskilled foreign workers cannot seek employment in Japan legally. The Immigration Control and Refugee Recognition Law restricts categories of legal employment for foreigners to commercial business, teaching, entertainment, technical assistance, and skilled labor. As a consequence, the official statistics show a very small foreign population in Japan. In 1985 there were 850,000 registered aliens, representing only 0.7 percent of the total population.[12] These foreigners are primarily Korean nationals who moved to Japan around the time of World War II. Additionally, it is estimated that there are thousands of unskilled foreign workers employed illegally, having come to Japan as visitors with no status or means of gaining legitimacy as labor force participants.[13] Most of these foreign workers are South Korean, Malaysian, Thai, Iranian, Taiwanese, Filipino, Pakistani, and Bangladeshi. Men find work primarily in manufacturing and construction. Women, on the other hand, work in the "water trade" as "hostesses," strippers, and prostitutes. It is estimated that only 12.5 percent of female migrant workers work outside of the "water trade."[14]

Japanese officials recognize the presence of illegal workers as testimony to the need for more labor by Japanese industry. In response, the law was amended in 1990. But the amendment reflects the Japanese policy of ethnic "purity." The law permits only foreigners of Japanese descent to work without restriction in Japan. As a consequence, the number of ethnic Japanese from Brazil immediately increased. Nonetheless, the law appears to have had its desired effect: The number of lawfully employed Brazilians of Japanese descent increased over fivefold from 1987 to 1990.[15] The amendment, however, did not stem the flow of illegal workers to Japan or stop Japanese employers from hiring them. Nor did the amendments deal with the issues of discrimination and exploitation of these workers. Because they are illegally present, the basic needs of unskilled foreign workers for job security and decent living conditions are unrecognized and unmet. These workers constantly feel fearful of detection and deportation. In 1990, 30,000 aliens were indicted for unlawful employment.[16] In these circumstances, it is doubtful these illegal foreign workers can be maximally productive.

Germany maintains foreigners as guest workers (Gastarbeiters), also rarely eligible for citizenship. Although allowed entry when needed by industry, they are without the rights and benefits of German nationals. Nor can they control their type of employment, place of employment, or length of stay. They have no mobility in the labor market; hence their allocation within that market is not optimal. The intent of the policy is to ensure that their residence in Germany remains temporary. If there is no job, the guest worker is expected to return home. Guest workers, unemployed for more than one year, are deported. It would be hard to imagine that these German or Japanese policies encourage productivity. Instead, we would guess, they leave the United States with the competitive edge.

Immigration policy in Germany focuses on economics. Immigration, when permitted, is in response to a labor shortage. Therefore, in 1973, because deteriorating economic conditions in Germany diminished the need for foreign labor, German officials brought a halt to immigration and placed a ban on employment of foreigners. The foreign population continues to grow through new births (who, unlike children born in the United States, cannot gain citizenship by virtue of place of birth) and the arrival of family members in Germany. The number of foreigners in the work force, however, has declined. Backes-Gellner and Frick calculated that foreigners represented 8.8 percent of the labor market in 1982, but 7.5 percent by 1987.[17]

The temporary status of guest workers and the uncertainty that accompanies their position does not encourage commitment to employers. Without the wages and benefits, opportunity for advancement or promotion afforded to nationals, and the ability to plan for their families' and their own futures, guest workers do not have the incentive to offer the optimal performance that typifies American immigrants.

Impact of Immigration Policies

The laws and practices in these two countries are in direct contradiction to the increasingly open quality of United States immigration legislation, which welcomes diversity. Immigration policies in Japan and Germany have caused a range of economic and social problems:

1. *The policies threaten economic health by restricting a needed supply of labor in the manufacturing and service sectors.* A large segment of the labor force in both of these countries is engaged in industry or manufacturing. The largest industries include steel, ships, vehicles, machinery, coal, and chemicals. In Germany 40 percent of all workers are in industrial jobs. Approximately one third (32 percent) of the Japanese labor force is in manufacturing and industry. Both percentages are

higher than that in the United States, where 25 percent of the labor force is involved in manufacturing.

Japan and Germany each experience a shortage of labor in services and manufacturing either because of a lack of workers or because their own nationals shun the available jobs. For example, in Japan the unemployment rate has dropped to 2.1 percent and, on average, for every person seeking a job there are 1.4 job offers. The situation is compounded by the fact that improved levels of education and earnings lead younger nationals to avoid manual labor and unskilled work.[18] Labor-intensive and small- and medium-sized companies are most affected. In 1988, 57 small- and medium-sized companies folded because they could not attract labor. In 1991, that number increased nearly sevenfold to 381. Even the manufacturing giants, such as Nissan Motor Company, Mitsubishi Motors, and Toyota, are struggling to fill labor shortages. For example, in an effort to attract workers, Nissan created a "dream factory" that replaces the assembly plant and paint shop with "pavilions" and the cafeteria with the "Harbor View Restaurant".[19] The hope is that the improved environmental quality will serve as a sufficient lure to potential workers who are reluctant to perform manual labor.

2. *These policies hurt productivity.* First, immigration policies in Japan and Germany foster discrimination against and exploitation of foreigners in the workplace.[20] Workers cannot look forward to citizenship and protected opportunities for themselves and their family members. Foreign workers typically work for lower wages and without health and other benefits. These workers may do the work, but they will not express commitment and loyalty to their jobs under such conditions. Second, migrant workers in Japan and Germany fill the least desirable jobs, those that nationals are less than willing to take. Foreign-born men most often find themselves in "3-D" jobs—dull, dangerous, and dirty. Such jobs, especially when they are handled as dead-end positions, do not encourage commitment to national goals or to the goals of the employing firm. Finally, the status of foreign workers makes it almost impossible for employers to establish work-group cohesiveness, even if they chose to emulate the United States in managing diversity. Native coworkers understand that foreign workers are temporary and, therefore, feel it unnecessary to accommodate to their differences. Native workers also feel that they are in competition with foreign workers for scarce jobs and resources. In Germany this sentiment has erupted into riots. Without cohesiveness among workers, commitment to achievement of group goals is impaired.

3. *The policies in Japan and Germany have led to an array of social problems.* The policies restrict access to housing, education, and health care

both implicitly and explicitly. Even when allowed entry, foreign workers are forced to live isolated from their families, who are denied entry, in substandard, deteriorated housing. They have inadequate access to medical care and education. The government policies carry a message to the citizenry that discrimination is tolerable and tolerated.

In short, the immigration policies in Japan and Germany, by not offering legal status to foreign workers or providing the opportunity of citizenship to guest workers, create tiered work forces that undermine group cohesion. Furthermore, the policies hurt the competitive edge of these countries by restricting a needed source of labor and by structuring the experience of foreign workers so that they have no incentive to perform their work optimally.

Women, Older Workers, and Workers with Disabilities

Women, older workers, and workers with disabilities are less welcomed as labor force participants in Japan and Germany than in the United States. Though workers from these groups have been assimilated to varying degrees, their participation is limited because of passive legal provisions and lack of enforcement. In both of these countries the problems are recognized; policies are articulated, but they have not resulted in solutions. For example, Haruo Shimada, a professor of economics at Keio University, comments:

> Corporate and social opinion is that workers are most useful from their late twenties to their early forties, and that the role of women is to assist men. These attitudes have been embedded in the system and reinforced by its perpetuation. Japanese business is incapable of responding to the recent changes that have occurred in the supply structure of labor, namely the shortage of young workers, the aging of the population and the entry of women into the work force.[21]

Japan passed the Equal Employment Opportunity Law in 1986 to reduce discrimination against women in relation to recruitment, employment, training, and retirement. Compliance with the law, however, is not mandatory. Women are far from approaching equal status to men. In 1989, average female full-time wages were 60.2 percent of average male wages (in the United States average female wages were 68.7 percent of male wages) and women do not have equal opportunities to advance. Many companies still limit their recruitment for clerical, sales, and technical positions to men. In Japan women comprise 85.3 percent of the part-time work force.

German women also face discrimination in the workplace. Although some protective legislation exists, Backes-Gellner and Frick quote one commentator who expresses its shortcomings:

> Community legislation has proved a necessary but not sufficient remedy against sex discrimination; while the Equality Directives have been useful in combating individual cases of sex discrimination, they have to date had no significant impact on the sex segregated labor market. In short, the socio-structural causes of sex discrimination lie beyond the reach of the existing Equality Directives.[22]

Like women in Japan, women in Germany tend to be in the service sector in occupations that reflect social stereotypes (most often in clerical jobs) and are characterized by low wages, unstable employment patterns, and little opportunity for advancement. Women are also significantly more likely than men to be in part-time positions. In 1984, 2 percent of men were part-time compared to 27 percent of women. Although some women may prefer part-time employment, such a large percentage probably represents underemployment rather than choice.

Following a demographic shift similar to that occurring in the United States, Japan and Germany are experiencing decreasing numbers of younger people and increasing numbers of older people. In Japan it is estimated that by 2010 25 percent of the population (31 million) will be over the age of 65.[23] Germany, too, is experiencing an aging labor force. Despite labor shortages or lack of skilled workers, older workers tend not to be well utilized in these countries. The economic burden of carrying a large nonproductive population will catch up with Germany and Japan even earlier than with the United States, unless they reverse their current policies.

Perhaps one of the clearest expressions of how cultural values operate to promote or limit labor force diversity is the employment policies for workers with disabilities. It is estimated that 5 to 10 percent of the working-age population in major industrialized countries is disabled.[24] Surely, the quality of life for these individuals is reduced when they are denied access to employment. Further, the economic costs associated with income replacement and health care are astronomical, spurring employers and legislators to find alternative ways to assist the working-age population with disabilities to maintain work connections.

To encourage employment of workers with disabilities, Japan and Germany have adopted quota/levy systems. Legislation defines the number of workers with disabilities an employer is obligated to employ (the quota) as a ratio of the total number of workers with disabilities to the total work force. If an employer fails to meet the quota, a levy is collected. When you think about it, you realize that a quota/levy system is a license to "buy out" from a firm's public responsibility. All it takes to be "rid" of the responsibility is to "pay off." How can anyone feel equal and valued as a member of a group covered by such provisions?

In Japan an exclusionary definition of the target population has been used. The population of workers with disabilities is defined as those who are employed or seeking employment—a relatively small percentage of the total number of working-age people with disabilities. Additionally, only recently have workers with mental impairment been included. Consequently, the quota for Japanese employers is very low (1.9 percent in the public sector and 1.6 percent in the private sector).[25] Statistics show that actual employment did not meet even this low quota. The actual private sector employment in June 1988 was only 1.3 percent.[26] It is estimated that more than half of Japan's employers pay a levy for failure to fill their quota obligations.[27] They certainly seem hesitant to include people with disabilities in the labor force.

The quota system has been more successful at employing people with disabilities in Germany. A 6 percent quota is required of German employers of more than 15 workers. As of 1987, approximately 800,000 workers with severe disabilities have been employed. Even with this success, the system is not without significant problems. In 1987, 70 percent of employers failed to meet their quotas and 30 percent were unable to list any workers with disabilities in their work force.

But something more significant seems typical of the quota/levy system. It does not try to change the attitudes and behavior of employers, supervisors or coworkers toward workers with disabilities. Additionally, this system does not try to maintain people at their usual work or at work commensurate with their skills. There is no suggestion of *equal* employment opportunity for qualified persons with disabilities. The lack of alternatives and flexibility creates a tremendous disincentive for workers with disabilities to seek employment. Finally, singling people out for a special quota does not intercept the attitude of employers that most workers with disabilities are not capable of maintaining normal employment, reinforcing the barriers to work for these people.

The quota/levy system stands in sharp contrast to the American efforts where policy embodied by The American with Disabilities Act (ADA) reflects the concept that all people have a right to participate in the mainstream of life including the world of work.[28] The American approach contrasts with sheltered work, which provides employment for people with disabilities outside of the mainstream in segregated work environments. Germany and Japan, on the other hand, are expanding this employment alternative, based on the belief that many people with disabilities can never be normalized.

In sum, legislation and practices regarding immigrants, women, older workers, and workers with disabilities in Japan and Germany work against equalizing opportunities and encouraging contributions by these workers, or they are relatively ineffective in overcoming cultural biases. (Differences in race do not generate a significant minority among workers in these countries.) The result is that productivity is limited by the lack of commitment of these workers to the workplace, a loss of skilled labor, a shortage of labor for the less desirable jobs, and the loss of a cohesive work force. There are further costs in relation to replacement and retraining and, in the instance of workers with disabilities, to income support and health-care costs.

As we turn to experience in the United States, we will see that we have made significant strides toward a more inclusive model by valuing, celebrating, and managing diversity. These exciting efforts represent a present and future competitive advantage.

Evidence of Managing Diversity

The Public Policy Arena

Legislation, as is apparent throughout this chapter, is the public expression of policy. Among the nations of the world, the United States has in its laws the earliest and firmest commitment to support for policies that promote equal opportunity both to emigrate to the United States and to participate in the workplace, and in the nation, regardless of personal characteristics. This legislative environment has been a driving force in encouraging business to come to grips with issues of difference among employees. For as Elias and Purcell have noted,

> Legislation can undermine the mechanisms which perpetuate patterns of gender inequality on two levels: it can improve women's *access* to the labour market and occupational opportunities, and it can seek to ensure the equal treatment of women and men *in* employment.[29]

The 1990 census confirmed that just under 20 percent of all Americans are foreign born. This reality reflects the operation of immigration laws as well as the positive way in which opportunity is viewed among those outside the United States, particularly in comparison with the situations in their own countries. Checkered though the provisions have been in relation to equal treatment, American immigration statutes have welcomed some entrants throughout our history. The most recent law, the Immigration Reform and Control Act (IRCA) of 1986, as amended, offered amnesty (i.e., legal entry) to all persons who could prove continuous residence since 1982, even though he or she had entered the United States without the legal right to immigrate (i.e., as an undocumented alien). It also contains provisions for family reunification and provides opportunities for immigrant status for people with needed skills, or those who are able to bring substantial investment into the United States, and others who queue to gain entry and are reached in numerical order. (At all times in our national history there have been special groups of refugees and asylum seekers who are exempt from numerical limitations.)

Under IRCA legislation, this last decade of the century is being characterized by a wave of legal immigration unequaled since the century's first decade. Most of these individuals enter the labor force. Whatever their basic motivation to work, their commitment to it is likely to be enhanced by their guaranteed access to citizenship status and by the promise that that status will afford to their children and grandchildren. Many bring valuable skills and knowledge to enrich the American workplace; others are willing to do necessary jobs that Americans choose not to perform.[30] As Senator Bradley has been reported to have noted, the work force's increased diversity "could be an enormous opportunity." It represents a plus for the economy for numerous reasons, including greater knowledge of languages and greater cultural affinities with markets overseas. Achieving this potential constitutes one of the imperatives driving diversity management.

The labor force, whether immigrant or citizen by birth, is protected by numerous statutes that encourage employers to hire and maintain a mixed employee population. The landmark legislation in this area was Title VII of the Civil Rights Act of 1964, which protected against discrimination in hiring, promotion, and discharge, on the basis of sex, religion, race, or national origin. Regulations have been issued by the Equal Employment Opportunity Commission (EEOC), and interpretations of both the law and the concomitant regulations have been issued by the courts over almost three decades. While the cases reflect employers' struggles with requirements, the outcomes have encouraged employers to find new ways to achieve compliance, again promoting interest in managing diversity.

Protection is also available to those who might suffer mistreatment because of age through the Age Discrimination in Employment Act of 1967. Except for a few exempt categories, (e.g., CEOs) workers may no longer be forced to retire on reaching a particular age. This means employers must engage their older employees in finding creative ways for them to contribute to the enterprise. Travelers Insurance has gone beyond that to create a pool of retirees who are "on call" for temporary work to fill in for any needs that develop. These Travelers' "temps" are knowledgeable concerning the workplace and are immediately able to pitch in, unlike the usual temporary worker sent by an agency.

The Americans with Disabilities Act of 1990 provides the same protection against discrimination coverage to otherwise qualified applicants and employees who may have a physical or mental disability. Its premise is that disability should not interfere with employment for "otherwise qualified" individuals who, with "reasonable accommodation" can perform the "essential functions" of the job. Even before this legislation many companies designed schemes to expedite the return to work of employees who may have become disabled. For example, Steelcase, a major office furniture manufacturer, set up a special work area where recovering employees can work, on flexible time schedules, repairing and cleaning the work gloves used by their fellow employees. Weirton Steel, anticipating the new skills that would be required as the mill computerized its production processes, brought workers experiencing disability back to work at the earliest possible time to train them in the use of computers.

Various state and local statutes have expanded these protections even beyond the levels defined by federal law. In all, a legal climate has been established which welcomes everyone to the workplace and expects that each person will be equally accepted. When combined with good business practices, that is, those practices that achieve the greatest productivity possible from each worker through work group cohesion and commitment to corporate goals, these legal requirements lead naturally to the diversity initiatives that have been developing.

Statistical Data

It has been said that demography is destiny. The once white male dominated labor force has been changing appreciably over the past two decades and promises to change even more in the future. The most remarkable of these shifts has been the increment in the percentage of working married mothers of children under the age of six, which moved from 18.6 percent in 1960 to account for 58.4 percent of all such mothers in 1989. It is noteworthy that the figures before 1960 were so small that the data was not even recorded separately. Women between the ages of 16 and 65 increased their labor force participation rate, from 37.7 percent in 1960 to 57.4 percent by 1989. Racial minorities, too, have vastly increased their proportions in the labor force. For example, the nonwhite share of the labor force, which was 11.1 percent in 1970, rose to 13.1 percent by 1985 and is projected to be 15.5 percent by the year 2000.[31]

The working population in 1985 included 7 percent immigrant workers, who along with nonwhites, accounted for almost a fifth of the labor force. More startling is the change projected to take place by the year 2000: of all *new* entrants to the labor force, 42 percent are projected to come from nonwhite and immigrant groups. More older workers will also be in the workplace. The median age of America's workers, which was 28 in 1970, is projected to be 36 by the year 2000.

Whether this increasingly diverse population will be a rich resource or a destabilizing, uncommitted force engaged in conflict and confrontation rather than cohesion and productive work is yet to be determined. Even in the past, the demography of the United States has certainly provided ample occasion for business executives, seeking to achieve a competitive edge, to develop skills in the effective management of diversity. Our measured progress to date may be the determinant of our competitive edge.

The reader, undoubtedly, has a nagging voice asking a hard question, to wit, "How can the relatively low earnings of women and minorities, and their inability to break out of their middle-management status, be reconciled with the claim that effective management of diversity has been achieved?" A twofold response is in order. On the one hand, we can all point to the Los Angeles riots, the glass ceiling, and intercultural conflicts. On the other hand, most managers are aware of the issue, a significant number of CEOs have made public commitments to managing diversity, and many work groups throughout the country are struggling with the meaning of the term.[32]

Furthermore, as reported in *The New York Times,* the gap between men's and women's earnings in the United States has been narrowing. From 1960 to 1980 the differential remained steady, with women earning 60 cents to men's dollar. This gap is clear evidence of discrimination in the labor market because only part of it can be explained away by lower educational attainment or by less work experience. By 1990, however, women's earnings had risen to 72 cents, and for younger women, ages 24 to 35, the figure reached 80 cents.[33] While women may not be "home" yet, these figures indicate an encouraging recognition of women's contribution and potential.

We suggest that this head start increases the attractiveness of working for American industry, and that as long as we remain on the cutting edge of the issue, we may continue to maintain our competitive advantage. The next section describes some of the American experience and suggests what still needs to be done to achieve the potential identified here.

Corporate Experience

The history of expanding the offer of opportunity reaches back, at least, to the passage of the Civil Rights Act in 1964. And yet, no one has identified a magic formula for achieving acceptance of diversity. Many organizations thought they were doing quite well when their recruiters went out and lured increasing proportions of persons whose differences were not well represented among the company's employees. But those new members were greeted with a welcome that included the suggestion that they not rock the boat. The message was clear: "Now that you are here, watch the way we operate, and learn how to fit into that."

It did not take long for the entrants to realize that it was uncomfortable to try to fit. One young African-American employed at a Fortune 100 firm told one of the authors, "They were so busy worrying about my hairstyle, they never even noticed the work I was doing. And I began to place more importance on keeping my hairstyle, as an expression of my personal image, than worrying about my work. Everyone lost out." The result was that the turnover rates equaled the recruitment rates. Rather than gaining from affirmative action, corporations were spending an estimated $50,000 to recruit and train each new professional only to have that investment walk out the door after an unproductive, blame-passing attempt at assimilation. The need for a better way became obvious.

As a recent Labor Department publication suggests, "Moving toward managing diversity calls for new rules for the workplace, new skills for managers, new ways to evaluate performance, and even new routes to the top."[34] Successfully reaching for diversity requires traveling an expensive and demanding road, marred with costly pitfalls and labyrinthian dead ends. Those companies that have traversed that road successfully are now beginning to realize an economic payoff. The road may not have been easy for corporate America, but therein lies the competitive edge, since a comparable experience seems not to exist in other industrialized nations.

Corning, Inc., is a successful traveler. It views its corporate headquarters, in the small town of Corning, New York, as a "global village." It has tried to have its work force mirror the global population, and its corporate culture incorporate that diversity. The experience of one of its scientist is telling: A Ph.D. researcher, the only geologist in her work group, suggested a novel research procedure, which grew out of her dissertation research, and was belittled by her fellow researchers, who were white men ignorant of her area of expertise. Management, sensitive to the reality that "threatened" men might react to an assertive woman in a way to thwart her creativity, promoted her to a better assignment in materials research.[35] To the men she left behind, the message was clear, and the behavior was unlikely to be repeated.

Corning, Inc., has made major revisions in its corporate vision. Its expectation is that employees who work in a "global village" will have a global outlook as a state of mind, fulfilling Corning's corporate slogan, "Imagine what we can do together." Each employee is expected to be skilled at communication, not just technologically but also interpersonally. The company instituted training for managers on gender interaction in the workplace and on racial diversity issues. The formation of groups and networks is encouraged. It has even financed a barbershop to serve the African-American community. Promotions and other rewards are linked to one's contribution to production, which is, in turn, reflected in one's effectiveness in managing diversity. Tucked away in its out-of-the-mainstream location in upstate New York, Corning needed to manage diversity for a very important reason. Its president has noted, "If we don't have the environment conducive to getting the best employees, we won't get them."[36]

For Avon Products, Inc., the issue was equally compelling for other reasons—it found its market changing and needed to stay competitive. Its president asked and answered a significant question: "Corporations and organizations of all kinds are awakening to the fact that a diverse work force is not a burden, but their greatest potential strength....Who can best understand and serve this changed [increasingly diverse] and changing market? Certainly not the 'old-boy network.'"[37] For Avon, this answer meant forming both a women's task force and minority task force to communicate with management and to act as support systems for women, African-American, Hispanic, and Asian employee networks.

As part of an overall effort to manage diversity Avon carried out research to understand where it was, and then formulated plans to reach the position it sought for itself. As an example of the new agenda, it recognizes that fairness is not treating everyone the same, (where it was), but rather treating each individual "appropriately," (where it wants to be). So, too, it replaced decisions made at high levels within the organization with "empowered associates making decisions at lower levels in the organization." In short, by managing diversity effectively, Avon is able to communicate more efficiently with its market and operate more productively in all aspects of its organizational functioning.

Xerox has been one of the most active companies in the search for a better way to handle diversity. The company has moved through the stages of affirmative action and managing diversity to a "balanced work force strategy." The concept recognizes that you cannot promote women and people of color from the bottom to the top without their gaining experience in the middle. The company identified a group of four "pivotal jobs" that anyone who reached the top had occupied at some time during his or her employment at Xerox. It purposefully moves women and minority group members into those jobs so that they have the knowledge and experience considered appropriate for eligibility for top managerial positions.

Wisely, Xerox's plan tries to head off any backlash resulting from its policy. It recognizes that balance requires fair treatment for all, including white males. It derived, and applies, a complex formula for its goal setting that combines eight factors. For each diverse population grouping the formula takes into account the available population in the company, labor market, and country weighted by estimates of the numbers from each grouping who have the requisite education and skills. Analysis indicated that white males were underrepresented at the entry level. Knowing that the feeder line must include sufficient numbers for the next levels to maintain balance, Xerox began a recruiting effort to attract white males. The company regards the issue of balance as not just necessary to meet government requirements but critical to Xerox's future success. As one vice president and general manager commented recently: "We know that the work force is going to continue to become more diverse by the year 2000. We have many more different employees and employee needs than we have had over the past years."[38]

The examples of corporate struggles with, and success in, managing diversity are countless. Each reflects back to the benefits of managing diversity itemized earlier in this chapter, which suggests that the gains to be achieved by managing diversity successfully are significant, multiple, varied, and idiosyncratic to a particular organization, its labor force, and its starting situation. As compared with the situation in the industrial nations with which the United States is in competition, our management of diversity provides clear evidence of our competitive advantage.

Conclusion

The true barriers to achieving a competitive edge in a global economy are suspicion, mistrust, intergroup rivalry, and armed hostilities. Conversely, the antidote is openness, trust, intergroup cooperation, and group cohesion. This chapter has asserted that the United States is closest to that idealized model by virtue of its leadership position in managing diversity. An aggregate of forces has encouraged this leadership: legislation, national values, population pressure, and corporate experience. In comparison with our major competition, management in American industry is best prepared to recruit the most skilled and committed immigrants to our country and then to utilize them, and all other members of our diverse population, in making the manufacturing enterprise second to none in international competition. Our diversity, when well managed, will improve recruitment, reduce turnover, empower and enable employees to be effective and efficient self-managers, decrease the need for costly supervision, and ensure that our products and market approaches are responsive to the needs of the equally diverse global market.

References

1. A. Pollack, "Japan Lures Auto Workers with 'Dream' Factories," *The New York Times,* July 20, 1992, A1, D2. The writer indicates that because Japan severely restricts entry, manufacturing sector employers are unable to meet their need for factory workers.

2. R. R. Thomas, *Beyond Race and Gender,* AMACOM, New York, 1991.

3. A. H. Maslow, *Motivation and Personality,* 3d ed., Harper & Row, New York, 1987.

4. D. C. McClelland, *Human Motivation,* Scott Foresman, Glenview, Ill., 1985.

5. F. Herzberg, "One More Time: How Do You Motivate Employees?" *Harvard Business Review,* 65, 1987, pp. 109–120.

6. F. J. Roethlisberger and W. J. Dickson, *Management and the Worker,* Harvard University Press, Boston, 1939.

7. F. W. Taylor, "The Principles of Scientific Management," in J. M. Shafritz and J. S. Ott (eds.), *Classics of Organization Theory,* 2d Edition, The Dorsey Press, Chicago, 1987, pp. 66–81.

8. E. Ginzberg, *Good Jobs, Bad Jobs, No Jobs,* Harvard University Press, Boston, 1979.

9. U.S. Department of Labor, "Managing the Move to Diversity," *Labor Relations Today,* VI(6), Jan/Feb/Mar 1992, pp. 1–2.

10. M. Loden, *Feminine Leadership or How to Succeed in Business Without Being One of the Boys,* Times Books, New York, 1985, pp. 106–209.

11. T. J. Peters and R. H. Waterman, *In Search of Excellence: Lessons from America's Best Run Companies,* Harper and Row, New York, 1982.

12. T. Hirotaka, "Immigration Reform for an Open Society," *Japan Echo,* XIV(4), 1987, pp. 19–24.

13. H. Shimada, "Now Hiring," *Look Japan,* August 1990, pp. 8–10; The Japan Institute of Labour, "A White Paper on Women Workers," *Japan Labor Bulletin,* 30(2), February 1991, pp. 1–2.

14. M. Selby, "Human Rights and Undocumented Immigrant Workers in Japan," *Stanford Journal of International Law,* 26, Fall 1989, pp. 324–469.

15. The Japan Institute of Labour, op. cit., pp. 1–2.

16. The Japan Institute of Labour, "A Record-high of 14,000 Foreigners Forced to Leave Japan: 30,000 Unlawful Employees Indicted," *Japan Labor Bulletin,* August 1991, pp. 3–4.

17. U. Backes-Gellner and B. Frick, "Discrimination in Employment in the Federal Republic of Germany," *Georgia Journal of International and Comparative Law,* 20, 1989, pp. 105–121.

18. H. Shimada, "The Labor Shortage and Workers from Abroad," *Japan Echo,* XVII(1), 1990, pp. 57–62.

19. A. Pollack, op. cit.

20. M. Selby, op. cit.; S. Hickox, "Labor Market Needs and Social Policy: Guestworkers in West Germany and the Arab Gulf States," *Comparative Labor Law Journal,* 8(4), 1987, pp. 357–397.

21. H. Shimada, "Now Hiring," *Look Japan,* August 1990, p. 8.

22. U. Backes-Gellner and B. Frick, op. cit., p. 105.

23. T. Ishii, "Growing Old," *Look Japan,* April 1991, pp. 10–11.

24. *Employment Policies for People with Disabilities: Report by an Evaluation Panel,* Organization for Economic Cooperation and Development, Paris, 1992.

25. Ibid.

26. Ibid.

27. M. Brodsky, "Employment Programs for Disabled Youth: An International View," *Monthly Labor Review,* 133, 1990, p. 12.

28. S. Akabas, L. Gates, and D. Galvin, *Disability Management: A Complete System to Reduce Costs, Increase Productivity, Meet Employee Needs, and Ensure Legal Compliance,* New York, AMACOM, 1992.

29. P. Elias and K. Purcell, "Women and Paid Work: Prospects for Equality," in A. Hunt (ed.), *Women and Paid Work,* London, McMillan Press, 1988, p. 218.

30. "The Immigrants—How They're Helping to Revitalize the United States Economy," *Business Week,* July 13, 1992, pp. 113–122.

31. W. B. Johnston, *Workforce 2000,* Hudson Institute, Indianapolis, 1987.

32. J. P. Fernandez, *Survival in the Corporate Fishbowl,* D.C. Heath, Lexington, Mass., 1987.

33. S. Nasar, "Women's Progress Stalled? Just Not So," *The New York Times,* Section 3, 1 October 18, 1992, p. 10.

34. U.S. Department of Labor, op. cit.

35. P. T. Kilborn, "A Company Recasts Itself To Erase Bias on the Job," *The New York Times,* October 4, 1990.

36. C. Skrzycki, "Bringing a Bit of City to the Company Town," *The Washington Post,* August 12, 1990.

37. R. R. Thomas, op. cit., pp. ix.

38. R. A. Friedman, *The Balanced Workforce at Xerox Corporation,* Publishing Division, Harvard Business School, Boston, 1991.

7
Women
Managers

Lyn Tatum Christiansen

Julie H. Hertenstein
Founding Partners,
The Argos Executive Group

Let me tell you about [Elaine]. She is acting plant manager for one of our plants right now and is just doing great. It was a terrible mill: the morale was terrible; the quality was so bad that the cost of [rejects] was 49 percent of sales. There was sabotage—a fire was set in the mill....Management was autocratic and there was no communication between groups. It was altogether a terrible environment.

Corporate woke up, removed the general manager, reassigned the mill manager to a job as a technical adviser and brought in Elaine. After six months, productivity was up 100 percent, quality was way up, morale was way up, participation was way up. The hourly workers were beginning to admit that things could be different.

Elaine isn't out of manufacturing, she had worked in HR and Finance, but she has excellent management skills and people skills, and that's what was needed. She listens, but don't mistake it, she doesn't just listen, she acts on what she believes is critical. She trusts people; but she makes sure big and little things that people say they'll do get done. She has an open door and means it. Communications in the plant are way up. But she is not a cream puff, she deals with the hard issues. She fires people and disciplines where necessary. But firing must be seen as fair—fairness is such an issue with her. She brings more integrity, honesty, and fairness to the job than anything. [**Manager, Quality, Fortune 100 Manufacturing Company**]

What's most unusual about this story isn't the disastrous business situation, nor the steps taken to turn it around. Rather, the story of Elaine, the acting plant manager, is striking because it illustrates a company that discovered that its women were a valuable addition to the pool of resources from which to draw managers with skills to solve critical problems in manufacturing. Although most manufacturing companies have traditionally looked to men to manage manufacturing operations, this chapter shows that many women managers in manufacturing also possess critical leadership skills needed for their companies' continuing prosperity.

In this chapter, we allow women manufacturing managers to present, in their own words, the skills contributing to their effectiveness including: a willingness to sublimate ego needs to meet important goals, a concern with the details of the process by which tasks are accomplished, and a focus on individuals and the quality of the relationships among members of a work group. The significance of the skills we will discuss lies in their usefulness for accomplishing tasks considered crucial for successful manufacturing operations in the 1990s—tasks such as building teams and developing cross-organizational linkages. In such circumstances, women managers provide a tremendous resource for filling manufacturing's need for a more multidimensional and strategically oriented leadership. By assigning women managers possessing the skills discussed here to solve critical problems, companies can leverage the opportunity they have in their women managers.

Why Women Manufacturing Managers?

At this point, some readers are wondering why they should take the time to read about women manufacturing managers. It is true that there are men who possess these skills too; however, companies traditionally have looked *only* to men as the source of skills necessary for manufacturing management. Many companies may not be aware of the numerous women who also possess skills and training necessary for meeting manufacturing needs. If one is not used to looking at women managers as sources of these skills, it is easy to overlook valuable potential. By failing to recognize this potential in women manufacturing managers, valuable assets are being underutilized. Just as hordes of cash should not be allowed to remain underutilized in non-interest-bearing accounts but should instead be invested in assets which yield substantial returns, so too should women with valuable skills be utilized in contexts where their skills are most needed and can be leveraged to greatest advantage.

As demand for effective manufacturing managers continues to grow, expanding the resources available to fill this demand can provide companies with advantages over competitors in the United States and abroad. Therefore, increasing the utilization of women managers in manufacturing is desirable for at least three fundamental reasons, outlined below and elaborated in the sections which follow:

1. Women, due to their historically low participation in manufacturing management, are a hidden resource that can be utilized to significantly expand the pool of highly qualified employees from which to draw leadership and innovation.

2. Women bring new perspectives to manufacturing, and the existence of diverse perspectives is valuable in many problem-solving situations.

3. Many women managers possess skills necessary for successfully meeting critical manufacturing needs.

Untapped Talent

The educated, experienced talent available for manufacturing management could be expanded by tapping the resource represented by women. Women now represent over 45 percent of the work force.[1] Further, women with the most education, and hence greatest potential, have the highest labor force participation. Projections indicate that the number and proportion of women in the work force will increase through the year 2000.[2] From a national perspective, including women in the pool of candidates for management positions increases the number of potential managers and the amount of talent to draw upon.

A key source for qualified new managers in manufacturing is trained and experienced managers from the company's nonmanufacturing departments, such as marketing or finance, or managers from other companies. Although the proportion of women managers in manufacturing has historically been quite low, the proportion of women managers in other functions has been significantly higher, thus providing a sizable pool with managerial experience.[3] Not only are these women experienced managers, but they have leadership skills appropriate to line positions.[4] As we will see later in this chapter, women from nonmanufacturing functions have performed well in manufacturing leadership roles. Another source of new manufacturing managers is the nonmanagement work force; here the numbers of women have increased dramatically.[5] A third source, which has less experience but high potential, is hiring women directly from college or graduate school.

One issue facing any attempt to utilize women more often is whether they are prepared. From a national perspective they are. Women are educated. Women now earn over half the bachelor's and master's degrees and one third of the doctorates. Women are approaching 50 percent of the MBA degrees earned and are increasingly opting for professional and managerial positions in manufacturing industries.[6]

Further, women are educated in fields valuable to the manufacturing workplace. It is a myth that women have only liberal arts backgrounds. Many women are educated in math and science, fields traditionally considered relevant for manufacturing. The kinds of knowledge and abilities needed to be effective in manufacturing are changing and increasing in variety, however, as manufacturing tasks become more complex and production processes become more computerized and electronically rather than mechanically controlled. Women are now highly represented in all fields except engineering and even here the number has increased steadily over the last 15 years.[7] Thus, women represent the range of expertise that will be required to meet future manufacturing needs.

As yet, women are not highly represented in manufacturing management. Given the qualifications, experience, and numbers of women available, they could be a significant factor. Indeed, their historically low participation increases the potential impact of their inclusion. If women's participation in manufacturing management increased to the level of their participation in the overall work force, the pool of talented candidates available for manufacturing management would nearly double. Tapping this heretofore underutilized resource has many attractions, including the opportunity for U.S. companies to gain an advantage over companies in other countries and to retain this advantage for a substantial period. The U.S. advantage results from having lower structural barriers to the use of women in manufacturing management than other major industrial countries and from the existing U.S. lead in utilizing women managers. We will look briefly at the situation in the United States, Japan, and Europe.

Barriers and Incentives
Compared

Evidence suggests that while some social adjustment will need to occur in the United States if there is to be greater utilization of its women managers, this adjustment will be notably less in the United States than in Europe or Japan. The United States has many structural incentives in place which can ease the task of attracting and retaining women in the manufacturing sector. Some of these incentives are externally imposed and thus more fragile, but others are part of the culture of the United States.

External incentives include legislation, such as equal employment opportunity and equal pay, and legal decisions supporting women's rights in the workplace. Momentum is building for additional external incentives, for example, federal support of day care. Manufacturers are beginning to join in support of these initiatives; in 1988 the National Association of Manufacturers backed federal legislation to support the establishment of day care.[8]

Cultural factors supporting women include general acceptance of women working full-time throughout their adult lives; increasing availability of day care; growth of formal part-time, flextime, and job-sharing programs; growing recognition of the changing racial, ethnic, and gender composition of the work force projected by the year 2000; and increased understanding of the value of a diversity of role models at all management levels.

The United States leads most European countries and Japan in the proportion of women in the work force by only a small margin.[9] The U.S. lead increases significantly when the proportion of *women managers* is compared to that of other countries, however.[10]

The proportion of women in the work force, and presumably of women managers, is expected to increase in most European countries and in Japan.[11] Yet, despite recent trends and legislation in many countries to end or reduce discrimination against women in the workplace, there remain many barriers to their participation. Examples of these barriers are Japan's Equal Employment Opportunity Law, effective April 1, 1986, which asks employers to "make efforts" to treat women workers equally with men in recruitment, hiring, and promotion, but provides no penalties for violators; the United Kingdom's laws against the use of quotas in hiring and employment; and strong preferences by men in some cultures, such as West Germany, that their wives not work.[12]

The United States, therefore, has the lead in utilizing women as managers. Existing structural barriers and incentives in the industrialized countries suggest that this lead will persist despite recognition by some other countries of the potential available from increasing their female work force and their stated desire to catch up. Since the United States could increasingly utilize women in manufacturing management, we need to consider the value these women would bring to manufacturing beyond simply increasing the pool of available talent.

The Value of Diverse Perspectives

Manufacturing continually faces the need for fresh insights, innovation, and solutions to vexing problems in order to meet—or beat—increasing competitive pressure. More ideas for new directions and better solutions to problems come from diverse groups, when those groups are well managed. As the CEO of Bell Atlantic recently stated:

> The diversity of America's labor pool is the key to beating the competition. If you take a roomful of Carnegie-Mellon engineers like me, you're going to get a particular slant on solutions. But with a diverse group in terms of race, age, and sex, you'll get a much better array of options.[13]

Diverse perspectives occur along dimensions other than race, age, and gender; they also occur because of ethnic or cultural heritage, educational background, or the specific work experience of individuals.

Women bring different perspectives to problem-solving efforts in manufacturing management. First, they bring the perspective of a new gender to a management group which has historically been male. For example, in many industries, women are more likely to have personal experience as the purchaser and consumer of a company's products than their male colleagues.

Further, women add another dimension to manufacturing management because there is a greater chance that their work experience differs from that of male manufacturing managers. Rather than spending the majority of their career as line managers within manufacturing, women spend more time as managers in staff, marketing, and finance functions, as we illustrate later in this chapter. The variety of experiences brought by women to manufacturing are an advantage because they provide enhanced understanding of the business as a whole, and of where and how to make needed interfunctional connections. Further, having spent a relatively brief time in manufacturing, there is less chance that women managers have internalized long-standing assumptions. Because they are not captives of tradition, they can more easily reexamine long standing—but perhaps no longer appropriate—practices.

Finally, women, as outsiders, bring fresh insight to an enterprise in a fashion similar to that of immigrants. (See Chapter 8 for a full discussion of immigrant characteristics.) Indeed, women managers and executives often refer to themselves as immigrants in U.S. corporations, because of the problems they confront and the advantages they bring to the workplace. As a female ex-CEO of a Fortune 500 company explained—to Lyn Christiansen in a 1990 interview:

Women are mirrors of the culture just as immigrants are. As new immigrants, they reflect the culture and respond to it in different ways. People came to the United States and really thought this was going to be the land of milk and honey and really thought the streets would be paved with gold. But 15 seconds after they arrived, they knew that the streets were not paved with gold and there was no milk and honey. Some couldn't take it and went back home; some stayed and were miserable; and some said, "Wow, what a challenge!" I don't believe it's so very different for women...I am by nature a change agent, and I knew that I would face enormous challenges personally. I wanted to face those challenges however, and that's what makes me like those immigrants that stayed and embraced their new world.

Meeting Critical Needs of U.S. Manufacturing

Bringing more women managers into manufacturing will add a rich resource for U.S. companies because the specific kinds of skills and talents many women managers have are particularly relevant to and important for meeting several critical needs in U.S. manufacturing companies for the 1990s. To support this contention, we must first understand what these critical needs are.

Increasing the competitiveness of U.S. companies is a popular topic; many authors have identified needs which must be addressed to turn around what they consider a deteriorating situation. Using the needs defined by respected researchers of manufacturing and operations, we highlight those needs that increased participation of women managers in manufacturing will most directly and usefully support.

There is a need for improved strategic and organizational linkages in manufacturing. For example, among the top five action plans on the agenda of the majority of U.S. manufacturing firms responding to the 1990 Manufacturing Futures Survey are "linking manufacturing and business strategies" and "developing interfunctional work teams."[14] In another study, describing the ideal manufacturing role in a "world class" company, Hayes, Wheelwright and Clark identified seven factors each of which had cross-functional attributes:

[In a world-class company] business unit strategy is based on information and issues provided by *all functions*; communication of strategy is *across functions* and organizational levels; there is deliberate *integration of functional strategies*; capabilities are consciously developed in *all functions*; numerous *cross-functional* teams exist;

talent is developed and located in *all functions* and combined with frequent lateral movement and *cross-functional* training; and general managers are drawn from *several functions* whose composition changes over time. [emphasis added][15]

They observe that these characteristics are not common among U.S. firms. Indeed, these needs reflect the central limitations that past management practices have placed on our manufacturing companies.

A New Breed of Manager

Leading researchers in manufacturing have noted that "the problems faced by American industry are largely the product of inadequate management...their solution requires a different approach to management. Specifically, it requires a different mind-set toward manufacturing and technology."[16]

"The new rules (of the competitive market place) require new players, or at least players with different skills, attitudes and beliefs. Manufacturing leadership...will be more successful if it can...see the factory as an instrument for competitive success, handling a continuous shifting of manufacturing tasks as changes [occur] in technology, the competitive situation, and the firm's competitive strategy."[17]

The answer for U.S. manufacturing companies is superior management. Superior management means the ability to innovate and to accept innovation particularly in organization and process areas; it requires an enhanced ability to solve problems effectively and efficiently; it calls for imaginative leadership who can handle a great deal of change, variety, and organizational learning.[18]

The answer for U.S. manufacturing companies is not just an issue of individual managers. According to a major study from M.I.T., the answer also "requires a change in company culture that encourages and supports participation, teamwork, and decision making at lower levels of the organization."[19]

In our research and experience working with companies on these issues, we have observed that women provide one source of the new energy and mind-set required in manufacturing and a proclivity to create the kind of flexible culture called for by manufacturing experts. To better understand the skills that women manufacturing managers bring to their work, and how these skills fit the needs claimed crucial for the reemergence of the U.S. manufacturing firm, we talked to women currently holding such positions, seeking their insights as they reflected on their jobs and careers.

Women Managers in Action

Our goal was to learn from women who currently were manufacturing managers and to gain their perspective on what they had experienced. When trying to discover new ideas in any discipline, it is important to listen to those whose experiences differ from the norm. The nine women interviewed were carefully chosen to represent a wide range of work experiences.[20] Thus, the experiences these women reveal reflect opportunities which are widespread. It is likely that these women are fairly effective in their roles, both because of the high levels to which most had been promoted, and because many were recommended to us by their colleagues. By seeking the insights of these women on their own experiences, there is a risk of self-reporting bias. Although this is possible, prior research suggests that women are more critical in evaluating their own performance than their male superiors are when evaluating them.[21]

We discovered numerous consistent themes in their responses, despite the variety of companies, industries, and parts of the country that these women manufacturing managers represented. Although we will discuss the themes we uncovered, because what we heard from these women was so compelling, we will let them illustrate the themes by telling their stories in their own words. The themes that characterized situations in which these women were particularly effective were building teams and using organizational and strategic linkages.

Building Teams That Work

Building teams, especially interfunctional work teams, requires managers who draw out, recognize, and encourage good ideas from all team members despite the possibility that these ideas will often diverge. No longer is the manager the one who "knows it all." Contributing to building and leading interfunctional work teams is a style characterized by some researchers of leadership as interdependent, connected to others and responding to them in their terms, as opposed to autonomous, separate from others and following nonpersonal procedures. Many women use an interdependent approach, as Belenky et al. found in their study of women students.[22] Other research has noted that interdependent leaders believe and value the fact that the people they lead are different and hold different opinions. Under their leadership:

> Plans of action emerged from the careful encouragement of a group's participation in articulating and "voicing" these differ-

ences and their ideas. In that process, listening is an activity of competence—following the reasoning of people, weighing ideas against other ideas, including one's own, and developing new options...[Also] at work...are other competencies:...most importantly, having a stance toward the self that allows the leader to hear and encourage others not at her own expense but with a special sense of relation to them as a leader.[23]

We observed that the women managers interviewed attributed their effectiveness in building teams to three factors: sublimating their egos, focusing on team dynamics, and focusing on team members.

Sublimating the Ego when Working with Teams

Most of the women managers we interviewed believed that to build effective teams, managers must encourage others to take initiative and provide leadership. This means not only that team members must be encouraged to provide their own ideas, but also that the team leader must objectively consider these ideas without preference for his or her own. Sublimating the ego does not mean that these women lack pride in their accomplishments, but rather that they view hearing and encouraging the contributions of others as an accomplishment.

[**Director, Technical Operations**] I don't have a big ego. People are very comfortable around me. I'm not just sitting there behind my desk saying to people "do this" and "do that" either. I'm out there doing it with them.

[**Director, Manufacturing**] We are building formal teams around materials issues. In fact I would say that I have been asked to do that because my bosses have always been able to count on me for it; I am consistent in my ability to build a good team. I am not out for myself first, but the team first, and they can count on me for that. I think the ability to lead teams well is a function of ego. To do it well you must sublimate your ego to the results. I think that, at least for the women [I consider my contemporaries from graduate school], with the kind of assumptions we began with, we tend to sublimate ego more [than men].

Focusing on Team Dynamics

The women manufacturing managers carefully chose their actions to facilitate team dynamics that were effective at eliciting contributions from all members. Including all members of a team in the generation

of ideas and then listening carefully to these ideas is central to achieving an optimal range of constructive solutions to problems. Nearly all
of the women we interviewed identified inclusion and listening as key
skills that made them effective in this role. Further, once the ideas had
been heard, these managers responded with encouragement and support for the workers' choice of actions.

> [**Manager, Engineering and Plant Services**] I am able to bring
> advantages to this organization because of my gender. Women are
> more approachable. All of my [direct reports] are male, but their
> people will bring me issues, for example, difficult medical issues. I
> am better able to listen and not judge. This is true for any sensitive
> issue. Yet, people view me as being tough, not soft or sweet.
>
> Women must establish relationships, must use every way to get
> the work done. They must involve everyone—anyone—they need
> help from all sources. By including everyone, they get everyone
> working, and thinking.

> [**Director, Technical Operations**] Many of [the people I work with]
> are scientists and engineers and that makes them very willing to
> experiment. They are experimenting all the time in the job, so they
> are willing to experiment with the process as well. They are not
> worried if the first try at a new process doesn't work. It doesn't
> mean the idea was wrong, but that we should try it again a differ-
> ent way. They are very challenging too. They don't accept any-
> thing because you say it. This is an environment where they are
> always asking questions, so if you have an idea they ask you
> everything about it until they understand it. So it takes some good
> skills of persuasion to lead a team here, but this process also leads
> to better end products because you've had to think through your
> positions carefully and in the end, your idea has broad ownership
> and there is more chance of success in the long run.

Focusing on Team Members

Finally, their effectiveness with teams comes from focusing on the
members of those teams as individuals. They show respect for their
work-related expertise and also for their lives outside work.

> [**Section Supervisor, Manufacturing Operations and Maintenance**]
> I'm here to make life better for these people. For me, the ends don't
> justify the means. The people I work for are the people under me. In
> my experience, men have an idea of where they want to go, and they
> will step on someone to get there. It's not that men are more ambi-
> tious than women. Women are just as ambitious and have just as
> high goals. It's just that for women, the means—the people along the
> way—are just as important.

[**Manager, Quality Systems**] [What makes you effective?] My will-ingness to engage with people, which is unusual here. People talk about *things* here, not people, and people become just another thing…I have an enormous, innate willingness to accept other peo-ple no matter who they are. It was the way I grew up: I lived a lot overseas and was in a lot of different cultures, so I got used to dealing with lots of new and different people. I'm amazed when people find it unusual the way I get along and accept other people, I don't see why that should be unusual.

A World without Boundaries: Building Linkages between Groups

To increase the effectiveness of the operations they managed, the women manufacturing managers built extensive links between the manufacturing domain and the wider corporation. These linkages served to reduce the divisive effects of intergroup boundaries and build a more organic, integrated company. The women managers built both conceptual links—between manufacturing plans, decisions, and corporate strategy—as well as operational links, connecting the people in manufacturing with individuals in related functions throughout the business.

Conceptual Linkages

The women we interviewed in manufacturing management positions focused on the big picture: a trait they share with effective male gen-eral managers. What was striking, however, was how often they viewed the process of linking manufacturing decisions to business strategies, market, and competitive issues as core to their job.

In addition, they saw the first step in effectively linking manufactur-ing and business strategies was to lead their organizations to an under-standing of the key elements of their business strategy and the forces influencing it. As a researcher of manufacturing companies, Wickham Skinner agrees, "Rather than always focusing the production system primarily on cost and efficiency, the manager must set objectives based on the strategic needs of the corporation. These objectives will estab-lish both priorities and tradeoffs."[24] This strategic understanding involves a working familiarity with relevant longer-term goals, com-petitors, and relative market positions and guides choices made within manufacturing.[25] The women manufacturing managers interviewed identified this area as one in which they were particularly effective:

[**Manager, Quality**] [To be an effective manufacturing manager] you have to give the sense of the context, so subordinates have some way to judge what they're doing. They need a basic knowledge of the customers and the competition. You need to make sure that they know this context and that everyone shares the same knowledge of the context.

[**Manager, Quality Systems**] I'm really trying to have all the employees here have a knowledge of the whole operation so they can make the right judgments in their area of responsibility to support the whole. I'm bringing them communications, a rich understanding of the context they're working in, trying to get them to understand the company. And I work to translate the goals into meaningful terms for the employees, "How do we do this in the polymer process?" It's really that, goals translation, an iterative process. It's getting people to talk top down and bottom up; both ways. And it's working. Recently a group of our supervisors had an opportunity to explain our operation to a group of visitors. These first-line people really could explain the business and how their operations fit into it.

To the surprise of some of these women managers, the need for all manufacturing employees to understand strategic forces and make the conceptual linkage between manufacturing processes and their company's business strategy was not already a norm. Indeed, they sometimes found a veil of secrecy surrounding strategy; strategic issues were supposed to be the purview of top management only. But the women managers interviewed knew manufacturing choices could not be linked to strategy if that strategy was secret.

For example, the quality manager quoted earlier found that the strategic planning process was secret in one plant she worked in and that the plan itself was kept in a secret storage place. She organized an ad hoc group of managers to run "grass roots" strategic thinking sessions to develop some sense of context for their decisions. "People have so little sense of the business context. To make good decisions, manufacturing people have to be able to see the connection between the daily tasks of manufacturing with the overall strategy, that utilizing resources to change the company's manufacturing culture in positive ways will also achieve business objectives."

Operational Linkages

Effectively linking manufacturing and the wider corporation requires not only conceptual but also operational links both among manufacturing functions and between manufacturing and other groups, including those outside the firm, where appropriate. Greater integration and interaction between functions (internal and external to operations) is required to optimize overall firm performance.[26] The women manufacturing managers identified building operational links as another key area of effectiveness. Linking groups requires more than connecting individuals. Emphasizing goals helps different groups pursue shared purposes; deemphasizing organizational boundaries makes it easier for them to work together.

When asked how they made effective connections between different operational groups and functions, these women manufacturing managers identified two critical factors: focusing on tasks to achieve goals and ignoring formal organizational and operational boundaries.

[**Manager, Engineering and Plant Services**] I'm encouraging my group to work with people outside this plant. For a simple example, we have guys who purchase materials and inventory. I asked some questions about, "Do we focus on key suppliers? Do we try to develop relationships with them?" The answer came back, "We should, but there is too much paperwork just to buy the stuff we need. We don't have time." I suggested that they talk to purchasing people in [other corporate subsidiaries]. I view the world beyond manufacturing. I don't see manufacturing as just driving a bus. I can see beyond the fence, my colleagues often can't. Their attitude is "Protect the plant—to the end." I look outside for what we have to do so that there will be a plant in 10 years.

[**Director, Technical Operations**] We were constructing a new wing of our building to enable us to move everything that is technology into one facility. [This firm combines manufacturing, R&D, and information technology into what they define as the technology area.] I was responsible for how to assign the space. We really looked at who needed to communicate to whom and how often, and worked to get these things close to each other. I literally was building the cross-functional linkages by putting people with different functional skills next to each other.

I developed a process needed to initiate new products. When a new product is developed in R&D, planning for its introduction needs to be linked between manufacturing and both the product groups and geographical regions. It is all about building liaisons between the different groups. Basically we put together teams on a new product that have the various types of expertise we need and they go about figuring out how to get all the information flows going. They're working in teams all the time and pretty soon the loyalty is to the team and the project goals, not to any organizational group. All the old loyalties disappear. In fact they don't remember anymore what department they technically belong to. All that old turf stuff doesn't matter any more. It's the outcome that's more important. They start to be guided from a business point of view.

The ability of these women managers to shape linkages among manufacturing functions and between manufacturing and the rest of the firm may have been facilitated by their own career paths. Time and again, they described their career paths as "unusual." They met organizational resistance to being placed in the core manufacturing positions and being moved straight up the line. Often they entered the firm in staff functions. They requested line jobs, jobs "close to the core business," but these were not forthcoming. Often, they were moved to other staff functions, or outside of manufacturing altogether, and given more responsibility. Therefore, by the time they got line positions in manufacturing, they had acquired a wide range of experience and expertise in the business, as well as extensive organizational connections. The women managers viewed their career paths, which had provided them with a breadth of experience, as unconventional compared to that of their male peers.

> [**Manager, Engineering and Plant Services**] When I was placed in this job, executives were still very hesitant to give the job to a woman. They expressed their concerns as, "You are qualified and capable. Our concern is that the organization you are going to is not ready for you and you'll be miserable and you'll quit." However, they really needed the position filled, and there were few other candidates with the extensive qualifications I had. The other candidates had been moved narrowly and did not have the range of experience I had.
>
> Plant services, my area, is viewed as a poor second cousin to operations; but I am increasing its credibility. I understand the business side—the making and selling of our product. My marketing experience comes in here. I also understand the services that support the business function. Because of my experience in a variety of these areas, I can see why all are important, how each contributes to the whole, and I can communicate this to people within my services organization.

Mining For Gold: Finding the Value Intrinsic in Women Managers

The two abilities evidenced by the women in this study—building teams and using organizational and strategic linkages—directly address the needs central to successfully revitalizing U.S. manufacturing discussed earlier: that is, the need for cross-functional communication and integration, developing interfunctional work teams, and linking manufacturing and business strategies. The widely recognized need for these skills, and the relatively few women manufacturing managers, suggest that there are many other situations where women with similar skills and abilities could make significant contributions to manufacturing management.

To earn the highest return on the resource that their women managers represent, companies need to place women into positions that require—and leverage the benefit from—these skills. This means looking at jobs not only in terms of *what* the goals are, such as increased productivity, but also in terms of *how* they are accomplished: for example, internalizing an awareness of how manufacturing tasks link to the overall business strategy. Leveraging the benefit from these skills may necessitate new ways of thinking about job requirements: that is, identifying jobs, tasks, and problems involving multifunctional approaches, teams, strategic partnerships, inter- and intra-group integration, and turnarounds. By assigning these jobs to individuals whose skills best meet the requirements, companies will find that they are providing more opportunities for aspiring women.

Further, to fully unleash the power of women for companies, companies must not only provide work opportunities that leverage women's skills and abilities, they must also recognize and value these needed contributions through goals and rewards. For example, specific goals reflecting company needs can be established, such as "Build an effective cross-functional new-product development team to reduce new product introduction time by 20 percent," or "Establish cross-functional linkages between engineering, manufacturing, and customer service to reduce customer complaints by 10 percent." As noted by one of the managers quoted earlier:

> [**Manager, Quality**] You've got to have clear measures that support what you want, what your goals are, with programs like TQM (total quality management). But our existing measures don't line up with our goals. They're out of sync with what we need now. It really is a systems problem. Can you change your expectations but still have the old measures and be measured in the old ways? I don't think so. And we have to get it lined up.

Once appropriate goals are established, companies must then recognize successful achievement of these goals through rewards such as bonuses, raises, promotions, and perks. Companies should view a successful track record in such assignments as appropriate preparation for senior positions, including general management positions.

In the process of discovering ways to value and reward the contributions of women which may, historically, have gone unrecognized, companies may also find barriers to the women's full participation in, and contribution to, the workplace. Frequently encountered barriers range from unintentional oversights like being left off the routing list for an important memo to exclusions which profoundly and directly impact career opportunities.[27]

Barriers should, of course, be eliminated for women to perceive that their contributions are fully valued. Addressing these issues requires not only careful monitoring of systems such as career pathing and performance appraisals but also careful analysis of and attention to all types of opportunities that establish qualifications for managerial positions to ensure that women are not only prepared but also have access to such positions.

The key to successfully eliciting and leveraging the best skills that women have to offer, nonetheless, is the open recognition that their skills are of value to the company. Unfortunately, such is not usually the case. We asked women managers, "How can companies better utilize abilities of women managers in manufacturing?" Here are some of the responses:

> [**Section Supervisor, Manufacturing Operations and Maintenance**]
> We need to educate companies on the value of motivated employees. If you want employees' brains, it requires more of a supervisor to keep them stimulated, thinking. My company is into quick fixes. They say, "if there is no rate of return in the next year, then I don't know if we can do it." These things I am doing are 5- to 10-year initiatives.

Another often iterated complaint was the lack of value senior management placed on the woman manager's ability to build cohesion and morale in her plant.

> [**Director, Manufacturing**] The president had no sense of the need in the plant for the better environment that I was creating. He certainly wouldn't recognize it publicly. If you asked him what he needs in the plant he would say something about productivity of the work force. But his lack of verbal support for what I am doing in the work environment is not an issue for me. I don't care if they value it or not, because I'm going to do it my way anyway. Top management values the results, and as we know, creating a good environment is how you get the results.

Not everyone is as self-confident as this manager was to do what she knows works, to follow her best judgment and focus on the quality of the processes and relationships between people. When the contributions of women are not valued, many come to the conclusion that their skills, abilities, and values are somehow inconsistent with the needs of the corporation, and they become discouraged. Women cannot do their best when things they value are clearly of little interest to others in their work environment, are not rewarded or worse, openly rejected. This reduces their ability—or willingness—to put forth the effort required to undertake those tasks the company desperately needs.

One woman described the dilemma as follows:

> [**Director, Technical Operations**] What I've seen with women that I have known is that when we first came out of school 15 or 20 years ago and started working, we said "OK, things at work are about work and that's separate." I, for one, evolved an attitude of "Here is my work person and here is my after-work person." The after-work person was my real self; that was me as a woman. So I lived this dichotomy. But then work got more and more demanding and the workday stretched and stretched, until there was less and less, maybe even no, real me. That wasn't going to last long, and so I started flexing the business person and stretching it and making it fit the real me. So you work to pull the two together and make what you are effective at work. That is quite a process. The younger women I'm working with are going through this process now and dealing with the question of whether they can do it— whether they can ever integrate the two.

That this process was sometimes unsuccessful or bore a great personal cost was evident in a comment made by one woman manager reflecting on several levels of women in her company.

> [**Manager, Quality Systems**] When I introduce groups to team processes I sometimes find it is actually harder for some senior women to adopt team approaches. I believe this is because they have had to repress so much of their natural selves. Our most senior woman was so much "the first" in everything she did that she had to bury her instincts, had to become totally individualistic in her approach to survive at all. She had to build an incredible shell around herself. We have all done that to some extent, but you can see the need for it declining as you go through the generations. With the younger women, they come to the team stuff much easier and their natural abilities come to the fore quicker.

Women care about the nature of the relationships among the people they work with; they care about how things get done, not just that they get done. As we have seen, many women are very innovative when it comes to the processes used to get tasks done. These qualities make good business sense for companies. They increase productivity; they increase profitability; they are strategically important. Companies that

recognize and value these abilities will be able to develop women who
are ready for senior management positions.

Leveraging the Opportunities Intrinsic in Women Managers

Leveraging the opportunity in women managers will occur not only
when they are more in number but when women are represented in
all aspects of manufacturing operations. The potential in women as
manufacturing leaders became clear to us as we came to know some
of them. They applied their abilities of focusing on the process and
people and building links not only to the more routine daily operational areas of building teams and interorganizational connections but
also to larger and more complex venues, such as leading organizations through times of crisis or through major transitions. In the past
women have rarely had the opportunity to hold such major responsibilities, perhaps due to lack of awareness of how well their abilities fit
the needs of these situations.

We share one example: Iris had been vice president for manufacturing for one company and was recruited to a similar position in another company with an entirely different technology and manufacturing
process. This is how she told her story:

> I am given responsibility for manufacturing whenever there are
> particularly difficult problems to confront. When no one has a clue
> about how to implement something, then they ask for me and I just
> go and do it.
>
> When they called me, the plant manager had quit. It was a real
> shock to come here because I found myself totally lacking in the
> most basic tools to work with either to get information about the
> operations or to do anything about problems when I did learn some-
> thing. The company had just consolidated all the operations into one
> plant, which involved closing a plant in Mexico and bringing the
> jobs back to the U.S. Previously, the plant manager had scheduled
> operations in his head and on pieces of paper. But now there were
> hundreds of shop orders and no system to handle them. I found a
> company 55 percent past due on the orders on its books and com-
> pletely out of control. I found an environment that was very anxious
> because it was not feeling successful. I found a punitive manage-
> ment style that said, "Do what you're told or you're out."
>
> We had to catch up so we wouldn't lose the sales we already
> had, and then meet new orders. I had to get this place going again.
> I saw my task as tackling management first, where there was a
> total need. The management problems were unusually big. So I

worked on the structure of management and the expectations I had for what each person should be doing. I tried to get everyone to understand what we were trying to do in this plant. I really didn't do anything unusual. I just got down and started working with the employees one-on-one and in groups. You know, "What will it take to do this task?" "What do we need to do to make this task manageable?" "Where are the bottlenecks?" "What is your problem?" Basically we just went from a yelling culture to a problem-solving culture.

I'm nonjudgmental about other people and their abilities. It is obvious where my expertise is and I put my energies there. I work on the process, and bring an intellect that is logical, if not technical, to the issues. I can see where the problems are and keep the focus on them and do not let irrelevancies get in the way. People always want to start pointing fingers and finding blame. I just cut that stuff and get on to constructive things and keep the focus on the future rather than the past. I come to people and say, "Well, if this is the problem, what are you going to do about it?" Then I give them positive reinforcement for their ideas.

When we interviewed Iris, she had been on the job for five months and felt she was far from completing the turnaround. But they had caught up on orders, successfully negotiated a confrontation with union leadership, completed a restructuring of the management systems, wiped out the environment of fear, and brought a sense of purpose to the plant floor. It seemed to us she was well on the way to a successful turnaround.

In many ways, Iris is like Elaine, whose story began this chapter. Their stories tell of managers who can lead in large operations in the tough times as well as the good ones. They focused on the future; they worked closely with their employees and took seriously issues of morale; they rarely fired individuals but held people accountable. Yet, as one woman plant manager commented, "We are noticed only because we are so rare."[28] In our discussions, we were struck by how isolated these women were. They saw some of their abilities as unique to them as individuals and rare in their organizations. Because they had few opportunities to work with other women, they were surprised to learn that they and their counterparts in other companies demonstrated many of the same approaches, abilities, and attitudes. We suspect there are many more Elaines and Irises and that by the Year 2000, they will no longer be surprising to discover.

As stated at the beginning of this chapter, these skills are not unique to women; there are men who are effective team builders, too. An interesting question is whether women are more likely than men to possess some of the skills we have discussed. While this is possible, and some feel it is likely, it cannot be proved or disproved based on our observations. As we have suggested, however, the firm that *values* skills such as team building through explicit goals and incentives will encourage the application of these skills by all managers with these capabilities. Women and men with these skills can be encouraged to help others, who are perhaps less capable in these areas, to develop and strengthen their skills.

We close this chapter by returning to the issue of leveraging the opportunity that already exists in women managers. It was heartening to find strong, impressive women managers in manufacturing. But what was disheartening was that these women had to find their way to their positions in an ad hoc way. To create a new competitive edge through their women managers, companies need a systematic process to search for and fully utilize the potential leadership in women employees. They need to create and regularly provide programs that support the development of women's leadership potential. Companies who learn how to tap this resource will gain advantages over competitors in the United States and abroad. Tapping the potential of women managers requires more than recognizing the special skills and abilities many women bring to their work. It also requires understanding the contexts where those skills are most needed and can be leveraged to greatest advantage.

Notes and References

1 U.S. Bureau of the Census as reported in Paula Ries and Anne J. Stone, eds., The Women's Research and Education Institute, *The American Woman, 1992–3: A Status Report*, Norton, New York, 1992, p. 312. In 1990, women were 45.4 percent of the full-time work force and 49.9 percent of the full- and part-time work force combined.

2. Labor force participation rates for women over 16 are projected to increase from 57.5 percent in 1990 to 62.6 percent in 2000. As reported in Howard N. Fullerton, "New Labor Force Projections, Spanning 1988 to 2000," *Monthly Labor Review*, 112, November, 1989, Table 4, p. 8.

3. According to the U.S. Department of Labor, "Statistics show that minorities and women are less likely to obtain positions in line functions—such as sales and production—which most likely affect the corporation's bottom line and are considered the fast track to the executive suite. Instead, many minorities and women find it easier to obtain (or are steered into) staff positions, such as human resources, research, or administration. The findings of the pilot reviews were consistent with these assertions." *A Report on the Glass Ceiling Initiative*, U.S. Department of Labor, 1991, p. 16. In their research on women in senior management positions, Catalyst

states that in durable and nondurable manufacturing companies, approximately 80 percent of the companies report women in senior management in human resources and 70 percent report women in senior management in communications while fewer than 5 percent report women in senior management positions in plant/facilities or production. Adapted from "Women in Corporate Management: Results of a Catalyst Survey," Catalyst internal paper, © 1990. By permission of CATALYST, 250 Park Avenue South, New York, NY 10003-1459, (212) 777-8900.

4. Based on a study by Russell Reynolds Associates, Inc. (New York), *Men, Women and Leadership in the American Corporation*, November, 1990, as described and cited in A Report on the Glass Ceiling Initiative, U.S. Department of Labor, 1991, p. 17.

5. Between 1983 and 1989, the number of women in the work force who were not administrators or managers increased from 26 million to 31 million, and the proportion of women in this segment of the work force increased from 40 to 42 percent. U.S. Bureau of Labor Statistics, Bulletin 2307. (See also Chapter 6 in this book for additional data.)

6. U.S. National Center for Education Statistics, *Digest of Education Statistics,* 1988.

7. In 1988, of the college degrees awarded at the Bachelor's level, women received 30 to 39 percent of degrees awarded in architecture and environmental design, computer and information sciences, philosophy, religion and theology, physical sciences, and protective services; 40 to 49 percent of the degrees awarded in business and management, mathematics, and social sciences; 50 to 59 percent of the degrees awarded in agriculture and natural sciences, areas and ethnic studies, liberal and general studies, life sciences, multidisciplinary studies, and parks and recreation; and more than 60 percent of the degrees awarded in communication, education, foreign languages, health sciences, home economics, law, letters, library science, psychology, public affairs, and visual and performing arts. The only categories where women earned less than 30 percent of degrees awarded were engineering (13 percent) and military science (5 percent). U.S. National Center for Education Statistics, *Digest of Education Statistics,* 1988. It should be noted, however, that the breadth of these categories masks some continuing deficiencies in some scientific fields such as physics where other sources indicate only 18 percent received bachelor's. Graduate degrees awarded to women in all science, math, and engineering fields not only continue to be low (except in psychology and medicine) but are actually declining as a percentage of total new degrees. See for example, Stephen Brush. "Women in Science and Engineering," *American Scientist,* 79, Sept–Oct, 1991, pp. 404–419. However, for managerial positions in manufacturing the above statistics for bachelor's degrees seems most relevant.

8. Sara E. Rix, ed., The Women's Research and Education Institute, *The American Woman, 1988–89: A Status Report,* Norton, New York, 1988, p. 63.

9. In 1982, the female share of the labor force was: United States—42.9 percent, France—38.6 percent, Germany—38.2 percent, Italy—33.8 percent, Sweden—46.2 percent, United Kingdom—39.1 percent. Isabella Bakken, "Women's Employment in Comparative Perspective," in Jan Jensen, Elisabeth Hagen, and Ceallaigh Reddy, eds., *Feminization of the Labor Force: Paradoxes and Promises*, Policy Press, Cambridge, U.K., 1988, p. 18.

10. According to one source based on a 1983 survey data, 11 percent of the working women in the United States are classified as administrative and managerial; in the United Kingdom and France only 2.4 percent and .2 percent respectively, are so classified. Angela Dale and Judith Glover, "An Analysis of Women's Employment Patterns in the U.K., France, and the USA: The Value of Survey Based Comparisons," U.K. Crown Copyright, Research Paper No. 75, Employment Department Group, 1990, p. 15. Another source, citing 1985 OECD data, reports the percentage of the female labor force in the administrative and managerial occupation is 5.9 percent—United States; 9 percent—United Kingdom; .2 percent—Italy; 1.5 percent—Germany; and 1.5 percent—France. Bakken, op. cit., p. 29. Considering the proportion of administrators and managers who are women, in 1984, only 6.1 percent of Japan's administrative and managerial workers were women as compared to 33.3 percent in the United States, 21 percent in Sweden, and 20.9 percent in the United Kingdom. Larry S. Carney and Charlotte G. O'Kelly, "Barriers and Constraints to the Recruitment and Mobility of Female Managers in the Japanese Labor Force," *Human Resource Management*, Summer, 1987, 26(2) p. 193.

11. V. Holton and V. Hammond, *A Balanced Workforce? Achieving Cultural Change for Women: A Comparative Study*, Ashridge Research Management, U.K., December 1991, pp. 6–7; Carney and O'Kelly, op. cit., p. 200–205.

12. Carney and O'Kelly, op. cit., pp. 194–195; "Hiring Women Managers in Japan," *California Management Review*, Spring 1988; "A Helping Hand for Women," *Financial Times*, December 11, 1991; "West German Women Make Presence Felt at Work," *Financial Times*, October 24, 1989. Also see Chapter 6.

13. Antony J. Michels, "How to Beat Japan," *Fortune*, November 18, 1991, p. 13.

14. Boston University, INSEAD, Waseda University, et. al., *Factories of the Future: Executive Summary of the 1990 International Manufacturing Futures Survey*, Boston University Manufacturing Roundtable, Boston, 1990, p. 5.

15. Robert Hayes, Steven Wheelwright, and Kim Clark, *Dynamic Manufacturing: Creating the Learning Organization*, The Free Press, New York, 1988, p. 354.

16. Hayes, Wheelwright, and Clark, op. cit., p. 15.

17. Wickham Skinner, "The Taming of Lions: How Manufacturing Leadership Evolved, 1780–1984," in Kim B. Clark, Robert H. Hayes, and Christopher Lorenz, eds., *The Uneasy Alliance, Managing the Productivity-Technology Dilemma*, Harvard Business School Press, Boston, 1985, p. 98.

18. Ibid, pp. 97–99.

19. Michael L. Dertouzos, Richard K. Lester, and Robert M. Solow and the MIT Commission on Industrial Productivity, *Made in America: Regaining the Productive Edge*, The MIT Press, Cambridge, Mass., 1989, p. 123.

20. The women interviewed came from six major U.S. companies, five industries, and most major U.S. geographical regions. Their titles ranged from first-line supervisor to vice president, and their responsibilities ranged from directing manufacturing operations to managing quality to managing manufacturing support services. In addition to asking them to describe their educational and work history, and the scale and scope of their responsibilities, we asked them to describe situations in which they had been particularly effective and to analyze why they had been so effective. We asked them to compare their approaches to those of their colleagues. Finally, we asked them what manufacturing companies could do to better utilize women managers.

21. See, for example, Nancy DiTomaso and George F. Farris, "Diversity and Performance in R&D," *IEEE Spectrum*, June 1992, pp. 21–24.

22. M. F. Belenky, B. M. Clincy, N. R. Goldberger, and J. M. Tarule, *Women's Way of Knowing*, Basic Books, New York, 1986, pp. 102–123, 144–146.

23. Carol Gilligan, Nona P. Lyons, and Trudy J. Hamner, eds., *Making Connections: The Relational Worlds of Adolescent Girls at Emma Willard School*, Harvard University Press, Cambridge, Mass., 1990, pp. 188–189.

24. Wickham Skinner, "Wanted: Managers for the Factory of the Future," *Annals of the American Academy of Political and Social Science*, 470, November 1983.

25. Janice A. Klein, *Revitalizing Manufacturing, Text and Cases*, Irwin, Homewood, Ill., 1990, p. 3.

26. Klein, op. cit., pp. 5–6.

27. Examples uncovered during these interviews included repeated rejection of women's requests to hold line positions in manufacturing; assigning women to small, seemingly unimportant projects or to small facilities or units; and restricting access to resources: "In the 15 years I've been here, I have had a total budget to spend on consultants of $50,000 while any man with my responsibilities and at my level in the company has spent hundreds of thousands of dollars on consultants," or "I wanted to go to Japan to meet with the firm who designed and manufactured the process equipment we would be using. I was told 'No.' The reasons for denial were smoke, like 'The Japanese won't accept you because you are a woman,' or 'The product won't work.' But we had already done trials of the process and made the product. I had to go three levels above my boss to finally get a 'yes.'"
    Other authors have identified many significant exclusions experienced by many women that impact career opportunities: for example, women's underrepresentation in skills and leadership training, in apprenticeship

programs, and in executive education programs held at top business schools to which companies send their promising managers; denial of access to developmental opportunities, such as corporate committees, task forces, or special projects, which provide visibility required for advancement; resistance met by women seeking line positions in key functions considered prerequisites for executive positions; or constraints imposed on the performance of women's job responsibilities but not on their male peers that limit women's effectiveness and their learning experience. For further discussion of these issues, see *A Report on the Glass Ceiling Initiative,* U.S. Department of Labor, 1991. See also, "Can the Feds Bust Through the 'Glass Ceiling'?" *Business Week,* April 29, 1991, p. 33 and "How to Keep Women Managers on the Corporate Ladder," *Business Week,* September 2, 1991, p. 64.

28. "The Success of Grace Pastiak," *The New York Times,* May 5, 1991, Section 3, p. 1.

8

Immigrant Entrepreneurs

Marion E. McCollom
*Assistant Professor of Organizational
Behavior, Boston University School of
Management*

Perhaps the most powerful theme in the American experience is captured in the museum on Ellis Island in New York harbor. Here are
tinted images of desperate adventure, of exhausted but wide-eyed
strangers arriving in a strange country looking for escape and opportunity. These photographs and the stories behind them represent a
profound truth about the American character, culture, and political
system.

What they also represent is the core of a powerful U.S. potential for
gaining and holding an economic edge in the 1990s. Recent scholar-
ship and journalistic analysis has shown that many of the people who
have come here with little have been, and continue to be, a source of
prosperity for this country. In this chapter, I argue that immigration
has created a major strategic advantage for the U.S. economy and that
U.S. manufacturing can benefit greatly from the resources generated
and represented by immigrant entrepreneurs.

The first step in this argument is to establish that in fact the United
States has a strategic advantage both in its rate of immigration and
also in the likelihood that immigrants to the United States will become
successfully self-employed. The next step, which is the crux of the
argument, lies in the demonstration that successful immigrant entrepreneurs from various ethnic backgrounds demonstrate common atti-

161

tudes and strategies in running their businesses: hard work and single-minded devotion to building the business, comfort with risk taking, strong community values, fresh perspectives on business opportunities, frugal deployment of resources, concentration on market niches, and close ties to customers.

This chapter shows that these characteristics can benefit U.S. manufacturing in two ways: in revitalizing the manufacturing sector via immigrant-owned start-ups and in providing powerful partners and in-house expertise to rejuvenate the management practices of manufacturing enterprises.

Give Me Your Poor...

Although U.S. immigration policies have been justifiably criticized as exclusionary for certain groups during certain historical periods (Jews during the 1930s and 1940s, Asians from the 1920s until the major overhaul of immigration laws in 1965), a recent *Business Week* article on the subject reports that U.S. borders are currently crossed by about a million people a year and that immigrants produced about 39 percent of the total U.S. population growth in the 1980s.[1] Recent legislation (the Immigration Reform and Control Act in 1986 and the 1990 Immigration Act) has created a trend toward more open borders, granting legal status to some illegal aliens, raising the ceiling for newcomers from certain countries, and granting access to immigrants who can invest $1 million in U.S. business. There is little question that the United States is the world leader in immigration.

What is more open to debate is the impact of these immigration policies on U.S. society. Despite the fact that new arrivals to the United States in recent years are more likely than U.S. residents to be college-educated,[2] immigration is widely perceived as a "problem." Researchers may argue that new immigrants help create as many jobs as they fill[3] and add significantly to tax revenues, but in the popular perception, immigrants are seen as a drain on public services, on housing, and on jobs that could go to working-class Americans (some of whom, inevitably, are other newcomers who got here first). While immigrant groups have been credited with the rejuvenation of urban downtown areas, inflows of racial and ethnic groups into some neighborhoods—Cambodians and Dominicans in the Boston area, for example—have caused resentment and violent backlash. Immigrants, for the most part, have not been easily accepted into local communities and local economies.

The good news for immigrants to the United States, however, is that despite racial discrimination, language barriers, and obstacles to entry into the traditional job market, the opportunities to jump into the mainstream are far greater in the United States than in any other society in the world. "Making it in America" is not a myth; and the successes experienced by family and friends continue to draw more immigrants. Specifically, the opportunity to acquire and accumulate capital appears to be the key to success; with capital comes access to housing and education. Moreover, despite a generally discriminatory climate, legal protections for all citizens (and most noncitizens) have helped immigrants climb the social and economic ladder. Although most first-generation immigrants are not prosperous enough to send their children to Ivy League colleges, enough *are* able to do this to make the immigrant success story more than a fiction.

In Europe, labor shortages are bringing floods of immigrant guest workers. However, government policy determines that the status of these workers is fixed. For example, in Germany, guest workers are not eligible for citizenship; those who become unemployed are deported. Observers are predicting even more restrictions on immigration into Europe, and violence against immigrants, particularly in parts of Germany, is on the rise.[4] In Japan, as reported in Chapter 6 of this book, foreign workers have few if any legal rights and are limited to low-paying, low-status jobs. Most immigrant workers enter Japan's homogeneous society illegally and never enjoy privileges of citizenship.

The advantage that the United States holds in immigration (and the rest of this chapter is devoted to developing the argument that it *is* an advantage) is not likely to be quickly lost to Europe or Japan. The key point here is not, ultimately, how many foreigners are admitted into these regions, but rather what happens to them when they get there. Do they remain ghettoized at the bottom of the socioeconomic ladder, or do they have access to mainstream society? In both Europe and Japan, public attitudes and government policies are likely to perpetuate the barriers that now effectively block immigrants out of membership in the social and economic mainstream.

It would be incorrect to imply that *all* immigrants to the United States are successful in joining the mainstream or that the success rate of all immigrant groups is equal; as we shall see, observers of immigrant entrepreneurship have noted clear differences in rates of self-employment and in successful business operation among different ethnic groups.[5] However, immigrant entrepreneurs are providing an important boost to the U.S. economy. What we will explore next is the relationship between immigration and entrepreneurship in the United States.

The Immigrant Entrepreneur

Theories of entrepreneurship suggest that the drive toward business development shown by many immigrants is not generated entirely out of economic necessity. In fact, researchers have argued that entrepreneurs are bred fundamentally from social dislocation; the psychological dynamics of the uprooting process are as crucial in business development as is the need to make money.

The Psychology of Entrepreneurship

Research has clearly shown that rates of entrepreneurship are higher among immigrant groups than among native-born individuals in a variety of countries.[6] In a study of Michigan entrepreneurs, 19.8 percent were foreign-born, compared to a figure of 5.9 percent for the total population. In addition, 35 percent were born in the United States but had a foreign-born father, versus 15 percent for the total population.[7] Interestingly, researchers suggest that it is ethnic and religious minority status, rather than immigration in itself, that spurs entrepreneurship.[8]

The explanations linking minority or immigrant status to entrepreneurship are varied. Some observers argue that dislocation produces an adaptive response in the form of a greater tolerance for ambiguity: "The very process of uprooting and resettling forces immigrants to become highly adaptive, ingenious, and persevering."[9] Others suggest that minorities feel pressure to prove themselves: "Minorities feel that the way to better themselves as a people is to be in business for themselves, and to help others do it too."[10]

Other researchers describe a deeper psychodynamic linkage between immigrant or minority status and entrepreneurship. According to psychoanalytically trained management researchers, the anger and mistrust that are generated by the upheaval (and usually downgrading) of social status can often lead the immigrant to retreat into a fantasy world. When a strong creative drive is coupled with the immigrant's natural desire to exert control over an environment which has proved so dangerous, the entrepreneurial personality emerges.[11] The enterprise becomes the entrepreneur's private world over which, as owner, he exercises control. The business often becomes infused with themes from the family's private saga of escape from poverty or brush with extinction.[12] "For refugees especially, getting into business is often a way to regain control over family destinies after years depending on...others."[13]

Profiles of the Immigrant Entrepreneur

Learning that the immigration experience tends to produce entrepreneurs does not tell us what kinds of people are successful business developers in the United States and what kinds are not. Most observers of immigrant entrepreneurship note that ethnic groups who bring traditions of self-employment to the United States are much more likely to start in and succeed at business upon arrival here: "Thirty percent of Greek male immigrants were self-employed in 1980, 28 percent of Israelis, and 25 percent of Koreans, compared to 11 percent for native (U.S.) male workers....Newcomers without capital and an entrepreneurial culture have much lower rates: 6 percent for Jamaicans...and 3 percent for Vietnamese."[14]

In addition to identifying a range of entrepreneurial traditions among ethnic groups, we should also recognize that there are at least two very different types of immigrant entrepreneurs in this country. This split is demonstrated in statistics on the educational preparation of immigrants: Immigrants as a group are more likely than native-born citizens to be college-educated, but they are also more likely to lack a high school education.[15] The road to business ownership is different for these different types of immigrants.

The first type is drawn to the United States because of the opportunities to acquire wealth, utilize talents, and live a cosmopolitan life. This person is college-educated (at home or in the States), ambitious, and often willing to give up a white-collar or professional job in his or her native country in order to earn more in the United States.[16] Many have sophisticated technical or scientific skills and turn to entrepreneurship because language barriers, regulatory restrictions, or discrimination prevent them from practicing their profession in the United States: "Behind the rise in entrepreneurship is both personal ambition and a feeling of frustration....Many Asians who came to study in American colleges and stayed on are now at a point where they want greater responsibility or financial rewards....another factor is that it is difficult for Asians to advance within established companies."[17]

The second kind of entrepreneur is the political or economic refugee who matches the more traditional stereotypes of the immigrant. Arriving here with nothing, these individuals are sponsored by family or members of an extended clan until they can survive by self-employment. They learn a business from others in their own ethnic group by working for them, and when they are ready, they are able to borrow capital to get started on their own.[18] Sometimes ethnic business networks link such new entrepreneurs to established suppliers and distributors to minimize risks in the start-up phase.[19]

An example may help illustrate how a refugee becomes a successful entrepreneur. Sol and Esther Katz came to New York in 1952. Without a command of English, the only job Sol could get was as a grocery delivery boy. To earn more, he soon began a tiny weekend business: he bought baby blankets and other basic children's products and sold them for a small profit at suburban flea markets on the weekends. After a few years, Sol and Esther found a partner in their tightly knit Jewish community who had a little capital; they opened a store together. The couple bought him out several years later and soon were running four small stores selling children's clothes. Most suppliers and customers were members of the Ashkenazic Jewish community in the Bronx and Manhattan. Later when Sol's sons took over the business, the same ethnic ties gave them access to credit, retail expertise, and capital to fund the growth of the business into an eight-store chain reaching into the New York and Connecticut suburbs.

The Heart of the Immigrant Enterprise

The crux of the argument here—that immigrant entrepreneurship in the United States represents a potential "edge" for U.S. manufacturing—rests in the *way* that these entrepreneurs do business, as well as in the *kind* of businesses that they create. We have seen that immigrants to the United States are likely to become entrepreneurs for a variety of reasons; now we can show that there are distinctive patterns, common to both immigrant types, in the way they approach self-employment. In some ways, these patterns are typical of all family businesses, especially those run by a first-generation owner-manager; however, they are intensified when that owner-manager is an immigrant. The argument here is that the American edge can be sharpened by the quicker percolation into mainstream manufacturing of this entrepreneurial management style and strategic approach.

Managerial Psychology

Observers of immigrant entrepreneurs agree on at least four psychological characteristics of immigrant managers: their "Protestant" work ethic, their willingness to take risks, the value they place on community, and their perception of opportunity.

The willingness of immigrant owner-managers to work hard is noted in every article or study on entrepreneurship.[20] This can be explained partly by the intense demands of owner-management.

However, the immigrant's single-minded commitment to the enterprise, revealed in anecdotes of the sacrifice of every available hour and penny to business development, has been called the product of the refugee mentality. It represents an ability to stick it out through hard times and to defer short-term gratification in favor of building a future: "The way I was brought up, I feel there is opportunity in hard times, that if we can be tougher and more durable, we will come out ahead. There are no failures in this world, just setbacks."[21]

In the same way, immigrant entrepreneurs appear to have a strong tolerance for risk. While every entrepreneur is by definition a risk taker, immigrants have opted for or been forced into a situation in which every path they take is risky. Therefore, the risks and the ambiguities of self-employment, a situation in which they have some control, may be preferable to employment that requires dependence on others. The first type of immigrant (the opportunity seeker) is a risk taker by personality, choosing a high-risk, high-return situation over the familiar course that people from their reasonably privileged backgrounds would normally pursue. The second kind of immigrant—the refugee—has no choice but to take chances: "Starting a business is a risk for most people, but it really isn't as much a risk when you're a refugee and don't really have anything to lose."[22]

Research and journalistic reports have shown that immigrant entrepreneurs are characterized by strong ties to their communities. (Interestingly, this dynamic is reflected generations later in the fact that closely held companies as a group contribute a greater proportion of profits, compared to public corporations, to community projects.) This may be explained in part because of the strong norms in many ethnic communities of helping newcomers arrive and get settled. Once this help is provided to you, you provide it for others; mutual assistance assures the success of the whole community, especially in an unfamiliar and hostile environment. It is easy to see how this commitment to community translates into business practice. It is not just that the viability of a local business depends on the proprietor's knowledge of the community;[23] it is that the entrepreneur and his family continue to rely on their status and good reputation in the community for access to community resources (e.g., pooled loans or help for newly arriving family members).

The final psychological characteristic that scholars and journalists find in the immigrant entrepreneur is his or her perspective on opportunity. They see opportunities where many U.S. managers and owners see nothing: "The newcomers have come to America with fresh eyes and fresh convictions, and with a willingness to face competitive industrial challenges that too many of our more established corporations hesitate to confront."[24]

As the quote suggests, this perspective comes in part simply from the "newness" of immigrants. However, it also comes from experience. Many ethnic groups bring long traditions of specialized expertise in particular industries from their own cultures (for instance, Sikhs in the transportation business).[25] Finally, the ability to recognize opportunity is also bred from a willingness to "bottom fish"—that is, to enter markets that U.S. managers avoid because the margins are slim or because the product is old-fashioned or because the technology is dirty: "Immigrants innovate and sacrifice in ways most natives are too comfortable or too despairing to try."[26]

Business Strategies

The immigrant enterprise often succeeds, if it does, by relying on a characteristic set of business strategies: the use of family labor, capital investment practices, market-niche development, and the focus on customer and quality.[27]

Observers have noted consistently that immigrant businesses tend to rely on family members as a source of labor. The rationale is obvious: Family members are motivated (they too are financially dependent on the success of the enterprise), loyal, and willing to work for low wages. Family cohesiveness is not compromised by one parent's long hours at work. The employment of family or extended family members also minimizes language barriers in company operations. When children come into the business, the training necessary for a smooth succession process begins early. It is important to note the potential risks associated with this and the other entrepreneurial strategies: In this case, one needs to consider the boycott several years ago in New York City of Korean grocers by African Americans. Immigrant businesses that employ only family members may appear ethnocentric or discriminatory, alienating other ethnic groups in the community. In addition, the company's later growth may suffer from the absence of fresh ideas and expertise.

Capital is also used in characteristic ways in immigrant enterprises. First, for obvious reasons, immigrants typically pick businesses with low initial capital requirements, then minimize the need to borrow (for example, by making and scavenging equipment rather than buying it new). Second, capital is *kept* in the business; costs are kept as low as possible and profits are reinvested, rather than used to improve the family's standard of living. In fact, many families deliberately keep their own living costs low long after they can afford a more luxurious lifestyle in order to put every available cent into the business.[28]

Access to capital is typically secured initially through community and ethnic ties. The Korean *kye* is only one example of the systems of pooled or revolving credit that provide resources to immigrant start-ups. Strong social ties within the funding group also assure a low default rate on these loans.[29] As the business grows, capital may be secured via more traditional banking or venture capital institutions, but often links into those organizations are made via ethnic networks.

To the degree that there is a negative side to these capital management strategies, it is that company growth may suffer from the immigrant entrepreneur's conservative attitudes toward capital. In the start-up phase, cost control is crucial; later, the unwillingness to spend unnecessarily can produce an attitude of unwillingness to spend at all. Thus, opportunities to enter new lines of business or to utilize new technologies or to attract key personnel with competitive salaries are sometimes forgone. In addition, entrepreneurs may be unwilling to borrow at commercial rates, even if the business can support the higher interest costs and the loan has a good chance of producing revenue growth.

The third business strategy typical of immigrant enterprises is the initial exploitation of a small and specialized market niche, often within the ethnic community. The niche is often defined by the popularity of a specialized ethnic product not widely available outside the community, by the group's particular expertise, or by the avoidance or abandonment of that niche by other businesses.[30] The concentration in small, local markets benefits the business owner (customers will often choose a store in which the proprietor speaks their language) but also benefits the local economy by recycling earnings within the community. Although some businesses get trapped in local markets and wind up undermining other small competitors, others, once they are established, are able to tailor their products to a wider market. For example, three Hong Kong natives developed bilingual computer software designed for Chinese restaurants that they are now adapting for and marketing to English-speaking restaurants.[31]

Finally, immigrant entrepreneurs tend to stay close to their customers. Clearly, if they are part of an ethnic community, they know what that customer wants and values, what he or she can afford, and how to sell to them. Moreover, the customer is likely to know them, both professionally and personally, if they are part of the same community. Thus, the quality of the product or service reflects directly, and personally, on the reputation and status of the proprietor and his or her family. Their success depends on their continued ability to earn customer loyalty. These overlapping social and professional relationships between customers and proprietors can also cause problems, however, if friends expect special treatment or if proprietors sacrifice good business judgment in trying to meet local needs. [32]

The American Edge

What emerges from this portrait of the immigrant entrepreneur and his or her enterprise is a model for management that has been overlooked too often and for too long. Business school curricula, the business press, and management consultants have kept the spotlight on large, publicly traded corporations. However, in the difficult environment of the 1990s, the companies that keep debt load low, watch costs, stay close to their customers, focus on quality, and do only what they can do well are finally being recognized. [33] And what we have seen here is that the immigrant experience typically produces exactly these management philosophies and business strategies, most of which are vital to success in the start-up phase and, if adapted successfully in the marketplace, can help create a platform for growth.

However, there are more questions still to be answered: What does the activity of these entrepreneurs mean for the American manufacturing sector? How can these enterprises benefit U.S. manufacturing as a whole, and how can individual manufacturers use them to realize an advantage?

Honing the Edge: Benefits to Manufacturing

We know that immigrant entrepreneurship has benefited the U.S. economy as a whole by contributing to employment, the GNP, and tax revenues. There is also good reason to believe that the specific characteristics of these businesses can help to strengthen and revitalize the American manufacturing sector in particular. In this section, I show that these benefits are available in two forms: (1) in the fresh perspectives and entrepreneurial talent that is being demonstrated by the immigrant owner-managers of manufacturing companies and (2) in the opportunity for manufacturing executives to use the immigrant entrepreneur as a partner (supplier, distributor) or as an expert to rejuvenate traditional management attitudes and practices. Evidence in the business press suggests that the first opportunity is beginning to be recognized; the second remains underexploited.

Immigrant Entrepreneurs in Manufacturing

Though most immigrants start businesses in the retail or service sectors (low capital requirements), the business press recently has reported numerous examples of the special contributions that immigrants have made on entering the manufacturing arena. The success stories include examples that range from heavy industry to high-tech to garment making. For example, *Inc.* featured a portrait of Vinny Gupta, a U.S.-educated Indian immigrant who recognized a business opportunity in a "dying" Midwest business. The foundry that he managed was largely ignored by the Connecticut-based conglomerate that owned it, and the plant was failing. He bought the operation, invested the time and energy necessary to understand the business in depth, and turned his new company into a profitable, three-foundry enterprise. Discussing his success, Gupta said, "Having an education in a dirty business is a unique asset. A lot of educated people don't want to work in a dirty business. There's always opportunity where the other guys don't want to go."[34]

Demonstrating that the refugee-type immigrant can follow the same strategic path, David Diaz was an illegal alien from Mexico whose successful manufacturing venture was reported in *Business Week* several years ago.[35] The company he worked for, a failing spring maker, fired him but gave him the chance to buy its manufacturing equipment. Solar Spring Co., Diaz's firm, is a revitalized and profitable supplier of springs for the aerospace and automobile industries.

In the high-tech arena, Asian immigrants, among other ethnic groups, have been utilizing a variety of strategies to operate successful manufacturing ventures. According to the Asian American Manufacturers Association in Menlo Park, California, Asian entrepreneurs in manufacturing have created thousands of jobs and generated over $1 billion in sales in the San Francisco Bay area.[36] Many of these business owners are Chinese-born and U.S.-educated people who have chosen to use their expertise to contribute to their adopted country. "We're getting an actual commitment to build products in this country, and to build them the way they ought to be built," commented one member of the California State World Trade Commission on these manufacturers.[37]

In one example, Solectron Corp., an Asian-owned business in the Silicon Valley, achieved sales of over $200 million in 1990 by specializing in the high-tech "dirty work" of assembling printed circuit boards and wiring computers—again, occupying a market niche that U.S. firms have abandoned.[38] Other firms have successfully utilized community ties across the Pacific, tapping into connections in Taiwan and Hong Kong to bring venture capital into their firms from overseas.

David Lee, founder of Qume, a manufacturer of computer printers in the Bay area, arrived in the United States as a refugee. His family was uprooted from China, Taiwan, and Argentina before they settled in the States. Lee used his U.S. engineering degree to help develop the daisy wheel printer. After founding and selling two computer companies, he bought one of them (Qume) back and now runs it. His explanation for why he left Xerox, the purchaser of his first company: "I don't think they even considered me as a manager....Even today, some large companies have a problem with Asian-Americans as managers."[39]

Immigrant manufacturers are also providing models of collaboration that more established manufacturers could learn from. For example, in order to beat overseas competition on delivery time and cost, a group of Chinese-American garment makers established the Metropolitan Fashion Center of New York. Pooling their manufacturing operations, they established an enterprise in a Brooklyn industrial park, where rents were lower and leases longer than in Chinatown. The company was set up to provide quick manufacturing and delivery of garments, plus a range of other services for fashion companies.

What these stories reveal is a wealth of talent in immigrant entrepreneurs, who have been driven to self-employment by a variety of circumstances and out of a range of backgrounds, creating successful manufacturing operations that match the general managerial and strategic profile of the immigrant enterprise. This anecdotal evidence suggests that the manufacturing sector is already benefiting substantially from the characteristic managerial approach of immigrant entrepreneurs, even though few of these companies have gained national attention.

Immigrant Enterprises as Models of Management

In a special issue of *Fortune,* author Stewart identified steps that the United States must take in order to compete more effectively.[40] Citing the need to strengthen the competitiveness of small manufacturers and service companies, Stewart identified single-minded focus on quality and responsiveness to customer needs as the key characteristics of stellar U.S. performers. Looking closely at the management style of immigrant entrepreneurs, it is apparent that we do not have to look far to find a model of the focused (even driven) managerial mind-set that is crucial to the revolution that Stewart calls for. Innovation is also key to competitiveness and, as one business journalist put it recently: "Make no mistake: innovation (in business) comes from immigration."[41]

The question is, must long-established, publicly traded manufacturers compete with owner-managed immigrant enterprises, or can these larger companies somehow take advantage of the immigrant entrepreneur's strengths? There are two ways to reap these benefits: (1) through partnerships with immigrant companies and (2) by bringing entrepreneurial talent in-house; neither strategy has yet been fully explored or exploited.

Manufacturers in the United States have moved closer to capitalizing on the first opportunity. *The Wall Street Journal* recently reported that larger companies facing cutbacks are discovering the advantages of subcontracting to outside companies certain functions that used to be done in-house (for example, manufacturing or freight forwarding).[42] While there are no reports that manufacturers are actively seeking immigrant enterprises as partners, the opportunity exists for companies to seek them out in partnerships and as suppliers, distributors, or subcontractors for their niche specialization, flexibility, and service and for cost savings.

On the second point, manufacturers so far have done very little to bring the skills and perspectives of the immigrant entrepreneur in-house. While they may exhort their subordinates to be "entrepreneurial," corporate executives typically don't understand the entrepreneurial mind-set and can't create an environment that would allow it to thrive in-house. Therefore, opportunities to recruit and retain immigrant entrepreneurs as middle and senior managers remain undeveloped.

Currently, immigrants are employed primarily in bottom-tier manufacturing jobs for a variety of reasons, ranging from their willingness to work for low wages to their poor English skills to their ability to focus on details. This essay suggests that many of these workers may be underutilized as laborers; companies that could break through language barriers could benefit from immigrants' knowledge of local markets, their experience with self-employment in other countries, or their ability, because they are "foreigners," to see opportunities to improve manufacturing processes and cut costs. Many of these employees could develop into talented middle managers.

As we have seen, anecdotal evidence suggests that immigrants at the more senior management level are exiting companies because they are not given the opportunities they seek. While increasing numbers of scientists and engineers in high-tech and pharmaceutical companies are foreign-born,[43] the potential benefits of the entrepreneurial mind-set they may possess are not being captured. What if manufacturers created conditions to retain future entrepreneurs in-house? For example, companies launching a new product or plant might deliberately recruit the "immigrant entrepreneur" in their ranks to run the venture as a spin-off. While the psychological profile of the entrepreneur will not allow every candidate to succeed in a corporate environment, some will, if given appropriate financial support and managerial autonomy. And, if they can be retained and promoted within the company, immigrant entrepreneurs can also be a valuable source of expertise for strategic problem solving and start-up management at the corporate level.

Is it really possible to bring the entrepreneurial mind-set into established companies? Granted, some of the capacity to focus unidimensionally on running a business comes with small scale and private ownership structure—it is easier to shape a smaller, closely held company around a core business than a large, professionally managed enterprise over which you have no ownership control. However, the specific characteristics of the immigrant entrepreneur create what we might call the "management model of the 1990s," which must be adopted by companies if they are to succeed:

- A primary focus on business survival; this means that the business does only what it can do well and profitably.

- A close connection to community (which includes customers and employees) as the primary source of capital, expertise, labor, and psychological support; seeing the business as embedded in society fosters responsible and responsive management.

- The development of a specialized market niche, which comes with the recognition of value in underserved markets.

- The forging of loyal customer relationships as the key to initial survival and also to long-term, sustainable growth.

- A tight-fisted attitude toward capital and a system of religious reinvestment: no extraneous spending even after profitability is well established.

- A future-oriented strategic mind-set, in which the long-term interests of the next generation (of family-owners, employees, and customers) weigh heavily in business decision making.

Cultivating these operating strategies will mean change for manufacturers, but most are already embarked down this road. Why not take advantage of the talent available in potential partner companies, in existing employee and professional ranks, and in demonstrated entrepreneurial success to find new management ideas?

Barriers to Immigrant
Entrepreneurship

Every step of this argument reveals obstacles that currently constrain the utilization of the advantage presented U.S. manufacturing by the immigrant entrepreneur. The first obstacles, and the hardest to address, are the pervasive negative attitudes and popular stereotypes about immigrants as a group. Journalists and politicians, riding xenophobic tides of anxiety about the economy, continue to argue that immigrants to the United States drain societal resources and steal jobs from native workers, despite substantiated and articulated evidence to the contrary. Somehow, the following view needs to be more widely circulated and understood: "Economists have shown that immigrants do not steal employment away from native-born workers. Instead, in the short run they mainly compete with slightly earlier arrivals from the same region. And in the long run, the new immigrants help create as many jobs as they fill, bringing skills and initiative to the U.S."[44]

In the same vein, public misperception about the value of cultural assimilation needs correction. Making immigrants into "Americans," at the expense of severing ties with their ethnic communities, is actually detrimental to their success: "Sociologists...argue that strong ethnic bonds, not rapid assimilation of individuals, continue to characterize immigrants who have moved farthest in mainstream society."[45] Thus, public education and training programs designed to "mainstream" children need to be reevaluated to be sure that links to native cultures and communities are preserved.

Another obstacle pointed out by researchers and journalists is that the above economic analysis notwithstanding, U.S. immigration policy still doesn't pay much attention to the entrepreneurial skills and ambitions of individuals who apply for entry (although the Immigration Act of 1990 created more than 100,000 new slots for specially skilled foreign immigrants).[46]

The success of immigrant entrepreneurs who do manage to enter the States depends to a large degree, as we have seen, on the economic success of at least some members of their ethnic communities. For members of those groups with less well-developed mutual support mechanisms or absent histories of self-employment, the possibility exists to do more to help them achieve entrepreneurial success. In general, policies could help promote small business development and better control discrimination against minority business owners.[47] More specifically, private or public agencies could provide apprenticeship opportunities and capital to immigrants via systems modeled on the successful ethnic capital assistance arrangements that now assist certain cultural groups: "Greater access to capital, employment, and training could help immigrants channel more of their extraordinary energy into productive enterprise."[48]

Finally, and perhaps most importantly, the current and future business community needs to understand in much more detail how an owner-manager thinks about running an organization. Even though small, closely held companies comprise 80 to 90 percent of the businesses in the country, business schools, the business press, and consulting organizations still rely on large public corporations as virtually the only models of management. While executives in those companies are casting around to learn other ways to run their operations, the image of the immigrant entrepreneur remains invisible to them. It will take wholesale revisions of business school and executive training programs before manufacturers can fully benefit from the model of management offered by the immigrant entrepreneur.

Conclusion

What we have seen here is that immigrants who find an ethnic community in the United States that is willing to sponsor them and that can provide capital and expertise are likely to try self-employment. And, importantly, this process takes place within a society that, despite its discrimination against people who are different on almost any dimension, uses financial success and educational achievement as measures of social status and acceptability. This means that immigrants can succeed and that their success draws others and helps fund their efforts.

Further, we have seen that the immigrant entrepreneur typically creates the type of business that 1990s gurus are lauding: a disciplined, focused, flexible operation that stays close to the customer. However, immigrant entrepreneurship is an underutilized resource for U.S. enterprise, especially for U.S. manufacturing. Describing the values and behaviors that made his foundry venture successful, Vinny Gupta says, "What we have found is the success formula for the next American revolution."[49] We need to study this formula and learn from it.

Notes and References

1 Michael Mandel, et al., "The Immigrants: How They're Helping to Revitalize the U.S. Economy," *Business Week,* July 13, 1992.

2. Ibid.
3. Michael Mandel, "Roll Out American's Red Carpet for the Skilled," *Business Week,* October 30, 1989.
4. Craig Whitney, "Europeans Look for Ways to Bar Door to Immigrants," *The New York Times,* December 29, 1991, p. 1.
5. Roger Waldinger and Howard Aldrich, "Trends in Ethnic Business in the United States," in Waldinger et al. (eds.), *Ethnic Entrepreneurs,* Sage, Newbury Park, Calif., 1990, pp. 49–78.
6. Ivan Light and Edna Bonacich, *Immigrant Entrepreneurs,* Berkeley, Calif., University of California Press, 1988.
7. Orvis Collins, David Moore, and Darab Unwalla, *The Enterprising Man,* Bureau of Business and Economics Research, School of Business Administration, Michigan State University, 1964.
8. Abraham Zaleznik and Manfred Kets de Vries, *Power and the Corporate Mind,* Houghton-Mifflin, Boston, 1975.
9. John Campbell, "The New New Englanders," *The Federal Reserve Bank of Boston Regional Review,* 2(1), 1992, p. 18.
10. Dena Coyle, Vice President of the National Minority Business Council, in "Entrepreneur Reports on `New Immigrants,' Minorities Fulfilling the American Dream," *PR Newswire,* June 30, 1989.
11. Zaleznik and Kets de Vries, op. cit.
12. Marion McCollom, "Saga and the (Re)Construction of Organizational History," Boston University Working Paper #91-17, 1991.
13. Vu Duc Vuong, Executive Director of the Center for Southeast Asian Refugee Resettlement in San Francisco, in Raymond McLeod, "Asian Firms Clustering in Bay Area: Census Report Finds Many Immigrant Entrepreneurs," *San Francisco Chronicle,* August 2, 1991, p. c1.
14. Campbell, op. cit., pp. 15–16.
15. Mandel et al., op. cit.
16. Timothy Noah, "Asian-Americans Take Lead in Starting U.S. Businesses," *The Wall Street Journal,* August 2, 1991.
17. Andrew Pollack, "It's Asians' Turn in Silicon Valley," *The New York Times,* January 12, 1992, p. D1.
18. John Kasarda, "Why Asians Can Prosper Where Blacks Fail," *The Wall Street Journal,* editorial, May 25, 1992.
19. Eva Pomice, "New Bootstraps for Today's Immigrant Entrepreneurs: The Ties That Bind—And Enrich," *U.S. News & World Report,* April 25, 1988.
20. For example, Light and Bonacich, op. cit.
21. Entrepreneur Steve Hui, in Joel Kotkin, "The American Way," *Inc.,* September 1991, p. 100.
22. Vu Duc Vong. (See Note 13.)

23. Jeremy Boissevain et al., "Ethnic Entrepreneurs and Ethnic Strategies," in Waldinger et al. (eds.), *Ethnic Entrepreneurs*, Sage, Newbury Park, Calif., 1990, pp. 131–156.

24. Kotkin, op. cit., p. 96.

25. Donatella Lorch, "Ethnic Niches Creating Jobs That Fuel Immigrant Growth," *The New York Times*, January 12, 1991.

26. Campbell, op. cit.

27. Failure rates for all small businesses are high; studies have shown that 8 percent of all firms in U.S. cities are lost each year (David Birch, *Job Creation in America: How Our Smallest Companies Put the Most People to Work*, Free Press, New York, 1987). The failure rate for smaller and newer companies is even higher, as 50 percent of new businesses do not last longer than five years (Light and Bonacich, 1988, op. cit.). While immigrant business failure rates are higher than average in some industries, the rate of business creation is also much higher. Thus, the population of immigrant-owned businesses in industries like clothing manufacturing is growing while the pool of native-owned businesses is shrinking (Roger Waldinger, Howard Aldrich, and Robin Ward, "Opportunities, Group Characteristics and Strategies," in Waldinger, et al. (eds.), *Ethnic Entrepreneurs*, Sage, Newbury Park, Calif., 1990.

28. John Kasarda, op. cit.

29. Campbell, op. cit.

30. Waldinger, Aldrich, and Ward, op. cit.

31. Campbell, op. cit.

32. Jeremy Boissevain et al., "Ethnic Entrepreneurs and Ethnic Strategies," in Waldinger et al. (eds.), *Ethnic Entrepreneurs*, Sage, Newbury Park, Calif., 1990, pp. 131–156.

33. Thomas Stewart, "The New American Century: Where We Stand," *Fortune*, special issue, Spring/Summer, 1991.

34. Kotkin, op. cit., p. 98.

35. Joyce Heard, et al., "The New Wave of Immigrant Entrepreneurs," *Business Week*, September 15, 1986.

36. Jonathan Peterson, "Asian Entrepreneurs: An Influx of Immigrants, Many Educated Here, Are Bringing Jobs and Innovation to the U.S. Market," *Los Angeles Times*, August 6, 1989, Business Section, p. 1.

37. Ibid.

38. Kotkin, op. cit.

39. Peterson, op. cit.

40. Stewart, op. cit.

41. Michael Schrage, "Innovation: U.S. Should Welcome the Best, Brightest," *Los Angeles Times*, December 14, 1989, p. D 1.

42. Michael Selz, "Small Companies Thrive by Taking Over Some Specialized Tasks for Big Concerns," *The Wall Street Journal,* September 11, 1991.

43. Mandel et al., op. cit.

44. Mandel, op. cit., p. 128.

45. Campbell, op. cit., p. 14.

46. Schrage, op. cit.

47. Roger Waldinger, et al., "Conclusions and Policy Implications," in Waldinger et al. (eds.), *Ethnic Entrepreneurs,* Sage, Newbury Park, Calif., 1990, pp. 177–197.

48. Campbell, op. cit., p. 18.

49. Kotkin, op. cit., p. 102.

9

Foreign Operations

Professor of Business Administration, Georgetown University, and Visiting Professor of Technology Management, INSEAD

What do IBM, Hewlett-Packard, Xerox, Kodak, Mars, Digital, Black & Decker, Corning, AMP, Ford, GM, Stanley Tools, and NCR have in common? The obvious answer is that they are all American companies; the not so obvious answer is that they know how to run factories outside the United States better than many other companies— American or not. They are not the only American companies that excel in this capability: Apple, Intel, Procter & Gamble, Du Pont, Monsanto, Honeywell, Johnson & Johnson, and many others are also good. For 40 years, American companies have been building a network of foreign operations that surpasses any other nation's. And they continue to expand this network at a fast pace. About a quarter of all foreign direct investment in the world is still done by American companies. Both in absolute value and proportional increase, American companies are investing more abroad than any of their competitors.

The full significance of these facts is not generally well appreciated. Consider, for example:

- About a fifth of the output of American firms is produced offshore.

- Stock of foreign assets of U.S. companies are substantial, more than

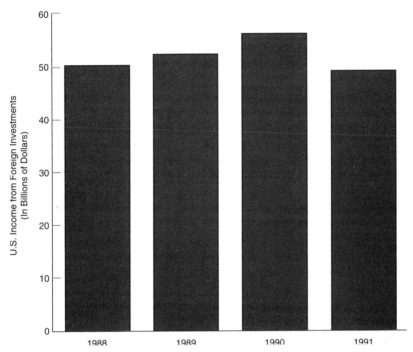

Figure 9-1. U.S. Income from foreign investments. (*Data from Fortune, July 27, 1992.*)

that of any other nation. In 1991 these assets stood at $457 billion (historical book value basis), and they are growing at a rate of about 7 percent a year.[1] The rate of return of these assets is generally good, almost $50 billion in 1991 (see Figure 9-1), and most of the profit is reinvested in the foreign affiliates (half of profits in 1986, two-thirds in 1987).[2]

- A quarter of all U.S. imports and a quarter of all U.S. exports are *intrafirm*—that is, between the foreign affiliates and the parent U.S. companies. The major share of these flows (about 40 percent) is in transfer of manufactured goods (as distinct from minerals, agricultural products, and services).[3]

- In 1985 American subsidiaries abroad shipped $294 billion to a third country (and $410 billion in the foreign country in which the subsidiary was located); by comparison, exports from the United States were worth only $216 billion that year.[4]

More statistics can be cited here, but they all support the fact that

manufacturing assets held by American multinational enterprises outside the United States are substantial and generally well managed;
more important, these companies have gained considerable experience
in running factories abroad. I argue in this chapter that, by choosing
strategies which build on their extensive international factory networks, and, more important, accumulated experience in managing and
expanding these networks, the U.S. multinationals can maintain a
decisive edge over their Japanese and European competitors. They can
stay ahead in this race in spite of the fact that others, particularly the
Japanese, are zealously expanding their production internationally.
The reason, as I will argue, stems from the relative advantage of
American multinationals in attracting and keeping foreign talent.

Using this relative advantage requires careful strategies. If foreign
factories are used essentially to employ cheap labor, to gain footholds
inside trade barriers, to obtain cheap capital (through loans and
grants), to enjoy tax benefits, or to lower transportation costs—all
good, pragmatic reasons—then the American multinationals would
not be exploiting this advantage. Others can do the same and catch up
eventually. To exploit their advantage, Americans must do more with
their foreign factories (as many of the companies named earlier have
done): They should use their extensive network of foreign factories for
tapping into local technological resources, advanced supplier infrastructures, and sophisticated markets worldwide. The achievement of
these goals requires highly qualified people who are comfortable
working *both* in the local environment and in the higher echelons of
the company. The advantage of American companies, as I shall argue,
is that, relative to their Japanese, German, or other major competitors,
they have a better chance to attract and hold these kinds of employees.
But they need to make their foreign factories places where such highly
qualified employees can thrive. I suggest how they can do this in the
last part of the chapter.

The Historical Advantage of
U.S. Manufacturing Abroad

In the wake of the Second World War, and the vacuum that resulted
from the devastation of Europe and Japan, healthier U.S. companies
managed to establish impressive strongholds outside the United
States. This was particularly true in Europe, where many of the companies mentioned at the beginning of the chapter established new factories or took over existing ones by acquisition or joint ventures.[5]

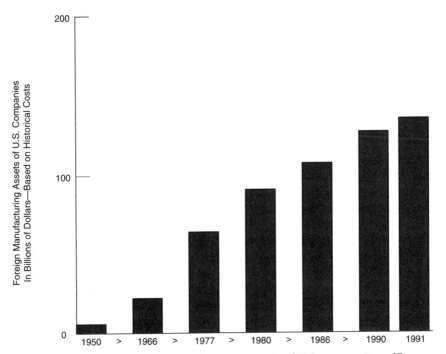

Figure 9-2. Stock of foreign manufacturing assets of U.S. companies. (*Source: U.S. Department of Commerce data. The 1990 and 1991 figures were computed on the basis of historical share of manufacturing in U.S. foreign direct investment.*)

Figure 9-2 shows the historical trend in the stock of manufacturing assets held by the U.S. companies.

Aside from the overall increase in the size of this stock, it is important to note that throughout this period U.S. companies have held the largest share of foreign manufacturing assets of all companies worldwide. In other words, if you add the foreign-owned manufacturing assets in all countries, you will find that by far the largest share—a fourth—is owned by U.S. companies (Figure 9-3). Although the U.S. share has steadily declined through the years (it was 50 percent in 1967[6]), a simple extrapolation of current trends shows that U.S. companies will continue to be the largest holder of foreign assets for quite a few years to come.

Moreover, and very importantly, most of these assets are in the highly industrialized countries of the world. In 1986, over two-thirds of the stock of foreign manufacturing assets of U.S. multinationals were in developed countries—primarily Canada, Britain, Germany, France, Switzerland, Holland, and Japan (Figure 9-4). Between 1980

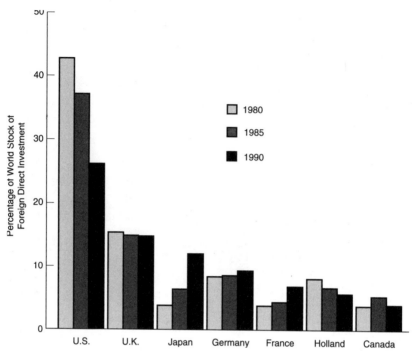

Figure 9-3. Shares of world stock of foreign direct investment. (*Source: U.S. Department of Commerce data.*)

and 1987, for example, American companies increased their stock of foreign manufacturing assets worldwide by 30 percent; but in Britain, Germany, and Japan the increase was over 40 percent.[7] New U.S. investment continues to go mostly into the highly industrialized countries. In 1991, over half of foreign direct investment by U.S. companies were in just seven countries: Germany, Mexico, France, Holland, Britain, Switzerland, and Canada (Figure 9-5). So while in certain industries or countries the American multinationals might have faced setbacks, in general, they have maintained a substantial manufacturing presence in most of the significant markets of the world. Their "beachhead" factories (those which were established before the onslaught of intense global competition) have been fortified and new ones have been added every year.

All this gives the U.S. multinationals a strong base to build on. History has given them a jump start in this race, and as such, a valuable advantage. The strong international manufacturing base of these companies, and the experience they have gained in running factories

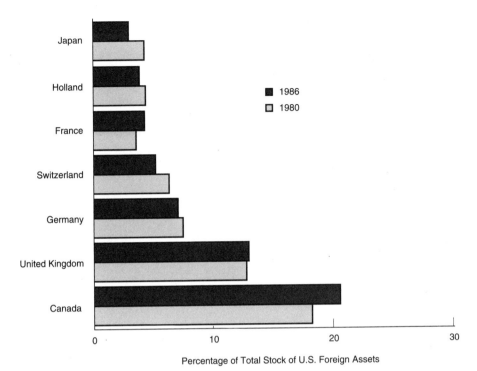

Figure 9-4. Major host countries for U.S. foreign direct investment. (*Source: U.S. Department of Commerce data.*)

outside the home base for so many years, are particularly precious in this age of ever-increasing globalization.

The Cultural Advantage of U.S. Manufacturing Abroad

An advantage based purely on having started earlier would be difficult to maintain in the long run. In more recent years, the Japanese and European multinationals have stepped up their rate of foreign production. The Japanese, in particular, sharply increased the rate of their foreign direct investment in the mid-1980s, raising their stock of foreign direct investment from $44 billion in 1985 to $201 billion in 1990.[8] This amounted to an average annual increase of 35 percent, three times the rate for the United States (11.2 percent per year) for the same period.[9] Many of the Europeans, too, have stepped up their foreign direct

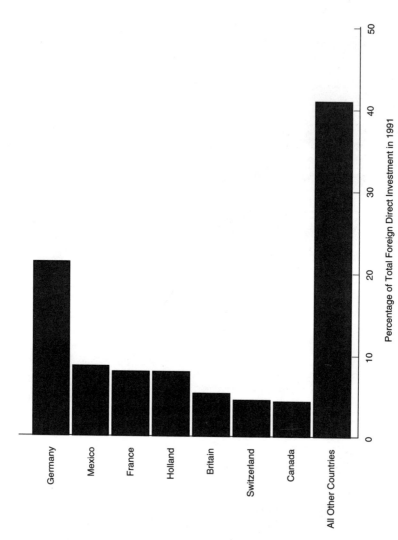

Figure 9-5. Major recipients of U.S. foreign direct investment in 1991. (*Data from Fortune, July 27, 1992.*)

investments. During the 1985–1990 period, Belgium, Sweden, Denmark, France, Germany, Holland, Italy, Switzerland, Spain, and Portugal, all increased their stock of foreign direct investment by over 20 percent annually—almost twice the rate of the United States. Therefore, the historical advantage of American multinationals is gradually eroding. But are there also other reasons why American multinationals might have an advantage in using their international network of factories—better than Japanese, German, French, or other multinationals?

· The answer is yes. My argument, presented in the next section, is based on a simple proposition: Upper echelons of American multinational companies seem to be more accessible to foreign managers than the upper echelons of Japanese, German, French, British, Italian, or almost all other multinationals. The perceived, or real, "glass ceiling" for promotion of foreign nationals seems to be generally higher in the American organizations. Unlike say the Japanese, Swedish, or French multinationals, the "inner circles" of American multinationals are generally more accessible to foreign managers.

Support for this proposition is partly anecdotal and partly based on logical inference; I have not been able to find reports of previous research addressing this issue. The rich literature on headquarter-subsidiary relationship only indirectly addresses the issue. The studies by Negandhi and Welge[10] (comparing practices in a sample of U.S., Japanese, and German multinationals), Hudlund[11] (comparing Swedish, U.S. and Japanese multinationals), Young, Hood, and Hamil[12] (a study of foreign subsidiaries of multinationals in the UK), Van Den Bulke and Halsberghe[13] (a study of foreign subsidiaries in Belgium), and Bartlett and Ghoshal[14] (an in-depth analysis of a sample of U.S., European, and Far Eastern multinationals), among others look into the relative influence of headquarters and subsidiaries in decision making in different areas, but data on differences in promoting local subsidiary managers into higher corporate positions do not seem to have been collected or reported.

Anecdotes, on the other hand, abound: For example, between January and April 1992, while I was writing this chapter, a Spanish national was promoted to vice presidency of General Motors (in charge of $30 billion worldwide purchasing), an Italian to the executive vice presidency of Xerox, a Frenchman to vice chairmanship of Pfizer, a German to presidency of Compaq Computers, a Swiss to presidency of Unisys, and a Britain to presidency of Next Computers. There were of course more.[15] They joined the ranks of many other foreigners already in the upper echelons of the U.S. multinationals. No other industrialized nation's multinationals, in particular the archrival competitors in Japan or Germany, seem to match such proportion of foreigners in high-ranking positions. And if there was a way to adjust for those managers who are naturalized citizens (probably more often found in the United States), the difference would be still greater. This is significant, because the issue here is really where the manager was raised and spent his or her early career, not the color of his or her passport. What is even more directly the issue, however, is the *perception* of a local manager working in a foreign subsidiary about the accessibility of the upper corporate echelon.

Why should upper echelons of U.S. multinationals be perceived as more accessible than the upper echelons of Japanese, German, French, Italian, Scandinavian, South Korean, or many other multinationals? One can cite many reasons: Immigrant origin of the U.S. society makes the foreign-born manager feel less alien. As Sheila Akabas and Lauren Gates show in Chapter 6 of this book, the United States, which has strict laws against discrimination due to national origin, has an advantage over Germany, Japan, and many other countries in dealing with diversity in the population. In Chapter 8, Marion McCollom argues that unlike Germany and Japan who rely on "guest workers" to supplement their work force, the United States embraces the immigrant as a member of society.

There are also practical reasons. For example, the ability to speak the language is crucial: Anything short of *mastery* of the language is indeed a serious handicap for reaching the upper corporate echelon. Even among educated and skilled individuals around the world, not many speak Japanese or German fluently; but luckily for American companies, many master English. And in general, more seems to be known about the United States than about most other countries. The American way of life, politics, and culture seem to be more transparent to outsiders. This is perhaps due to the very strong U.S. print and visual media—television in particular. The sheer volume of books and research available on U.S. managerial practices (compared to that of other nations) reduces the mystery of what goes on in the inner circles of high corporate offices. The large number of foreigners studying in the United States provide a continuous stream of qualified managers who are familiar with the U.S. system in different corners around the world. And, the mobility of U.S. managers (in moving from one company to another), inhibiting formation of impregnable high-level corporate circles, also promotes the perception of openness in U.S. organizations.

In short, there are many reasons why foreigners perceive American organizations to be more open than organizations in other countries (barring a few minor possible exceptions like Canada or Australia). Of course, Americans pay a price for this openness. U.S. multinationals cannot generally match the tacit understanding which exists among groups of Japanese, Swedish, German, French, or Italian senior managers. The managers in these countries generally come from more homogeneous backgrounds; they work together and rise in the same company through their formative years. Their relationships are based on trust and mutual recognition, and they can accomplish a lot through informal systems. This ease of administrative transaction can be enormously valuable, but there is also a drawback: It is difficult to bring outsiders into the high echelons of these companies, especially outsiders from different cultures. Only mavericks, like Sony, seem to be able to do that. Among all Japanese multinationals, Sony stands out in its efforts to let "the foreigners infiltrate the structure."[16]

Which one of these capabilities is more valuable in running a global network of factories in the future: easier assimilation of foreigners into the company or a close-knit inner circle? I submit the former. While the benefits of a close-knit inner circle are more visible and immediate, the long-term potentials of the ability to attract and hold qualified foreign employees are even greater. I base my argument on the implications of three trends in global manufacturing:

1. Trade in manufactured goods is increasing every year and tariffs are declining.

2. Foreign manufacturing assets in highly industrialized nations are increasing fast.

3. Technologically intensive industries do more intrafirm transfer of manufactured products than those industries with less sophisticated technologies.

Trends in Global Spread of Production

Among the many factors which have shaped the spread of production internationally, the three trends listed above are particularly relevant to our analysis. Let us examine the support for each of these and their collective effect on foreign factories.

- Trade in manufactured goods is increasing every year and tariffs are declining.

GATT statistics show that for the last 40 years trade in manufactures has consistently outperformed both growth of trade in general and growth of world output.[17] In other words, while worldwide output of manufacturing goods has been on the rise, every year a larger share of it has been crossing national boundaries. More materials are bought internationally, more components are made internationally, more sub-assemblies are transferred internationally, and more final products made are sold internationally. Surges of nationalism and protectionism, while they might have grabbed the headlines, do not seem to have been strong forces affecting global trade in manufactures. And the growth in manufacturing trade is likely to continue for the foreseeable future. In fact, in the light of the recent economic pacts—EC (European Community), EC with EFTA (European Free Trade Agreement), NAFTA (North American Free Trade Agreement)—it would be safe to assume a higher rate of growth in the future. These pacts accelerate the reduction of tariffs, which have declined steadily in the last 40 years (see Figure 9-6).

Together, increasing trade in manufactures and decreasing tariffs mean that there are increasing options for location of factories. To elaborate, because global trade in manufactures is increasing every

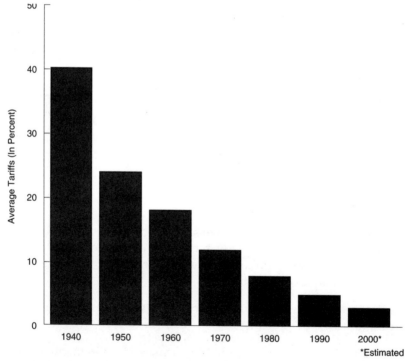

Figure 9-6. Average tariffs.   (*Source: GATT, IMF, as reported in The Economist, September 22, 1990.*)

year, companies are more likely to spread their factories globally, and because tariffs are coming down, they have fewer constraints in where they may put their factories. The world is becoming a more open arena, with more choices for locating factories.

More choice means more strategic potentials, and more foreign production means more strategic significance for the firm's foreign factories. To understand this better, it is useful to look more closely at where the multinationals are putting their foreign manufacturing investments. Are they chasing the cheap labor? In spite of hot political debates about relocation of factories to countries with low labor costs, in reality such relocations comprise only a minor portion of the global outward manufacturing investment. This becomes clear when you examine the second trend.

- Foreign manufacturing assets in highly industrialized nations are increasing fast.

Available statistics depict this trend clearly. Figure 9-7 shows the

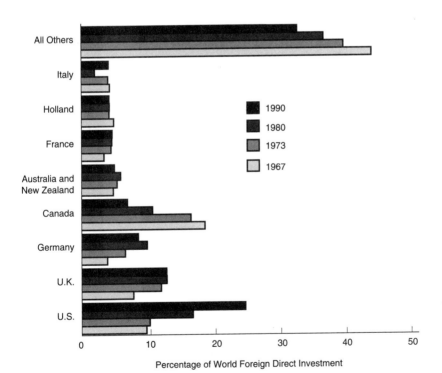

Figure 9-7. Shares of major host countries of total world stock of inward direct investment. (*Source: U.S. Department of Commerce data.*)

trend in investment in 9 countries which have been the largest recipients of global foreign direct investments for most of 1967 to 1990. (The breakdown for the part of the total foreign direct investments which were in the manufacturing sector is not available unfortunately. In general, around a quarter to a third of all foreign direct investments are usually in the manufacturing sector.)

Clearly, the overwhelming share of the foreign direct investments worldwide has been going into only a few highly industrialized countries. In 1990, four countries alone, United States, United Kingdom, Germany, and Canada received an astonishing 50 percent of all foreign direct investments; if we add six more, France, Holland, Italy, Australia, Spain, Switzerland, we have the list of countries which received *two-thirds* of the world's foreign direct investment that year.

Looking at the patterns of foreign investment by the largest current investors—the United States and Japan—shows this trend even more clearly. The pattern for the United States, still the biggest investor, was mentioned earlier (please refer to Figures 9-4 and 9-5); most of U.S. money continues to go into a few highly industrialized countries.[18] Figure 9-8 shows the pattern for the Japanese in 1989 and 1990. If we add the shares of various countries shown in this figure, it becomes

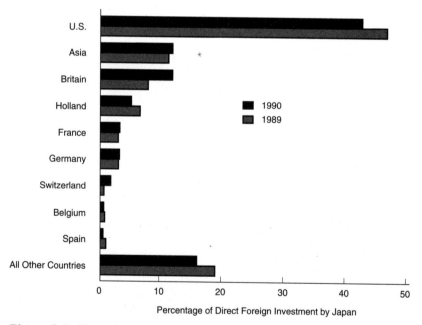

Figure 9-8. Major destinations of Japanese direct foreign investment in 1989 and 1990. (*Source: Japan Ministry of Finance data.*)

clear that over *two-thirds* of all Japanese foreign direct investments in these two years went into just five countries: the United States, the United Kingdom, Holland, Germany, and France.

What is the implication of this trend for the way the foreign factories are going to be used and managed? More foreign factories in the advanced regions mean more strategic potential for these assets. A company's foreign factory which happens to be in Germany has more potential than a factory which happens to be in the Philippines, Chile, or Nigeria. Why? Because the German factory can be used not just as a site for production, but also a place to collect critical marketing, technological, and competitive information; moreover, it can be a place for developing new processes, products, technologies, or management systems *for the entire company*. In short, it can be a "factory" that not only produces goods, but *generates knowledge*. The traditional roles of foreign factories—producing for specific geographical markets, supplying low-cost components, providing a hedge against foreign exchange fluctuations, getting inside trade barriers, or reducing the transportation costs for raw materials, components, or finished goods—are still important, in fact essential. But those companies which manage to go beyond them and are able to use their foreign factories to also collect information and generate knowledge will be doing more. Nowadays, hardly anyone disputes the significance of this ability in creating competitive advantage.

Since knowledge is transferred essentially from person to person, the best employees for these factories, especially for the managerial positions, are those who are comfortable working in *both* the factory's local environment and the rest of the company. To just produce a product, a nonlocal manager transferred from the home office or a local manager, even if he or she might feel isolated from the rest of the company, can do an adequate job. So the Japanese might be able to run their foreign factories very efficiently. But to get the latest ideas from the suppliers, customers, competitors, research centers, universities, and government agencies, to develop new processes and products, and to extend the firm's technological knowledge, and *to diffuse this knowledge in the rest of the company*, we need managers who can work easily in the "inner circles" of both their local environments and the company.

All this becomes more important with faster changes in technology. Firms engaged in industries experiencing rapid changes in technology—such as computers, cameras, telecommunication equipment, and fine chemicals—have a greater need to use their factories as a source of knowledge than firms engaged in industries with less dynamic changes in technology—such as beverages, dairy products, ferrous metals, or leather products. Or, as a corollary, firms that choose to compete on the capability of faster adoption of new technologies—regardless of the industry in which they operate—will have a greater incentive to learn from their foreign factories. Why? There is of course the intuitive logic: knowledge is the driver of technology. There is also some empirical evidence. To examine that, let us look at the third trend.

- Technologically intensive industries do more intrafirm transfer of manufactured products than those industries with less sophisticated technologies.

The best evidence for this is a study by J. K. Kobrin.[19] He has measured what he calls the "transnational integration index" for 56 manufacturing industries (classified according to the 3-digit SIC). The index is the proportion of international sales that are intrafirm. More specifically, it is the ratio of all intrafirm transfers across national boundaries over the total sales of all foreign affiliates plus exports from parent.[20] Figures 9-9 and 9-10 show the top and bottom 10 industries according to this measure.

Even a cursory look at the two figures shows that the industries with higher "transnational integration" are generally coping with faster changing technologies. The 10 industries shown in Figure 9-9, in which intrafirm transactions account for more than 25 percent of international sales, are motor vehicles, communications equipment, electronic components, computers and office machinery, farm machinery, photographic equipment, engines and turbines, scientific instruments, optical goods, and industrial chemicals. The least integrated industries, Figure 9-10, are paper boxes, leather products, ferrous metals, fabricated metals, a variety of food products, and nonelectrical machinery. More careful analysis confirms the impression from the "cursory look": The top 10 industries, as Kobrin shows, have spent a much higher percentage of their revenues on research and development than the average (of the 56 industries). Greater R&D intensity— normally associated with faster changing technologies—seems to demand or promote greater international transactions within the firm.

It is therefore safe to assume that the more a multinational manufacturer engages in faster development and adoption of new technologies, the more it would tend to transfer materials, components, semiassembled products, and finished goods among its units across national boundaries. In other words, each stage of production would tend to become concentrated in fewer places, forcing the factories to specialize.

Plant-level production economy of scale is *not* a significant force behind this. Increasing technological sophistication often does not raise

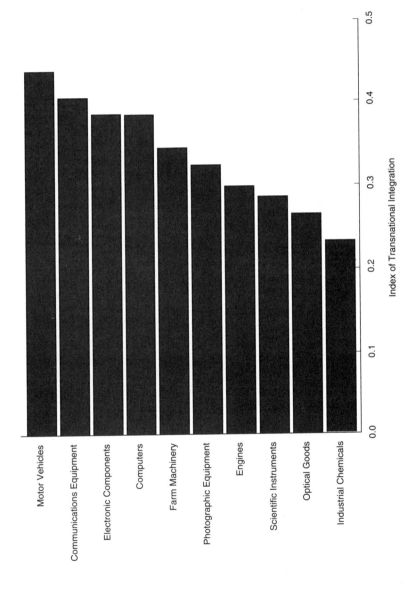

Figure 9-9. Most transnationally integrated industries (among 56 total industries). (*Data from Kobrin, op. cit.*)

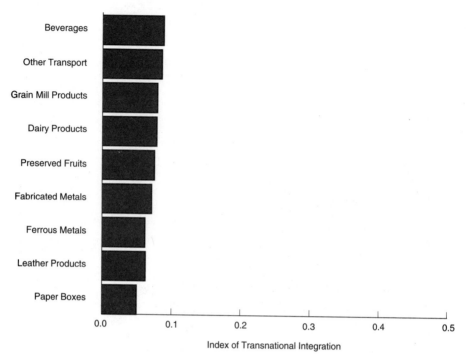

Figure 9-10. Least transnationally integrated industries (among 56 total industries). (*Data from Kobrin, op. cit.*)

the minimum efficient size of the factory, and in fact some of the new technologies, especially computer-driven process technologies combined with more versatile equipment and a multiskilled work force, actually reduce the minimum efficient size for the factories.[21] So instead of economy of scale, it must be the increasing levels of knowledge and expertise required to produce more technologically advanced components, semifinished goods, and different models of finished products and to master specific product or process technologies, which drive the factories towards specialization. So, again, those multinationals with factories in proper places staffed purposefully to maximize generation and transfer of knowledge are in a better position to use technology more aggressively.

To summarize, increasing global trade of manufactures, higher concentration of factories in highly industrialized countries, and greater technological intensity all point to greater potentials for the use of foreign factories. The traditional roles of foreign factories—such as, producing for a specific geographical market, supplying low-cost components, providing a hedge against foreign exchange fluctuations, getting inside trade barriers, or reducing the transportation costs for raw materials, components, or finished goods—are still important, but the potential roles go beyond them: The factories can also be used as a tool for collecting information and generating knowledge for the entire company. A global manufacturer must of course have well-run factories; but those with factories in the advanced regions of the world, and management systems which focus on deliberate use of these factories to learn and generate knowledge, can create a competitive advantage that is more difficult to match.

Leveraging the Advantages of U.S. Manufacturing Abroad

Compared to their archrivals, the U.S. multinationals, on the whole, have a competitive edge. They have more factories abroad, many of these factories are in sophisticated industrial regions, and, as I have argued, they have a better chance of attracting highly qualified local talents on whom knowledge generation depends. But these benefits will not accrue automatically. Because of the enormous complexity of management of an international network of factories, without a clear vision it would be difficult to stay on a course that would exploit this advantage. A shift in foreign exchange, a tax break, a grant or low-interest loan, a bargain acquisition opportunity, and many other things are powerful temptations to deviate from a well-conceived strategy.

How can a company develop a global network of factories which is economically viable and which at the same time maximizes exchange of knowledge? We have many models for factories effective in *producing things,* but not many models for factories effective in *generating and exchanging knowledge.* How would the latter factory look, especially if it were located in a "foreign" country?

The NCR factory in Dundee (Britain) provides a few clues. This factory is the center for managing a $1 billion business in automated teller machines (ATMs) for this American company.[22] This represents a third of the Western world's installed base of ATMs. Competing with the combined forces of IBM and Diebold (the two merged their ATM operations in 1989) and Fujitsu, the plant exports over 80 percent of its output to almost a hundred countries. Until a few years ago a second source for NCR's ATMs, Dundee is now its single worldwide center.

How has all this come about? In the early 1980s, like other NCR plants, Dundee was challenged to survive by developing a world-class manufacturing ability and creating a globally valuable business competence. To meet the challenge, Dundee has emphasized the powerful programs employed by many other factories—programs such as extensive education and training, total quality management, employee empowerment, just-in-time, automation, integration of information systems for production planning and control, order processing, cost accounting, and the like. But they have also done a few other things that are not as common. Chief among them:

1. Dundee has expanded its research and development department at the *factory site*. Most of the new hires in recent years have been for this department. In 1990, 250 persons (out of the 1400 total work force) were in research and development.

2. Like other NCR plants, *the factory* in Dundee maintains strong ties with local educational establishments. For example, it has funded a Department of Mechatronics at Dundee University.

3. The factory is remarkably close to its final customers. In 1989, the factory hosted 187 financial institutions from 23 countries, and went out to meet a further 307 from 18 countries. "When the bankers want to discuss the latest trends in banking, they head north to visit NCR in Dundee."[23]

4. Production of certain parts (like some PCB assembly, sheet metals, and bar stocks) has been retained in-house, primarily to enhance the factory's know-how in critical processes and technologies.

5. While the number of suppliers has been cut drastically (from 480 to 165 in the last five years), the value bought from *local suppliers* has increased from 45 to 80 percent of the total purchases. The factory works very closely with its suppliers, especially the local ones. Although NCR now employs less than a quarter of the 6000 people it used to employ in the 1960s, it contributes as much to the local economy as it ever did.

6. The factory has been essentially *self-financing* its phenomenal growth and development. It appears that the factory has managed to get into the "virtuous cycle" of generating enough funds to fortify and advance its leadership position, resulting in even more funds to repeat the cycle.

In short, the factory in Dundee is serving NCR not only as a site for production of ATMs (as good as it is in doing that) but also as a center of expertise for ATM market, customers, product development, supplier base, and process technology. Being such a center helps production, of course, but its value to the company goes beyond that. This factory is a "machine" that feeds on its ability to attract qualified people and to engage them profitably into a growth cycle. The focus is not on aggressive and continuous pressure to prune the "overheads"; it is on finding useful challenges for the people at the factory so that employing more qualified people is justified.

Remarkable as it is, NCR's Dundee factory is not alone. Hewlett-Packard's plants in Grenoble and Lyon in France, Böblingen in Germany, and Bristol in Britain are in many ways similar; the factories of the Mars Group in Strasbourg and Orléans in France, and Veghel in Holland, IBM's factories in Havant (UK), Sindelfingen (Germany), and Montpelliers (France), 3M factories in Cergy-Ponoise near Paris are but a few of many other factories which also share many of the similarities. In one way or another, more than production seems to be going on at these sites. The organization in these factories seem to be more "extrovert"—with more direct links to outside the factory—than usual. More process engineers, development engineers, sales technicians, computer experts, production planners, purchasing managers, maintenance mechanics, human resource professionals, distribution and shipping managers, quality management professionals, cost accountants, and other "overhead employees" seem to be working on these sites. The atmosphere is dynamic, interesting, and challenging—precisely the conditions needed to attract highly qualified individuals. And the best of these qualified people seem to have stayed with the company for a long time. Surely, an important reason why they stay is because they see that the scope of what they can do in the factory is not limited, that neither the factory's strategic charter nor the culture in the company is putting tight constraints on their potential in the company. Being a "foreigner" does not seem to be a significant handicap in having access to the circle of real decision makers in the company, and eventually being promoted into it.

So, what is the model for a foreign factory in which employing an increasing number of highly qualified local people would be justified? To start, the mission for that factory should involve building up a world-class specialty—a useful competence. The process of determining the exact nature of this specialty should ideally be kept fluid and self-correcting, letting each factory grow into its chosen area of competence step-by-step and justify every step. Top management's role is to create the right conditions in the factories and to ensure that major duplications of efforts are avoided. Creating the right conditions generally involves a tendency toward:

- Having more process engineering, upgrading of equipment, machinery installation and commissioning, or even process technology research done at the factory site.

- Doing more product customization, product upgrade, and product development at the factory site.

- Allowing more direct interaction between the factory staff and the suppliers.

- Whenever possible, increasing the value added in the factory (and less outsourcing and subcontracting of key components and operations, even if they bring marginal cost saving).

- Allowing more direct contacts between the factory and the distribution channel—all the way to the end users of the company's products.

- Encouraging more direct interaction between the factory staff and universities, technology centers, environmental agencies, machinery suppliers, and other sources of ideas and knowledge.

- Institutionalizing more direct contacts between the different factories of the firm (without having to go through a central staff).

All of the above aim at removing the barriers between the factory and its environment, both inside and outside the company. The premise here is that removal of these barriers not only results in better production in the long run, but also allows the company to use its factories as intelligence-collecting outposts, learning grounds, and mechanisms to attract good talent into the company. Maintaining a highly qualified staff at the factory is a key to making this strategy work. That is precisely where the potential American advantage lies.

Leveraging this advantage demands an unshrinking commitment. There are many temptations and obstacles on the way, which are not easy to overcome:

- The dazzling power of financial subsidies, tax reliefs, grants, subsidized energy and utility costs, and other incentives usually offered to convince the company to go to locations far from the centers of technology, sophisticated markets, or advanced suppliers, or generally where it would be difficult to attract highly qualified people.

- The urge to shift location of production in direct response to fluctuations in foreign exchange. This is a source of great insecurity for the employees of the foreign factories.

- The fear of relying on a "foreign" factory for a critical skill or technology, and the aversion to learning from one's own "foreign" factory.

- The tradition of treating the factory as a "cost center." This has generally deprived the factory of decisive power in reinvesting its own earnings and getting itself into the "virtuous cycle" of improving itself further and further.

Overcoming these obstacles is difficult during normal times; in an economic recession, the task is almost daunting. So in these difficult economic conditions of the early 1990s, my prescription may be hard to follow. Worse, aggressive, and sometimes indiscriminate cost-cutting programs, can easily destroy the valuable momentum in some of these factories. That would be a great pity. A factory, especially a foreign factory, can be a potent strategic asset, but it takes years to shape it into its full potential. Because it is not easy to do that, the competitive advantage it creates is more defensible. Many American multinationals have already benefited from their investments in foreign factories. Given the trends in manufacturing trade and the spread of production around the globe, they have a chance to benefit even more. The key is to use their extensive foreign manufacturing assets to attract and profitably employ local talents of the highly industrialized nations. The future in global manufacturing belongs to those who can staff their foreign factories with the largest number of these sought-after employees.

Notes and References

1. *Recent Trends in International Direct Investment,* U.S. Department of Commerce, Office of Trade and Economic Analysis, August 1992.

2. "America Still Buys the World," *The Economist,* September 17, 1988, p. 87.

3. *Transnational Corporations in World Development: Trends and Perspectives,* UN Center for Transnational Corporation, New York, 1988.

4. "U.S. Firms Grow Abroad at Record Pace," *International Herald Tribune,* May 21–22, 1988.

5. A notable exception was investment in manufacturing in Japan, where—perhaps due to restrictions by the Japanese government at the time—even some of the companies that had operated before the war, like Ford and GM, did not go back.

6. *International Direct Investment: Global Trends and the U.S. Role,* U.S. Department of Commerce, 1988 edition.

7. "America Still Buys the World," *The Economist,* September 17, 1988, p. 87.

8. According to the Bank of Japan, foreign investment by the Japanese surged from less than $10 billion in 1984 to over $55 billion in 1989, before coming

down to $36 billion in 1991. The share of this investment which went into the manufacturing sector was about 25 percent in 1991.

9. *Recent Trends in International Direct Investment,* U.S. Department of Commerce, Office of Trade and Economic Analysis, August 1992.

10. A. R. Negandhi and M. K. Welge, *Beyond Theory Z: Global Rationalization Strategies of American, German and Japanese Multinational Companies,* JAI Press, Greenwich, Conn., 1984.

11. G. Hudlund, "Anatomy of Subsidiaries and Formalisation of Headquarter-Subsidiary Relationships in Swedish Multinational Enterprises," in L. Otterbeck, (ed)., *The Management of Headquarter-Subsidiary Relationships in Multinational Corporations,* Gover, New York, 1981, pp. 25–78.

12. S. Young, N. Hood, and J. Hamil, "Decision Making in Foreign Owned Multinational Subsidiaries in the United Kingdom," Working Paper No. 35, International Labor Organization, Geneva, Switzerland, 1985.

13. D. Van Den Bulke, and E. Halsberghe, "Employment Decision Making in Multinational Enterprises: Survey Results for Belgium," Working Paper No. 32, ILO, 1984.

14. C. Bartlett, and S. Ghoshal, *The Transnational Corporation,* Free Press, New York, 1989.

15. See "Foreign Accents Proliferate in Top Ranks as U.S. Companies Find Talent Abroad," *The Wall Street Journal,* May 21, 1992, p. B1.

16. Guy de Jonquieres, "How Sony's European Managers Are Exercising Their Prerogative," *Financial Times,* October 4, 1989, p. 10.

17. See, for example, "Thriving in a Cold Climate," *The Economist,* September 26, 1987.

18. It is interesting to note that Japan is not among the recipients of large U.S. foreign direct investment.

19. J. K. Kobrin, "An Empirical Analysis of the Determination of Global Integration," *Strategic Management Journal,* 12, 1991, pp. 17–31.

20. In other words, the index is the ratio of (a) foreign affiliate sales to foreign affiliates, plus (b) affiliate sales to (U.S.) parents, plus (c) parent exports to affiliates, to (a) all foreign affiliate sales plus (b) parent exports to affiliates. The sample was restricted to American manufacturing multinational companies. For more details, see Kobrin, op. cit.

21. For example, in most of the highly transnational industries listed in Figure 9-9—namely, communication equipment, electronic components, computers, photographic equipment, scientific measuring instruments, optical goods, industrial chemicals—plant-level scale economies are generally becoming less important as a force for global integration. For more evidence, see Kobrin, op. cit.

22. The data on the NCR factory in Dundee are from public sources, in particular, "NCR," *Management Today,* November 1990.

23. *Management Today,* November 1990, p. 62.

PART 4
Technologies

10

The Environmental Advantage

James E. Post
Professor of Management and Public Policy,
Boston University School of Management

All great truths begin as blasphemies.
—GEORGE BERNARD SHAW
(Annajanska, 1919)

As the twentieth century began 100 years ago, Americans celebrated a "new dawning." For them, technology and industry held enormous promise. The nineteenth century had given birth to powerful forms of industrial capitalism, unleashing the ferocious energies of entrepreneurs in the emerging steel, oil, and chemical industries. North America had been spanned by the transcontinental railroad; public and private investment poured into agriculture, mining, manufacturing, and transportation. At the dawn of the twentieth century, newspapers and magazines heralded a new coming of economic opportunity. It was an age of optimism.

The outlook could hardly be more different as the twentieth century closes. New doubts arise daily about the vitality of global economies, the quality of life, and economic disparities that are even greater today than they were a century ago. The world's wealthiest individuals and nations have more than quintupled the economic fortunes of their grandparents; the world's poorest are no better off than their grandparents, and many are suffering serious problems of famine and disease. There is pessimism, an overriding sense that the future is bleak, and fear that 100 years from now human beings will be unable to gather in parks or gardens to enjoy a breeze or bask in the sunshine. There is a sense of progress lost as we view the paradox of economic prosperity that has eviscerated human happiness.

It is our understanding of global environmental degradation that seems to capture these feelings more clearly than any other. The great blasphemies of twentieth century capitalism have been that "externalities matter," that "exploitation is not sustainable," and that "stewardship is as crucial to human happiness as growth." But those blasphemies have become the new truths of social, economic, and political decision making.

The cumulative effects of a century of economic growth have touched a sensitive chord in the public consciousness. Even before the 1992 Earth Summit meeting in Rio de Janeiro, more than three-fourths of Americans called themselves "environmentalists." In Europe, green political parties flourish as established and potent political forces. In the nations of the old eastern bloc, ecological political parties were among the first to be formed in the era of liberal reform. In Japan, a small but vigorous environmental movement and the pressure of international political and economic developments have prompted Japanese industry and government to seriously address environmental problems. Japan's posture at the Earth Summit signaled to many observers a major commitment by government and industry to create clean technologies, provide development funds, and actively shape the economic and environmental future for its many trading partners.

Developing nations are paying attention as well. Taiwan has announced a dramatic commitment to environmental cleanup; Brazil has set aside millions of acres of rain forest for indigenous peoples; China has begun to reduce ozone-depleting chlorofluorocarbon (CFC) emissions. As Vice President Albert Gore, Jr., has written in his book, *Earth in the Balance* and reiterated at the Earth Summit meeting, where he headed the U.S. Senate delegation, the environment is becoming a new organizing principle for international relations.[1] The world now faces both numerous local environmental problems and serious global environmental problems. And as the twentieth century closes, more and more of the earth's population knows it.

Global environmental problems are a legacy of the twentieth century and a promise for the twenty-first. Science and politics have converged to highlight the needs. The next step requires the use of political and economic resources to address the problems. Before the twenty-first century actually arrives, global investment will have turned sharply upward to support public and private responses to environmental needs. Europe, Japan, and the United States are devoting more resources to the task of coming clean. Before the decade of the 1990s ends, for example, more than one trillion dollars will have been spent in the United States alone to address environmental problems. For the planet and its inhabitants that may be just a down payment on what is ultimately required.

America's Environmental Progress

Americans have increasingly come to accept the view of environmental expert Lester Brown that whereas for decades economic trends shaped the environment, in the 1990s we are witnessing the reverse: environmental trends are shaping economic trends.[2] More than 50 major pieces of federal legislation articulate the nation's environmental commitment. These are supplemented by no less than three major statutes (water, air, land) in each state. The net result is a regulatory thicket composed of thousands of pages of statutory language, tens of thousands of pages of regulations, and hundreds of thousands of pages of rulings and decisions by tribunals at every level of government. And the cost of this commitment is staggering: according to Environmental Protection Agency (EPA) figures, 1990 spending on pollution control exceeded $100 billion (1986 dollars) and is forecast to grow by more than 60 percent to $160 billion (in 1986 dollars) by the end of the decade. Most experts believe these figures greatly *underestimate* true spending by 25 to 50 percent because they do not include related services, technology development, and government spending on environmental research. It is very likely that environmental spending substantially exceeds official estimates of 2 percent of U.S. gross domestic product (GDP).

Is all of this spending simply a drag on the productive capacities of U.S. industry? For much of the 1970s and 1980s that view prevailed among U.S. manufacturing executives. With relatively few exceptions, business leaders have argued that environmental protection was "nice, not necessary," rather like a luxury collective good.

That view changed in the 1990s for several reasons. First, there seems to be an acceptance of the permanence of the nation's environmental commitment as seen in law and regulation. The business leaders of the 1970s have mostly retired from the scene and have been replaced by a new generation, whose executive education frequently included stints in the corporate Washington office. These chief executives realize the depth of the nation's political commitment to environmental protection. Change is likely to occur, but most likely in the direction of more, not less stringent regulation.

Second, as the modern environmental movement matured during the 1980s, experts began testing alternatives to traditional command and control regulation. "Carrots not sticks" became a familiar theme in congressional debates and EPA meetings. The results included the "bubble" concept, pollution charges, and tradable emissions rights introduced by the Clean Air Act of 1990. Flexibility gives managers room to experiment, to test alternatives, and to find the most efficient way to meet performance standards. Advantages can be created because imagination can be employed for productive gain.

The third factor has been the changing economics of environmental protection. Regulatory compliance costs are but one part of the economic picture. Environmental liability claims have soared in number and cost. Billions of dollars of claims have been settled in each of the past five years, and contingent environmental liabilities are a significant item for companies in virtually all manufacturing industries. Risk avoidance through risk management has become a central activity in most manufacturing firms. Most importantly, once aggressive environmental risk management begins, there is often the discovery of new operating efficiencies as time-consuming and resource-consuming practices to deal with toxic materials, for example, are eliminated. Waste reduction and the elimination of toxic materials represent two of the most impressive areas of American industrial achievement in the past decade. The Minnesota Mining & Manufacturing (3M) Corporation's "Pollution Prevention Pays," or 3Ps program, helped the company save more than $500 million in a 10-year period. Dow Chemical's Waste Reduction Always Pays (WRAP) program has achieved impressive returns on investment too—in 1989, for example, capital projects in waste reduction produced more than a 200 percent return. For American manufacturing, those are rates of return that far exceed traditional levels.

America's Environmental Advantage

In 1900, the critical weapons for the competitive battles of the twentieth century were natural resources, human resources, and technology. As we look ahead, the critical weapons for the competitive battles of the next century will be human resources, technology, and decision systems that enable a population of nearly 6 billion people to live together on the planet. Ironically, where the exploitation of natural resources was a key to wealth in 1900, prosperity in the next century may depend heavily on the preservation of natural resources. Cooperation may become as important to success in the twenty-first century as competition has been to the twentieth century.

America has an advantage over the rest of the world in dealing with environmental problems. It has found ways to harness the enormous potential of people and technology to address ecological issues and natural resource problems. This has produced three distinct types of economic advantage.

First, the United States has the operating systems and processes that can meet or exceed world standards for "green manufacturing." American industry is either doing, or is capable of doing what political leaders in Rio de Janeiro were calling for: namely, achieving economic development that is compatible with ambitious efforts to protect and enhance the natural environment.

Second, the United States has technology that the rest of the world will need to use in meeting its environmental agenda. In the treatment of waste, recycling, pollution prevention, and remediation of old environmental problems (e.g., toxic dumping sites), the United States has an array of technologies that will prove critical to creating the type of environmental future set forth by political leaders at Rio.

Third, the United States has companies that are comfortable with the environmental ethic. Many American firms are in the vanguard of businesses that are showing the way to successful integration of economic goals and environmental protection. Across a broad spectrum of manufacturing, service, transportation, and retail businesses, environmental programs are yielding innovations and initiatives that are cost-effective and competition-enhancing.

These factors add up to a national competitive advantage that should be managed with a strategic purpose. Other nations cannot escape the need to address their environmental problems, and hence, must travel the experience curve of dealing with technical and human obstacles to a clean environment. These needs are creating opportunities for American industry to provide the goods and services required to meet these challenges. There is a boom occurring in an emerging global environmental products/services industry and it is far from having reached maturity. Many clean-up projects in Europe and the United States are projected to continue for 40 or 50 years, well into the twenty-first century.

Another reason for the United States to think in a strategic manner about its national advantage is its political role in shaping the international decision-making processes that will address the global environmental agenda. The experience of U.S. industry in negotiating and implementing the Montreal Protocol to reduce CFC emissions has prepared many companies and industries to grapple with international negotiations on global climate change, ocean resources, and the environmental aspects of free trade agreements. Although widely criticized for its position at the Earth Summit meeting in Rio, the United States government has developed considerable diplomatic expertise in negotiating the global and regional frameworks (e.g., North American Free Trade Agreement) in which future environmental and economic relationships will evolve. Thus, in both economic and political terms, the United States is ready to play a major role in creating the sustainable economy called for by the delegates to the Earth Summit.

Strategic Assets in the Environmental Sector: Six Factors That Make a Difference

As illustrated in Table 10-1, the United States fares well in comparison to Europe and Japan on six critical dimensions of environmental competitiveness. These factors represent the human, technological, and decision-making elements that are vital to mounting effective responses to local and global ecological problems. Each of these factors is discussed in more detail below.

1. Environmental Technology Base

In both size and quality, the United States has an environmental technology advantage over all world-class competitors. The core businesses, which are the underpinnings of a vibrant environmental technology base, include electronics, computers, instrumentation, and chemical processing. While Germany and Japan are well equipped to compete head-to-head with the United States in some of these industries, the number and experience of U.S. firms applying these technologies to environmental problems is a strategic asset for the United States. Figure 10-1 illustrates the linkages that are emerging in the United States between environmental needs and the supply of environmental

Table 10-1. Factors Contributing to an Environmental Advantage

Factor	Relative Strength		
	United States	Europe	Japan
Environmental technology base	Large, innovative vibrant; many small and large firms involved	Fairly large; significant large firms; modest small-firm base	Strong large firm base; modest small-firm base
Industry and regulatory infrastructure	Well developed; world class in most respects	Evolving in EC; disagreements over future governance	MITI now involved; stronger role for government
Private and public investment	Extensive; major investment by private and public sectors	Significant spending to date; major investment required in former eastern bloc states	Significant domestic spending; new international commitments
Large firms supporting environmental investment	yes	yes	yes

Table 10-1. Factors Contributing to an Environmental Advantage (*Continued*)

Factor	Relative Strength		
	United States	Europe	Japan
Large numbers of entrepreneurial firms in energy / environment field	yes	yes	yes
Record of multisectoral partnerships, alliances, consortia	yes	yes	yes

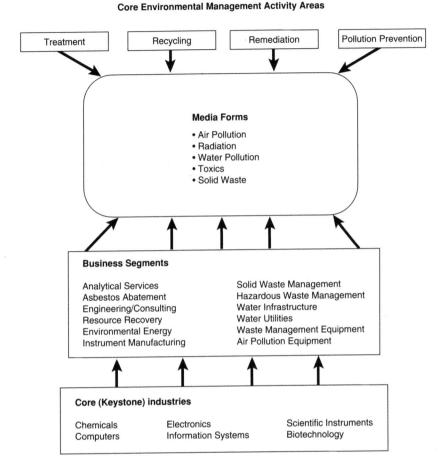

Figure 10-1. Linkages in the environmental sector.

services, products, and technology. The breadth and strength of what I term the "keystone industries" in the environmental sector can be effectively tapped by the multitude of entrepreneurial companies now competing in the environmental technology and services segments.

One weakness is the relatively small size of many of the most entrepreneurial U.S. firms and their limited export experience. The rapid development of trade groups to assist this industry is also capable of making a difference, however, as seen in the 1991–1992 experience of the Environmental Business Council's efforts to link New England environmental firms to business opportunity in Mexico. The existence of thousands of environmental technology companies in the United States represents an important clustering of technical knowledge, market information, and collateral business services that can make the nation a premier provider of environmental technologies to the world.

Japan has been making rapid progress in finding Asian markets for its environmental technologies. As part of its 1992 Earth Summit preparations, the Japanese Ministry of International Trade and Industry (MITI) offered impressive plans for developing future clean technologies. To U.S. industry experts who attended the Rio meeting and the industry trade show in São Paulo, Japan's commitment to creating new generations of clean manufacturing technologies points to a more competitive marketplace, and a shrinking U.S. advantage in the field of environmental technology.

For now, the competitive advantage lies with the United States. Many observers feel that Europe's needs and Japan's commitment to an environmentally sound industrial system bode ill for the United States unless more governmental and industry attention is given to the strengthening of the technology base. There has been a marked failure to think strategically about the environmental sector as an industry that can set and meet world-class standards. As Harvard's Michael Porter has suggested, someone is going to create a "Hollywood of the environmental industry." Why shouldn't that be the United States?

2. Industry and Regulatory Infrastructure

The EPA is the most capable public environmental agency in the world. Its technical assessments generally define world-class standards, and its policy making and administration is sophisticated. More than two decades of developing and enforcing regulatory policy has produced one of the most elaborate, expensive, and effective environmental regimes in the world.

The combined efforts of federal and state environmental agencies have produced impressive results. Water, air, and solid waste problems have been vigorously addressed. Industry after industry has achieved new levels of environmentally safe operations. The size, power, and importance of this infrastructure has been costly. Responding to critics at the 1992 Earth Summit meeting, President Bush asserted that the U.S. government alone has directly spent more money than any other national government to clean up the environment in the past decade. These costs do not take into account many billions more of indirect costs associated with regulatory compliance. But there has been both an environmental and an economic payoff for this expenditure.

Vigorous regulation has stimulated industry innovation and created a new environmental industry, directly leading to new jobs and indirectly promoting changes in education, consumer behavior, and public understanding of the relationship between human beings and the environment. In his book, *The Competitive Advantage of Nations,* Michael Porter has argued that regulation can create and strengthen a nation's economic base as well as weaken it.[3] In the environmental arena, regulation has actually stimulated the development of an environmental industry that is certainly "world class," and arguably *the* world leader.

American industry has also become highly sophisticated in dealing with EPA regulations and regulatory staff. The highly adversarial relations of the 1970s and 1980s seem to be giving way to a more cooperative, flexible form of regulatory administration. To a surprising extent, EPA and industry representatives are increasingly free to discuss global competitiveness, free trade agreements, and cooperative agreements in tackling environmental issues. In 1991, for example, the EPA announced the Public Private Partnerships (P[3]) Initiative. According to EPA Assistant Administrator, Charles Grizzle, "We have set several goals for the initiative over a five-year period, including fostering an increase in private sector investment in environmental projects, corporate voluntarism, and partnerships with states, local governments, and the private sector." Specific plans included strengthening state and local capacity to finance environmental programs and mobilizing industry, academic, and governmental resources to cooperate in addressing critical environmental resource needs. By 1992, more than a dozen P[3] projects were under way in six EPA regions of the United States.

The evidence of comparable public-private cooperation in Europe and Japan is limited. Despite a less adversarial regulatory approach in the United Kingdom, for example, the British government is not supporting industrial sector attempts to comply with regulatory standards. Despite its showing at the Earth Summit meetings, Japan has yet to demonstrate a clear harmony of business, government, and activist interests in the environmental policy arena.

The European Community has shown great promise for building an extremely large and potentially powerful environmental regulatory infrastructure in Brussels. The effectiveness of this bureaucracy, and its ability to catalyze environmental technology and industry development is still unproved. For now, the United States remains the world leader in terms of an environmental regulatory system. That is a strategic asset as we move into the twenty-first century.[4]

3. Private and Public Investment

The amount of private and public investment is a telling indicator of competitive advantage. Such investment is also a reflection of national and industrial priorities. Competitiveness is affected by three aspects of the investment picture: the absolute and relative magnitude of the investment, the balance between public and private spending, and the assignment of priorities and allocation of investment funds to various types of problems.

The United States has been allocating approximately 2.0 to 2.5 percent of GDP to environmental investment during the 1990s. As illustrated in Table 10-2, investment rates in both the European Community and Japan have been closer to 1.0 to 1.5 percent of GDP.[5]

Environmental constraints appear to have been a heavy burden for U.S. industry and for the U.S. economy during the past two decades. Many regulations have specified the type of technology, the process for its use, and standards of performance. But, in the 1990s, it is increasingly likely that environmental investment is being managed by private sector managers rather than bureaucrats from regulatory agencies. Shifts in regulatory approach have given more discretion to managers to assess the relative costs and benefits of different courses of action.

Two points are noteworthy. First, as a percentage of GDP, the U.S. rate of investment in environmental protection should be declining by the year 2000. Japan and Europe's environmental investment should continue to rise as a percentage of GDP until well into the next decade. Although the United States will spend more on capital and operating

Table 10-2. A Comparison of Annual Public Sector Environmental Spending in United States, Japan, and the European Community, 1975–2000.

(In $ Billion)

Year	United States	Japan	European Community
1975	18.4	7.6	
1980	29.0	2.5	
1984	35.0	2.8	13.3
1985	37.0	2.9	
1987	42.7	2.0	20–25
1990	50.0		
2000	88.0 (est.)		32–40

SOURCE: Reports of national governments prepared for United Nations Conference on Environment and Development, 1992.

Table 10-3. U.S. Environmental Spending on Capital and Operating Costs Compared to Two Tier-1 European Community Nations
(Percentage of GDP)

	1980	1985	% Change	1990
United States	1.60	1.44	− 10.0	2.00
West Germany	1.45	1.52	+ 4.8	1.80 (est.)
Netherlands	1.11	1.26	+ 13.5	3.20 (est.)

Table 10-4. U.S. Environmental Resource Allocation by Type of Media

	1987 ($77 billion total cost)	1997 ($134 billion est. total cost)	Projected percentage change 1987–1997
Air and radiation	28.9%	35.3%	+ 22.1
Land	26.0	30.1	+ 15.8
Water	42.9	31.7	− 26.1
Chemicals	1.2	1.7	+ 41.7
Multimedia	1.1	1.3	+ 18.2

SOURCE: Derived from data provided by the Environmental Protection Agency.

costs in absolute terms, countries such as Germany, Netherlands, France, and Spain are likely to increase both absolute and relative spending to meet environmental goals in the next decade. (See Table 10-3.)

A second point of note is that extensive U.S. private and public investment has already occurred in areas that remain as major challenges for European and Japanese societies. Table 10-4 indicates the allocation of environmental investments by type of environmental problem. In the 1990s, the United States will shift more resources to air and radiation problems and away from water pollution. This signifies high levels of water quality improvement that neither Europe nor Japan have yet been able to achieve. Europe will remain focused on water quality, an area in which the United States has extensive technology and experience to offer. Meanwhile, the United States will continue to innovate and should be able to lead the world in air pollution and radiation technology.

Public and private investment in meeting pollution control, prevention, and remediation needs is critical to the nation's environmental health and to the building of a successful environmental industry.

Compared to its European and Japanese competitors, the United States has the capacity to create a real and sustainable competitive advantage into the next century.

4. Large Firms Support Environmental Investment

The EPA estimated that more than $100 billion was spent in 1990 to protect the environment. Of this amount, 60 percent was paid by private interests, 25 percent by state and local governments, and 15 percent by the federal government itself.

Of private sector spending, business accounted for nearly two-thirds (62 percent) while personal consumption accounted for the remainder (38 percent). This amounted to more than $36 billion of industry spending in 1990. Within the private business sector, the burden of environmental cleanup has fallen most heavily on five basic industries: utilities (20 percent); petroleum (15 percent); chemicals (13 percent); pulp and paper (11 percent); and mining and metals (9 percent). The EPA estimates that nearly 70 percent of all spending by private industry comes from firms in these key industries.

In general, each of the "big five" is a capital-intensive and an energy-intensive business. Not surprisingly, each of these industries is also dominated by a relatively small number of large firms. This structure yields several advantages. The EPA has learned that it is possible to focus its regulatory enforcement efforts on leading firms in these key industries. And, in recent years, a number of leading firms have emerged in these industries to chart pathways to more environmentally sustainable practices. For example, a number of utilities have pioneered "demand side" management programs in which conservation measures are encouraged and rewarded. This reduces the demand for additional energy, and hence the construction of new power plants. In the chemical industry, a number of firms have undertaken massive voluntary waste reduction programs to reduce toxic air emissions. This leadership has now produced a major industrywide initiative called "Responsible Care" under the auspices of the Chemical Manufacturer's Association. The pulp and paper industry has also seen significant initiatives by manufacturers: recycled paper stock, for example, is now being used in manufacturing paper products, a commitment which has necessitated the building of expensive de-inking facilities. Many pulp and paper mills have replaced the chlorine bleaching processes, which are required to produce white paper, with alternatives that eliminate dioxin by-products. The primary metals industry has likewise been making strides in reducing its air and water waste streams.

One of the clear advantages for U.S. firms has been the integration of green manufacturing standards into the commitment to total quality management. Waste reduction programs in the U.S. chemical industry have set the standard for pollution reduction in the global chemical industry. Waste reduction has become a significant source of cost savings and productivity enhancement. Chemical firms from Germany, the United Kingdom, Japan, and Korea, among other nations, still largely trail the U.S. chemical leaders in this area. And, to the extent customers are influenced in purchasing decisions by practices such as "product stewardship," a concept of cradle-to-grave product responsibility, U.S. chemical firms have created a competitive advantage.

One of the weaker links in the effort to use more recycled materials has been market demand. In late 1992, however, the National Recycling Coalition announced the formation of the "Buy Recycled Business Alliance" to expand the use of recycled materials. Twenty-five major corporations, including Coca-Cola, Anheuser-Busch, Sears Roebuck, McDonald's, and Kmart pledged their efforts to expand purchases of recycled materials. To the extent the United States is able to develop a more robust domestic market for recycled materials, it has an opportunity to encourage entrepreneurial activity, achieve improved environmental performance, and enhance the domestic economy.

The United States has a further advantage. Many of the world's leading industrial firms are U.S. multinationals. They are experienced in meeting U.S. environmental standards, in creating and using clean technologies, and in devoting significant managerial effort to the creation of environmentally sound manufacturing. As national governments build on the commitments made in Rio to improve air and water quality, the experience and commitment of the multinational firms become a public asset.

Alternative pathways to "sustainable development" have been charted, but not yet traveled. The differences go well beyond differing political visions of conservative and liberal idealogues. The huge gathering at the Non-Governmental Organizations (NGOs) Global Forum in Rio pointed to a sustainable development pathway that relies less on large-scale industry and more on small-scale economic activity that is less damaging to the environment. The continued vitality of the vision E. F. Schumacher set forth in his book, *Small Is Beautiful,*[6] will challenge the vision of the multinationals. Politically, the United States continues to provide the global model of open, democratic approaches to the marketplace that encourage rapid dissemination of ideas and technologies. The multinational manufacturing, service, and retailing firms that have integrated environmental performance objectives into their business operations may provide examples of environmentally sustainable large-scale enterprises. Much depends on the vigor and sustained effort to meet ambitious environmental goals. To date, U.S. firms have been at, or near, the forefront of that development. It is where they belong and must be if they are to prosper in the business climate of the twenty-first century.[7]

5. Large Numbers of Entrepreneurial Firms in the Energy/Environment Field

The United States has been among the most successful of nations in spawning the development of new enterprises dedicated to meeting environmental needs. Throughout the United States, but especially in the technology-academic research incubators of California, Massachusetts, Minnesota, Texas, and North Carolina, thousands of entrepreneurial start-up ventures are under way. They range from low-technology recycling operations to high-technology toxic waste disposal firms. They populate niches of the market for waste treatment, recycling, remediation, and pollution prevention. It is a dynamic and growing segment of the economy.

The Environmental Business Council, an association of several hundred so-called enviro-tech manufacturing and service firms located in the northeast part of the United States, has estimated that in that region alone more than 55,000 jobs are directly connected to environmental technology and services. Moreover, the industry has sustained an annual job growth rate in excess of 9 percent during the 1990–1992 recession, down from a 15 percent annual growth in earlier years.

The vitality, entrepreneurial spirit, and competitive skill of such enterprises are illustrated by the example of an entrepreneurial company called Molten Metal Technology (MMT). Cofounded by a young, highly successful entrepreneur named William Haney and former U.S. Steel chemical engineer Chris Hayes, MMT is now developing and marketing a catalytic extraction process to heat toxic chemicals to temperatures at which they separate into their chemically elementary form. In this form, they can be extracted and recycled for future use. They describe their business as "elemental recycling." Despite superficial similarities to incineration, the young company has been able to tread the political minefields to secure regulatory and community approvals for its research and development facility; begin prototype operations with two large industry partners, Du Pont and Rollins Environmental; and form strategic alliances with L'Air Liquide in

Europe and Eco Administracion in Mexico. Throughout its development, the company's officers have maintained a dialogue with EPA officials and state regulators. The company virtually defines the unique mixture of technological, administrative, and political capabilities that are required for success in this complex industry.

6. Record of Multisectoral Partnerships, Alliances, and Consortia

Openness and activism are inherent elements of the political system in the United States, features which are sometimes cited as obstacles to doing business. The United States is likely to remain a society in which activism flourishes and political challenges to business are common occurrences. The environmental arena is a fertile ground for such conflicts, especially given the intense community opposition to projects that imply increased environmental risks.

Ironically, the experience of U.S. companies in such a climate constitutes an advantage of sorts. Successful companies have learned to build support in communities, responding in creative ways to the need to preserve or build public credibility and legitimacy. The climate of environmental politics, which was highly adversarial in earlier times, seems to have evolved toward a less contentious, more cooperative approach in the 1990s. While major political battles do occur on matters such as the Clean Air Act, mining rights, and wilderness preservation, and while there remain powerful NIMBY ("not in my backyard") forces, there is also a strong theme of collaboration emerging between the private, public, and nonprofit sectors. Some environmental organizations such as The Nature Conservancy have long operated in a nonconfrontational manner. For others, such as the Environmental Defense Fund, cooperative experiments with companies such as McDonald's and General Motors represent a new frontier. Indeed, across the spectrum of environmental activist organizations, more and more are experimenting with industry and government agencies to find creative solutions to environmental problems.

The President's Council on Environmental Quality detailed a list of more than 200 multisectoral partnerships, consortia, and alliances in 1992. In addition to numerous cooperative research arrangements with universities and technical institutes, these partnerships and alliances clearly are, and hold great potential to be, a strategic asset to American industry in addressing environmental issues.

Conclusion

America faces a number of challenges as it attempts to strike a new balance between growth, economic development, and protection of the environment. We are a nation that accounts for 5 percent of the global population, yet consumes well over 25 percent of global resources. Our twentieth-century manufacturing and resource-driven economy has operated on the convenient myths that air and water are free goods and that externalities need not be treated as real costs. The twenty-first century is certain to shatter what remains of those myths. A central challenge facing American enterprise is that of adapting to these new realities. Much progress has been made in doing so; much remains to be done.

The type of industrial change that must occur has been taking shape—in public policy and corporate behavior—for two decades in America. It has been painful and it has been costly. But American industry is emerging from this experience in far better shape to face the requirements of an environmentally sustainable economy than its counterparts in many other nations.

As we assess America's economic prospects for the twenty-first century, we should recognize our strengths as an environmental leader. Simply stated, America has an "edge" in the environmental arena. The six areas discussed above comprise a national competitive advantage that can be significant for our manufacturing and service sectors. Knowledge is the unifying theme of these factors—knowledge of our environmental problems and their causes and knowledge of the methods and means to the solution of those problems.

But action must be taken to nurture and enhance the competitive advantage offered by this knowledge. The Earth Summit in Rio demonstrated that Japan and Germany, our principal rivals for global economic power, have committed their industries to meet the world's environmental needs. The advantages that America enjoys will be temporary if wise policies do not guide their development. Corporate and public policies are required that recognize the economic potential for America in cultivating these capabilities. Strategic thinking is essential to any effort to achieve America's environmental advantage.

Action is especially vital in three areas: technology, management systems, and environmental values. The existence of a large, healthy environmental technology base is vital to continued U.S. preeminence. Critical keystone industries such as scientific instrumentation, electronics, computers, and chemicals are a wellspring of ideas that can be applied to the global needs of environmental preservation and restoration. The research and development programs in these industries contribute to the vitality and strength of the environmental industry. They must be enhanced. The enviro-tech industry of service and manufacturing firms must be supported with adequate capital, an educational system that effectively trains future employees, and a blend of regulatory and market policies that allows entrepreneurs to solve environmental problems in efficient and effective ways.

Environmental management systems and techniques must continue to be improved by manufacturers and service sector firms. Major challenges include the redesign of manufacturing systems to minimize waste, eliminate toxics, and reduce risk exposure for employees and communities. This agenda embraces total quality management approaches proved effective for achieving environmental as well as quality objectives in American manufacturing.

Systems improvement involves external parties as well. Linkages with customers, communities, employees, activists, researchers, and a multitude of other stakeholders must be strengthened. They can lead to more information sharing, cooperative management of risk, and preparedness for emergency situations. Cooperation will also involve sharing of information and knowledge via benchmarking, cooperative ventures, strategic alliances, and multisectoral partnerships.

Consciousness of the business imperatives of sustainable development must continue to be raised. Leading firms in the United States are demonstrating ways to harmonize economic mission with environmental protection. The mission statement of the 3M company, for example, speaks of "sustainable economic development" as "economic development which sustains the environment for future generations." There is a need to involve more companies in thinking about and discussing the practical and philosophical implications of environmental responsibility.

There is an ethical framework that ultimately guides the common view of what business enterprise is all about. "New age" companies such as Ben & Jerry's and Body Shop have been founded on principles that require their businesses to be compatible with environmental values. Companies like Molten Metal Technology also display a high degree of "fit" with environmental realities. The challenge for other firms, and for most large manufacturers and service firms, is to refine their concept of progress to one that fits with the realities of the new century.

The common theme of "stewardship" unites our concerns for the environment as individuals, business executives, and community leaders. No one wants a community that is unsafe, nor do they want a community besieged by unemployment and economic hardship. At the end of the twentieth century, our concept of "progress" requires that economic prosperity and environmental protection be achieved together.

Beneath the rhetoric surrounding the environment lies a deep human recognition of the need to preserve the support systems that enable human life to exist on this planet. The twentieth century will stand as an era in which people and organizations ignored environmental side effects in the name of economic growth. But it may also stand as the century in which we learned how to harness nature to human purposes *and* developed the wisdom to recognize the limits and consequences of that power. If so, it will stand as a testament to the ability of human beings to recognize how, in George Bernard Shaw's terms, some "blasphemies" do indeed become truths.

References

1. Albert Gore, Jr., *Earth in the Balance*, Houghton-Mifflin, Inc., Boston, 1991.
2. Lester Brown, *State of the World, 1990*, Worldwatch Institute and Norton, 1990, p. 3.
3. Michael E. Porter, *The Competitive Advantage of Nations*, The Free Press, New York, 1990.
4. For a contrary view of the value of U.S. regulation, see "America's Parasite Economy," *The Economist*, October 10–16, 1992, pp. 21–24.
5. *United States National Report for United Nations Conference on Environment and Development (UNCED)*, 1992.
6. E. F. Schumacher, *Small Is Beautiful: Economics As If People Mattered*, Harper & Row, New York, 1973. See also W. Edward Stead and Jean Garner Stead, *Management for a Small Planet: Strategic Decision Making and the Environment*, Sage, Newbury Park, Calif., 1992.
7. See Stephan Schmidheiny and Business Council for Sustainable Development, *Changing Course: A Global Business Perspective on Development and the Environment*, M.I.T. Press, Cambridge, Mass., 1992.

11
Remanufacturing

Robert T. Lund
Professor of Manufacturing Engineering
and Research Professor of Technology and
Policy, College of Engineering,
Boston University

Americans today have a growing conviction that their children are not likely to live as well as they. Many have already seen that their own standard of living has changed little from what it was in the 1970s. Real income of the American blue-collar industrial worker has actually declined over 8 percent in the period from 1979 to 1992.[1]

Part of our current uneasiness about the future stems from our unprecedented affluence during the 1950s and 1960s, when the rest of the world was trying to recover from the devastation of World War II. Toward the end of this period, when other countries had regained economic viability, a combination of forces began to choke our economic growth. Manufacturing activity—our prime source of wealth and income—began to decline. Concern for public safety, employee safety, and the environment were imposing new constraints and costs. Overseas producers entered many of our markets and gradually came to dominate them. Sapped by enormous defense expenditures and foreign trade deficits, and misled by a generation of executives intoxicated by acquisitions, buyouts, and high-risk borrowing, the American economy lost much of its resilience.

Now the United States faces the prospect of growing competition not only for markets but also for the dwindling energy and mineral resources of the world. Even though the United States is richly endowed with such resources, other nations are increasingly able to bid for and buy these resources at prices that serve to increase our domestic cost of living.

Meanwhile, Americans have become accustomed to buying products with shorter and shorter lifetimes. The "throwaway" generation has evolved into the "disposable" generation, in everything from diapers to surgical equipment. More rapid product innovation and shortened product life cycles are common phenomena. Hewlett-Packard, for example, has stated that about 60 percent of its product line is less than two years old.[2]

In the light of these trends which seem to be carrying us further into economic trouble, is there a solution relative to the products we buy and use that offers some hope? There is, and it has been with us for some time. The new-but-old paradigm is to conserve our wealth by making products live longer. Several strategies can be employed, one of which is a secret weapon: remanufacturing. The underlying philosophy is thrift.

The goods in our economy tend to fall into two categories: durable goods, that are made to last for a considerable length of time such as household appliances, industrial machinery, or buildings; and consumable or perishable goods that are used up quickly, like newspapers or food. There is little that can be done to prolong the life of products in this latter category. Last week's newspaper is no longer news. Wrappings of yesterday's hamburger have little value as wrappings today. We can recycle such products in the hope of recovering some value or at least reducing waste disposal problems, but many of these items are destined for short life.

Not so for the more durable products in our economy. These durable goods, plus the human assets of this country, constitute the real wealth of the United States. Modern materials, modern product design, and modern industrial practice make it possible for many products to live virtually forever. It is possible, therefore, to preserve and even enhance our physical wealth by the straightforward means of extending the lives of our products.

Alternatives for Extending Product Life

If you wish to make durable products live longer, several complementary approaches are possible: Products can be designed to be more durable, or they can be made more easily repairable or renewable. Finally, when the end of life appears inevitable, they can be remanufactured.

To make products more durable, materials can be used that are stronger, more resilient, more corrosion-resistant, and less subject to wear. Rugged, miniaturized, solid-state controls and robust assembly techniques further enhance product durability, as do modern protective coatings and lubricants. Given the materials and technologies available today, for example, it should be possible to make automobiles that, barring accidents, routinely last for hundreds of thousands of miles or for 20 years or more. A bridge should last for 100 years or more—why should we have to replace our highway bridges after only 30 to 50 years of use?

Products can be made more readily repairable. In those parts of a product where wear or corrosion are unavoidable, designing the parts for low cost and ease of replacement will encourage owners to continue using a product rather than discarding it when a relatively minor part fails. Often a product is thrown out because the cost of repair is large relative to the price of a comparable new product. Older products often have to be discarded because replacement parts are no longer available. Modular construction for ease of disassembly, better servicing instructions, and improved modes of customer service and availability of replacement parts are all approaches that can reduce maintenance and repair costs and keep products working longer.

Keeping the cost of repairs down would do much to prolong the lives of many capital goods. Public policy incentives are possible. In the same manner that we permit industrial firms to deduct the cost of maintaining their plants and equipment from their taxable revenues, we might allow private citizens to deduct the costs of maintaining their capital goods—their homes, vehicles, and equipment. Companies that manufacture durable products would be encouraged to maintain stocks of replacement parts for greater lengths of time if they were able to write off the older parts and yet retain them in inventory. Carrying costs, particularly the cost of keeping money tied up in parts inventories, constitute an important component of replacement part prices. Even at a modest 8 percent annual carrying cost (most firms consider 25 to 35 percent more appropriate), the cost of a part that is kept in inventory for 10 years more than doubles. By being able to carry these parts in inventory at zero value, companies could eliminate a major factor in the cost of parts.

Product appearance, a major reason for product discard, can be renewed. When a product's exterior is worn, damaged, or out of fashion, but the product still functions, it is possible to make cosmetic changes. We frequently do this with buildings, rather than tear them down. The multiple reincarnations of VW Beetles in a variety of sports car garb is a further example. The internal "workings" of many products are (or can be) designed to last many years longer than their external shells. This tends to be true of many household appliances, where changes in color or style, or superficial wear often bring about discard. Such products could be made to live longer if manufacturers made and sold replacement panels or entire jackets that simply replaced worn or outmoded shells.

In those instances where product performance is determined by computer or computerlike controls, it is sometimes possible to upgrade operating characteristics merely by changing software or by adding a few integrated circuit chips. When a product is designed with this strategy in mind, its useful life can be not only renewed, but enhanced. Computer companies have used this technique to enable users to stretch the capabilities of older machines. A recent example of this is Intel Corporation's introduction of its OverDrive Processor(TM) that boosts a personal computer's speed merely by adding a chip.

All of these alternatives are applicable to durable products around the globe. Because of America's enormous stock of capital goods, however, these strategies can have a much greater impact on living standards here than they would in a poor country with relatively fewer capital goods.

However, it is when a product is finally ready for discard that America's secret weapon, remanufacturing, comes into play. This industrial activity appears to be peculiarly native to the U.S. economy, for reasons we will explore later. It is a secret weapon in the sense that it is largely unknown and unrecognized, even though it is widely practiced.

Remanufacturing

Remanufacturing restores a nonfunctioning or discarded durable product to like-new condition. The remanufactured product's performance is at least as good as when it was new, and it is often enhanced. The process is both resource-conserving and economically sound.

The remanufacturing cycle begins when a user relinquishes a product to the system that collects and forwards such items, called "cores," to a remanufacturer. Often cores are the trade-ins accepted by dealers when a new product is sold, but cores also arise in salvage operations, such as those found in automobile junkyards. In some instances, the original owner of the durable good retains title to the core and merely contracts with the remanufacturer to restore the product to a specified condition. Machine tools are frequently remanufactured in this manner.

Cores are typically brought to a factory environment, where they are completely disassembled. Disassembly, cleaning, and refurbishment are key remanufacturing activities that differ from normal manufacturing operations. During disassembly and cleaning, parts are examined for damage or wear. Those that cannot be salvaged are discarded; those that can be reused are sorted by part and model number. If the volume of a given product is sufficiently large, the parts will be processed in batches.

Refurbishment may take a variety of forms. Parts may merely be stripped of paint, checked for soundness, and refinished. Worn areas on metal parts may be built up by welding, after which the parts are machined to original dimensions. Out-of-round holes may be bored to accept bushings that restore the original hole diameters. Bent shafts are straightened, surfaces are reground or scraped. Electrical components are cleaned, tested, and given new protective coatings.

Remanufacturers are intimately aware of weaknesses in a product that can cause failure. Frequently they will redesign a failure-prone part and substitute a more reliable replacement.

The possibility of upgrading a product beyond its original capability is also exploited by many remanufacturers. Machine tool rebuilders very often will add numerical control or computer controls to machines that were originally controlled manually. Relay-type controls are replaced with solid-state controls, and improved, fast-change tool holders will be substituted. The resulting machines are as accurate as they ever were, but more reliable, and more productive.

Measurement, testing, and quality control methods used during refurbishing are similar to those used in original manufacture. The one important exception is that inspection must be made on a 100 percent basis. When all parts must be presumed faulty until proved otherwise, sampling plans are inappropriate. Quality control is essential throughout the remanufacturing process. Every person working on the product must be alert for possible faults in the parts that are being used. This requirement obligates management to train all employees in rudimentary inspection techniques, to provide appropriate measuring and inspection equipment, and to motivate people to maintain high quality standards. The reputation and the ultimate success of the remanufacturer rest almost entirely upon the quality of the finished product.

Role of Remanufacturing in the Economy

Remanufacturing may be known to some people by other names, such as rebuilding and reconditioning. The essential characteristic of a remanufactured product is that it has been restored to at least the capability and appearance of the product when it was new. Remanufacturing differs from repair, in which only the product fault is found and corrected. Repair continues the original life of a product; remanufacturing gives it a new life. Modernization or upgrading of a product further distinguishes remanufacturing from repair.

Remanufacturing differs from recycling also, most importantly because it makes a much greater economic contribution per unit of product than does recycling. The essential difference arises in the recapture of value added. Value added is the cost of labor, energy, and manufacturing operations that are added to the basic cost of raw materials in the manufacture of a product.

For all but the most simple durable goods, value added is by far the largest element of cost. Even in a product as simple as a beer bottle, the cost of the basic raw materials (sand, soda, and lime) is much less than 5 percent of the cost of a finished bottle. The rest is value added. For a product such as an automobile, the value of the raw materials that can be recovered by recycling is only in the order of 1.5 percent of the market value of a new car.[3]

Value added is embodied in the product. Recycling destroys that value added, reducing a product to its elemental value—its recoverable raw material constituents. Further, recycling requires added labor, energy, and processing capital to recover the raw materials. When all of the costs of segregation, collection, processing, and refining are taken into account, recycling has a significant societal cost. Society undertakes recycling only because, for all nondurable and many durable products, the societal cost of any other disposal alternative is even greater.

Because it restores products to their original functioning state, remanufacturing preserves much of the original value added. The labor that went into making the parts, the energy used to produce the materials and form the parts, and the contribution of machines and processes remain in the product. Approximately 85 percent of the energy used to produce an automotive component such as an alternator can be recaptured.[4]

Figure 11-1 portrays the system of durable product manufacture and use, and shows the four value-salvaging loops, from repair through recycling. The larger the loop, the less value is recovered. If a product can be repaired simply, value is restored with minor cost. Reuse (selling a used automobile to a new owner, for example) likewise preserves much value at small additional cost. When neither of these alternatives is economically or technically feasible, then remanufacturing is, from an economic point of view, the option of choice. Only when none of the preferred approaches is possible should a product enter the recycling loop.

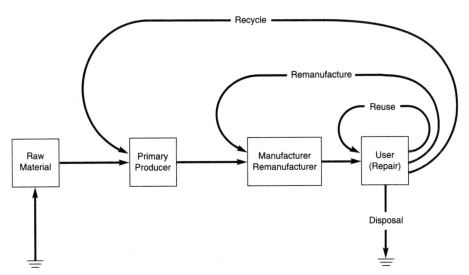

Figure 11-1. Materials resource system. (*Robert T. Lund, "Remanufacturing, The Experience of the United States and Implications for Developing Countries," World Bank Technical Paper Number 31, The World Bank, New York, 1985, p. 7.*)

Only a few parts are normally affected to the point where they cannot be salvaged. Technology exists that can restore, repair, refinish, or even replicate worn or damaged parts. A high percentage of parts in many assemblages need only to be cleaned and inspected. A 1980 study of remanufacturing found that between five and nine pounds of parts in a product can be salvaged for every one pound of new parts (gaskets, bearings, bushings, controls, etc.) needed to replace unrecoverable items.[5]

The cost of remanufacturing is such that restored products can be resold at 55 to 65 percent of the normal market price for comparable new products. Even at these prices, a remanufacturer can make a decent profit. The reason for this is that a nonfunctioning product, such as an electric motor that has failed, has a very low market value, despite a significant amount of recoverable value added in the core. A remanufacturer is able to buy these cores at a small fraction of the value that can be recaptured.

Remanufacturers typically offer warranties on their products that are as good or better than the original warranties. Some remanufacturers maintain that "experienced parts" are more reliable than new ones. Only well-designed parts survive. When remanufacturers discover which part is likely to fail in a given model, and replace that part with a better-designed part, product reliability is enhanced.

What Products Are Remanufactured?

Products that are remanufactured can be found in consumer, commercial, and industrial markets, but the range of acceptance of such products by consumers is far smaller than the potential in that market. The major remanufactured consumer products are automobile components, such as alternators, carburetors, water pumps, and engines. Remanufacturing has a dominant role in the automotive replacement parts market. About 85 percent of all replacement starter motors sold in the United States, for example, are remanufactured.

In the area of transportation equipment, virtually all types of equipment—autos, buses, subway and transit vehicles, trucks, aircraft, locomotives, and component assemblies for each—are remanufactured. The Automotive Parts Rebuilders Association in McLean, Virginia, has a membership of approximately 1000 remanufacturers of auto components. It estimates that there are an additional 6900 automotive parts rebuilders throughout the country. The typical APRA member has fewer than 20 production employees. Only a handful of companies have sales approaching $100 million or more.

Arrow Automotive Industries, with headquarters in Framingham, Massachusetts, is a large national automotive parts remanufacturing company. With sales that have been in the vicinity of $100 million since 1984, Arrow employs approximately 1500 people. Its operating plants are in South Carolina, Arkansas, and California. Established in 1929 as Speedometer Repair Company, Arrow was one of the first remanufacturers in the automotive and heavy-duty vehicle area. Its current product line includes starter motors, alternators, carburetors, water pumps, clutches, distributors, rack and pinion steering systems, wiper motors, brake units, and other related items. Products, marketed largely through wholesale distributors, are sold under the Arrow brand name, although units with private brands are also marketed through other channels. Arrow's products have a 12-month, unlimited mileage warranty. With the proliferation of foreign and American car models and rapid year-to-year changes in components, Arrow is continually making decisions about additions and deletions to its product line. Automobile downsizing has further complicated Arrow's remanufacturing efforts. Components that formerly had cast-iron or steel housings, for example, now may have thin-wall aluminum or plastic shells that are difficult to remachine or otherwise salvage. Highly profitable from 1975 to 1985, Arrow has encountered strong competition from other automotive remanufacturers in recent years. It has maintained a leadership position by emphasizing cost containment, quality, and marketing strategies.

Typical products remanufactured for the commercial sector include computers, computer disk memories, telephone switchgear, toner cartridges for computer printers, laundry equipment, soft drink dispensers, and vending machines, plus the commercial transport equipment mentioned above.

Magnetic Data, Inc., a wholly owned subsidiary of Applied Magnetics, Inc., is an example of a highly successful company specializing in computer components, particularly magnetic disk drives ranging from $3\frac{1}{2}$ to 14 inches, and computer circuit boards. When the company was launched in 1982, its customers were computer owners who needed replacement units. Now its customers are largely computer original equipment manufacturers (OEMs) who contract with Magnetic Data for remanufacture of components that they assemble into equivalent-to-new products.

Operating under the theme of "reutilization," Magnetic Data directs its R&D efforts to increasing the amount of value that can be recovered from a product. At present about half the number of parts in a disk drive can be reused; the value of these usable parts, however, is much greater than that. Annual sales of the 10-year-old firm are approximately $45 million. Its plants are in California, Minnesota, and Belgium. Worldwide employment is 500.

When it started up, Magnetic Data encountered resistance from computer OEMs, who raised questions about remanufactured product quality as a means of discouraging competition. Once these companies realized the business potential from remanufactured equipment and became customers, their resistance changed to advocacy. Magnetic Data now has at least half of the top dozen computer firms as customers. Optical disk remanufacturing is now being done in Belgium, and other new product avenues are being pursued.

Morrison-Knudson Corporation (MK), a major engineering and construction contractor with headquarters in Boise, Idaho, remanufactures locomotives and urban transit vehicles. Normally, MK will contract to remanufacture a locomotive for a customer, but they will also purchase locomotives, rebuild them, and either sell or lease them. In 1992 they had a fleet of 20 rental locomotives. The price of a remanufactured locomotive is in the vicinity of $800,000. If new, a comparable 3000-hp locomotive would cost $1.4 million.

Subway and transit cars are remanufactured by MK in Hornell, New York, and in Chicago. An additional assembly plant is planned for northern California in 1993. Plant sites are dictated by the location of customers: New York City, Philadelphia, Boston, Chicago, and San Francisco/Oakland. Between 40 and 50 percent of the New York fleet of transit cars have been remanufactured by MK. In the 10 years that the company has been in the transit car business, they have remanufactured over 3000 vehicles. Current capacity is 20 cars per week. At a price of "under $1 million" per car, MK is able to save municipalities between $1 and $2 million per vehicle and still make a profit. The company also manufactures new subway cars—the only U.S.-owned company in this business.

Another company, Equipco, Inc., of Monmouth, Illinois, remanufactures soda dispensers for Coca-Cola for use in restaurants, cafeterias, and the like. Equipco has just the one customer, and they are doing as much business as their capacity (which has been expanding) will allow. The company began as a service and repair agency in 1982, refurbishing Coca-Cola's dispensing machines. In 1985 the company persuaded Coca-Cola to have them remanufacture the units. Seven years later they were remanufacturing 8000 units annually, upgrading them when necessary. There are 56 employees. With a steady year-round demand from their customer, Equipco is a profitable small company within a unique niche.

A wide variety of products are remanufactured for the industrial sector. Typical of these are compressors, electrical generators, machine tools, power switching gear, food processing machinery, pumps, refrigeration systems, power transformers, and industrial valves. Many of these products are restored by their original manufacturers. Caterpillar Tractor, for example, remanufactures its diesel engines in plants in Iowa and Mississippi. Other companies arrange for independent contractors to do the remanufacturing for them.

Sometimes a remanufacturer of an industrial product performs a service to its customers that an original equipment manufacturer is unable to do. A fairly typical remanufacturer of refrigeration compressors, Dallas Hermetic Company, makes immediate availability of replacement units a major selling point. Often a customer seeking replacement for a unit that has failed is in a situation where a long downtime can be very costly. Dallas Hermetic maintains an inventory of remanufactured compressors and components for essentially all of the major brands. Quick delivery and product quality have been key factors in the company's 17-year growth. One-year warranties are equal to those of original equipment manufacturers. The president of the company, Bob Powell, reports they have good warranty experience: "We also offer extended warranties. We make money on them. If a compressor runs well for the first month, it is likely to continue without trouble for years."

Sunbelt Transformer, of Temple, Texas, remanufactures large transformers and switchgear used in substations for manufacturing plants, hospitals, office buildings, warehouses, military installations, and the like. The 10-year-old company has 45 employees, and sales in the vicinity of $6 million. As in the case of Dallas Hermetic, Sunbelt uses its large inventory of replacement units as a competitive advantage. Customers frequently seek replacement units for equipment that has just failed, and Sunbelt has built a national reputation for fast response in emergencies.

Engineers specify how each transformer is to be remanufactured. Randall Maddox, Sunbelt's president says, "We design for efficiency, not for lowest cost." Using techniques such as changing windings from aluminum to copper, or improving the quality of insulation used, Sunbelt can increase the performance of a transformer to 110 to 115 percent above original specifications. Prices of their remanufactured transformers vary. Smaller units tend to be sold at about the prices charged for comparable new units. Larger transformers are priced considerably lower than new equipment. A 10,000-KVA unit, for example, sells for about 55 percent of the price of a new unit of the same rating.

The company went into the recent recession with a strong financial position, and they found that this allowed them to bid for and acquire a number of transformers at distress prices. Consequently, they came through the recession with a larger, better inventory at a lower dollar investment. The company has started marketing new transformers in addition to its line of remanufactured products.

Dayton Machine Tool Company, Ohio, is a typical remanufacturer of industrial metalworking equipment. With engineering capability to modernize and upgrade machines, the company can convert units to computer numerical control, add parts handling systems, make special fixtures, or even combine old and new machines into complete manufacturing cells. About 90 to 95 percent of their projects involve upgrades; 95 percent require some engineering. Because of their high standards and the amount of engineering and inspection required, DMT has found that machines having a replacement cost of less than $100,000 are generally not economic candidates for remanufacture. Of their 60 employees, 12 are engineers. Having designed and built special new equipment for earlier customers, DMT also has a line of new proprietary products in niche markets.

The U.S. Department of Defense is a major remanufacturer on its own. It has, for example, a tank remanufacturing facility in Alabama, and a helicopter remanufacturing facility in Texas. Many of the higher-echelon maintenance operations in each of the services could actually be classified as remanufacturing facilities because their overhaul practices are so comprehensive.

An American Secret Weapon?

If remanufacturing is so well established in our economy, why should we consider this a "secret" weapon? The nature of the activity provides some answers. Remanufacturing does not lend itself to a great deal of publicity. It has very low visibility. There are few recognized remanufacturers' brand names, no new model introductions, no technological product breakthroughs to boast about. Remanufactured products are not even accounted for separately in national statistics, so it is even impossible to determine the size of this part of the economy. Independent remanufacturing firms typically are small to medium in size. Few of the largest firms exceed $100 million annual sales. Original equipment manufacturers who also remanufacture their products do not emphasize this aspect of their businesses, because their primary objective is to make and sell new products. Even in terms of trade associations, remanufacturers are underrepresented. The consequence of all this is low awareness on the part of the American public.

Remanufacturing is not unique to the United States, but American remanufacturing appears to be significantly more extensive than that of other industrialized countries. All countries have some activity in this area, but the total volume of durable goods in use in this country is enormous, so the supply of cores and the markets for remanufactured products are correspondingly large. In addition, the prejudice against used equipment in Europe, for example, is reportedly even greater than in the United States.

Less-developed countries have their own forms of product restoration. These restorations take place not in organized factories but in tiny shops, where individual workers craft make-do repairs or replacements that are contrived to keep a product running. Older equipment kept in use in this manner tends to become a hybrid patchwork of parts and pieces adapted to the peculiar problems of that item. Even though this approach provides the most product life possible under the circumstances, the process does not fit what would normally be called remanufacturing.

Remanufacturing then, is an unrecognized asset of significant importance to the American economy. It is a competitive weapon in that it reduces demand on the world's resources while it enhances our standard of living.

Criteria for Remanufactured Products

In 1980 I directed a study to determine the characteristics of a durable product that make it a prime candidate for remanufacture. The more important of these characteristics are the following:

1. The durable product fails functionally rather than by dissolution or dissipation. Something that melts away or corrodes away is obviously not a candidate. There must be a core—a discarded, malfunctioning, or used product that becomes the remanufactured product.

2. The technology must exist that can restore the product to its original shape, condition, and function.

3. The product is factory-built, standardized, and made with interchangeable parts.

4. The recoverable value added in the product is a high percentage of the product's original market price.

5. The cost of obtaining a core is low relative to its true economic value (i.e., the recoverable value added and materials in the core).

6. Product technology is relatively stable. Rapid technological obsolescence dooms otherwise remanufacturable products. The electromechanical calculator of the 1950s was remanufacturable, for instance, but the electronic calculator made it obsolete.

It is also helpful if the product is one that is serviced or installed by an organized service agency or distribution network. There must be an efficient way to maintain a continuous return flow of good cores.

Many of our durable products meet these criteria for remanufacturability. Many are being remanufactured to some extent. Many others could be added to the growing list, most notably in the consumer durables area. There are many benefits, and there are also some barriers to remanufacturing. The benefits that can be gained through remanufacturing are summarized below. Then the barriers are examined.

Benefits of Remanufacturing

- Of primary consideration is the fact that remanufacturing restores or even upgrades product value and life. Product function is as good or better than when new.

- Conservation of raw materials and conservation of energy have already been discussed. For every kilowatt-hour of energy spent in remanufacturing, about 5 kilowatt-hours are recaptured. Only activities such as coal mining and petroleum production fall in to this category of producing more energy than they consume.

- Likewise, remanufacturing recaptures original labor spent in making the product. It also recaptures the value of capital plant and equipment that entered into manufacture of the product.

- Remanufacturing also reduces the size of the solid waste stream. Because of the enormous volume of packaging and other perishable goods in the waste stream, however, the percentage reduction potential is small. The volume, nevertheless, is millions of tons per year in the United States. For all of the foregoing reasons, remanufacturing can be said to be very much an environmentally friendly activity.

- Employment opportunities are provided by remanufacturing, because it tends to be a labor-intensive activity. Relatively low-skilled people can be employed, and there are opportunities for training and advancement. Remanufacturing tends to be a rather portable industry, so it can be located in areas of high unemployment and economic distress. Remanufacturing also brings income to other suppliers of goods and services in the area.

- Lower product prices, typically in the range of 45 to 65 percent of comparable new products, give buyers a greater range of product choice and the opportunity to obtain items that might not otherwise be affordable.

- Finally, remanufacturing is a profitable private enterprise that returns tax dollars to the American economy. This is not a public cost activity; it is a viable industrial activity run by entrepreneurs and managers justifiably proud of their businesses.

Barriers to Remanufacturing

If we have all these benefits from remanufacturing, why has it been so invisible? Why is it not a larger factor in our way of life? There are barriers to remanufacturing, and some of these are deep rooted.

In the United States, perhaps the most pervasive and intractable problem is the fact that product newness is valued so highly. When a buyer lacks the expertise to evaluate the durability or reliability of a product, newness becomes an important criterion. As long as buyers consider a not-new product to be inherently inferior and unreliable, remanufacturers face a difficult hurdle. This predilection toward newness has carried over into public policy. There are laws that require remanufactured products to be so labeled. Even "new" products that may contain only one or two remanufactured components must inform the public of this fact.

The task of establishing a flow of remanufacturable cores can be formidable for a firm entering into a product area where no remanufacturing has been done before. One frequently used route to remanufacturing for small independent firms has been to start out as equipment retailers offering repair services. This starts the flow of potentially remanufacturable products. Distributors who take trade-ins as part of their business also are in a good position to initiate a remanufacturing enterprise.

Original equipment manufacturers (OEMs) can make it difficult for remanufacturers to obtain the replacement parts they use or to provide design specifications that would facilitate manufacture and testing. Obviously, the remanufacturer can be considered a competitor and is likely to be treated as such. OEMs that make frequent design changes in their products tend to discourage remanufacturers from dealing with their products. OEMs try to discourage their suppliers from selling parts to remanufacturers, but a recent U.S. Supreme Court decision (June 8, 1992) offers possible relief. In that decision, the Court allowed a suit to go forward that contests the actions of an OEM to limit the availability of parts so as to control the aftermarket service of its products.[6]

Remanufacturing's invisibility, the feature that makes it one of our secret weapons, is possibly remanufacturing's greatest barrier. Neither the consuming public nor public policy makers are fully aware of the contributions this activity makes. There is no American Remanufacturers Association to lobby for recognition and public encouragement of the industry. There are no subsidies, tax breaks, or national centers to provide technical assistance. There are no national statistics being collected that can even identify the current importance of this activity to our economy.

When an industry can make as many positive economic and environmental contributions as remanufacturing, public policy makers should recognize its value and find means to encourage its growth. At the very least, the government should not put more roadblocks in its way. So-called anti-piracy legislation has been proposed that would require product owners to buy parts exclusively from OEMs. This would effectively bar independent remanufacturers from the market. It is special-interest legislation of the worst kind.

Summary

One of the greatest legacies that one generation can leave for the next is a strong capital base. A country rich in useful durable goods, from steel plants to sewing machines, from locomotives to lasers, has the means to support a high standard of living. If we can make our current plant and equipment base live longer, using all of the various strategies available to us, we can continue to expand America's assets with minimum expenditure of human, material, and energy resources. We can provide future generations with the rich legacy of a healthy capital base, but only if we adopt practices for sustaining it.

References

1. Charles Stein, "Fraying of the Blue Collar Worker," *The Boston Globe,* April 28, 1992, p. 1.

2. Robert D. Hof, "Suddenly, Hewlett-Packard Is Doing Everything Right," *Business Week,* March 22, 1992.

3. Robert T. Lund, "Making Products Live Longer," *Technology Review,* 79(3) January 1977.

4. Lynn Bollinger et al., "Remanufacturing Survey Findings," M.I.T. Center for Policy Alternatives Report #81-12, Cambridge, Mass., January 1981.

5. Lynn Bollinger et al., "Energy Savings Through Remanufacturing: Final Report of Pre-Demonstration Study," M.I.T. Center for Policy Alternatives Report #81-13, Cambridge, Mass., 1981.

6. T. Smart, "Kodak Takes a Shot in the Mug," *Business Week,* June 22, 1992, p. 40.

PART 5
Conclusion

12

The American Edge

Each of the 10 preceding chapters stands alone as a constructive contribution to the competitiveness debate. But our task will not be complete until we answer two questions raised by their existence as a collection. Do the "secret weapons" identified in each chapter add up to more than the sum of their parts, that is, to an American edge? How can the American edge, if it exists, be used by manufacturing companies as they respond to the challenges of global, functional, and technical integration identified in Chapter 1?

As we began to ponder these questions, we ran across the following story which seemed to capture the important elements of each of the chapters in personal terms. The story illustrates that there is an underlying American edge that comes from adding up the strengths we had been investigating. It helped us understand that the edge is in the people who capitalized on those strengths.

> When it comes to designing cars, Mimi Vandermolen knows how to get the men at Ford Motor Company to take her seriously. To sensitize her mostly male design staff to the needs of women drivers, she had them work in fake fingernails. The result: a hot-selling 1993 Ford Probe with less bulky radio knobs and door handles. The Probe also has a lightweight trunk door and a lowered front end, to give shorter women a better view of the road. Says Vandermolen: "I've threatened to make our men designers wear skirts while getting in and out of a car."

Vandermolen, 46, is trying to take some of the macho out of Motown. As the highest-ranking woman designer in the auto industry, she's using her position to draw attention to the many frustrations female drivers face—from seat buttons that entangle skirts and rip panty hose to bulky gas and brake pedals that defy women in high heels. Traditionally, cars have been designed with men in mind. But with women making up 49 percent of new car purchases, many auto makers are reevaluating their market.[1]

This vignette depicts more than a portrait of another successful woman manager in manufacturing. The Ford Motor Company has a diverse work force and a rich management heritage dating back to Henry Ford. The technical ability to design a car has long been a hallmark of Ford automobiles. But Vandermolen's story exemplifies that all of this technical, market, and organizational knowledge must be pulled together by someone like her and used creatively and constructively. Her story represents one of many stories which could be told about companies and individuals who have instinctively taken advantage of what we have concluded is the American edge in manufacturing.

Throughout the previous 10 chapters there have been two interwoven themes that identify important elements of this edge. First, American manufacturers and their employees are uniquely positioned in their ability to acquire and generate knowledge from multiple sources of information, opinion, know-how, and data. Second, the nation has evolved many highly developed knowledge-processing capabilities to store, manage, and retrieve this storehouse of knowledge. These two factors combined provide the *potential* to discover new processes and products to enhance the country's competitiveness in manufacturing. The ability to convert this potential into an edge, however, depends upon people like Mimi Vandermolen. Only they can convert this edge into discoveries that make teams, business units, companies, and nations competitive.

Multiple Inputs and Perspectives

As Wick Skinner noted in his chapter on production managers, U.S. manufacturers have a wide variety of places to go to get new ideas or answers to current problems. They have universities where they can tap the latest academic thinking. They have countless consultants in every field imaginable eager to vend advise. They can turn to other companies to benchmark best practice, or they can attend conferences to learn from others' successes. In response to this desire to exchange ideas, numerous networks have been organized to provide forums for managers and employees to share experiences.

But beyond this myriad of institutional sources of knowledge, U.S. manufacturers can also turn to its "outsiders" for new ideas. For in addition to the multiple inputs they provide, they also bring new perspectives or different interpretations of existing ideas and knowledge. Part 3 on America's outsiders suggests that despite the country's failures, the U.S. industry is much more open to multiple inputs and perspectives than competitors from countries such as Germany and Japan.

The United States is a land of outsiders; other than native American Indians, its population comprises descendants of immigrants. Many of those original immigrants left their homelands because of their desire to be valued for their individual views; they sought a place where their religious, political, and economic rights would be honored. As a result, American society is relatively open to outsiders and, for the most part, there is a fundamental assumption that its organizations can learn from these outsiders.

American managers tend to listen and learn more from outsiders than from people internal to their organizations. In this regard, U.S. manufacturers keep looking globally for answers to improve the country's manufacturing competitiveness. Kasra Ferdows in his chapter on foreign operations showed the special skill that U.S. multinationals have developed that enables them to tap into offshore knowledge about markets and local supplier conditions. Marion McCollom, in her chapter on immigrant entrepreneurs, identified immigrants as another resource of foreign knowledge available within the country, which has yet to be tapped by most large manufacturers.

Traditionally, managers have attempted to take foreign ideas on how to manage manufacturing and mold them into their existing practices. This has tended to parallel the country's initial melting pot approach to managing work force diversity. As Sheila Akabas and Lauren Gates noted in their chapter on work force diversity, early efforts at managing diversity attempted to assimilate different groups into the majority view. But, as with integrating multiple people and their cultures, it is insufficient to merely mold new ideas to fit existing frameworks.

In Chapter 1, we noted that the world of manufacturing is undergoing radical changes that require organizations and individuals to become adept at global, functional, and technical integration. These changes are so fundamental that they cannot be accomplished by simply adding a few new ideas to existing ways of thinking. Major paradigm shifts are required, and research has shown that paradigm shifts are most often made by outsiders.[2] Mimi Vandermolen was an outsider, and it is clear that her fundamental role was to help shift the paradigm, or the way of thinking, of the Probe design team. The organizations that can identify and make these shifts most adroitly will have an important advantage.

Part 3 on America's outsiders also illustrates that America's richest resource is the large number of nontraditional sources available to provide new insights into alternative paradigms. The nation's outsiders are in the best position to observe inconsistencies in traditional ways of doing things, many of which have become commonplace to insiders. Furthermore, multiple inputs provide an opportunity to choose between competing alternatives or possibly an even better option which incorporates the best of each. Multiple inputs create synergy; one idea builds upon another, providing a new slant. As a result, much of the invention noted in Chapter 2 has been facilitated by the country's open access to multiple sources of knowledge about cultures, organizations, tastes, trades, and practices both within the population and from the global community.

Knowledge-Processing Capabilities

Having multiple inputs and perspectives is useful provided there is a mechanism to sort the good ideas from the bad or to combine or create good ideas into new products or processes. In other words, knowledge has little value unless an individual or organization also has the ability to process and manipulate it. The value inherent in outsider perspectives places a burden on the nation and its organizations to find ways to preserve and capitalize on differences while integrating diverse knowledge and skills into a unified entity which can function despite its heterogeneity.

The United States has developed a scientific and academic infrastructure which excels in such knowledge processing. Jane Fedorowicz, in her chapter on the information incubator, identified the enormous information infrastructure that provides American competitors with a special ability to transmit, store, and retrieve knowledge, regardless of whether it is technical, social, or organizational in nature. The information infrastructure in America helps to ensure not only that information is available but that it can be accessed rapidly and at a relatively low cost.

The United States has also developed unique managerial systems to process multiple inputs and perspectives. For example, the chapter on production managers noted that American corporations are developing a cadre of manufacturing managers who are skilled at integrating diverse functional expertise into the manufacturing operation. And, as Lyn Christiansen and Julie Hertenstein noted in their chapter on women managers, U.S. manufacturers have a largely untapped portion of their work force possessing skills to build effective teams and manage cross-functional and cross-organizational linkages.

The U.S. model for empowerment, the small business teams (SBTs) described in Chapter 4, also provides a way for companies to integrate multifunctional skills within a team. By narrowing the scope of a team's activities to a particular product or process, multiple inputs and perspectives are focused on solving specific problems or discovering new methods of improvement. The SBT structure also recognizes the importance of preserving the individual strengths of a diverse work force while integrating individuals into a team where the whole is greater than the sum of the parts.

Discovery

Multiple inputs and perspectives, coupled with highly developed knowledge-processing capabilities, enables discoveries to be made. As Pieter VanderWerf described in his chapter on invention, the United States has developed a scientific and educational infrastructure that produces technical knowledge at a rate unsurpassed by any country or region in the world.

But the American competency to acquire and utilize knowledge produces more than technological inventions. It also produces organizational discoveries. The United States has a tradition of discovering and advancing many of the premier managerial and administrative systems. For example, Frederick Taylor's notions about the division of labor and industrial engineering have been implemented throughout the world. Furthermore, many of today's quality control techniques, such as statistical process control, were born at AT&T's Bell Labs. Edward Deming and Joseph Juran introduced these concepts to Japanese manufacturers and a quality revolution, now known as total quality management (TQM), was born. Even Toyota's just-in-time inventory system was copied from Henry Ford; Ohno has noted that he first got the idea when touring a Ford operation in Detroit. More recently, Americans have led the way in coupling producers, suppliers, distributors, and customers with integrated information and communication systems.

In an earlier time, America's instincts for discovery might have been called "Yankee ingenuity." But that would be both misleading and a gross oversimplification of the nation's core competency. It would be misleading because *Yankee* denotes a white male Brahmin born in Boston. The chapters in this book bear witness to the fact that a critical component of the American edge is the diversity of the human and technical resources which the nation can bring to bear.

America's human resources are from Hanoi, Moscow, Jamaica, and Brownsville, and some were born and still live in Paris and Tokyo. They are male and female, old and young, black, brown, and white. The Yankee ingenuity label is an oversimplification because it implies that the edge lies in some inborn talent for clever thinking that is apparent in American newborns, but not in their overseas cousins. In fact, the ingenuity is the product of skills to acquire and apply knowledge which the country has learned and which the nation must work to sustain.

Unfortunately, foreign competitors often recognize the power of American managerial systems and technology more quickly than do U.S. manufacturers. The United States has discovered many break-through concepts, but learned to *value* them only after outsiders did. As a result, the United States has continually missed the opportunity to exploit its edge. A prime example is the way the ideas of Deming and Juran were received in Japan, but neglected in the United States. Another is the invention of semiconductors and how to make them which was, in essence, given away to foreign competitors. The challenge in the future is to recognize and value the nation's discoveries before competitors do.

Heritage + Outsiders + Technology = Opportunity

America's tradition of open markets and an open society means that all nations have access to America's strengths. Its multiple sources of inputs and perspectives, its knowledge-processing capabilities, and its discoveries have been widely used, most notably by Japan. But the United States still has an edge by virtue of its proximity to its strengths, its advanced understanding of them, and the sheer magnitude of multiple sources of input and perspectives available. With the proper motivation, the United States can leverage the American edge better than foreign competitors.

The "secret weapons" identified in this book point to the opportunities available when the country's administrative heritage and outsider perspectives are combined with its technological base. These weapons are not secret because too few people are exposed to them, but because too few have stood back and tried to understand how these

traditional sources of strength have matured and how American manufacturers can capitalize on them in the future.

Part 4 on the environmental advantage and remanufacturing illustrates how American technological know-how can be employed to
address business opportunities and social responsibilities. There are
many more aspects of American technology and know-how that could
have been included in this book. But, these two technologies are particularly important because they contrast very different aspects of the
nation's technological base. The technological opportunities described
in Chapter 10 by Jim Post are generally "high tech" in nature. They
involve the exploitation of America's vast reservoir of environmental,
scientific, and engineering knowledge. By comparison, remanufacturing, as described by Bob Lund, is a "low tech" application of technology that exploits the nation's sophisticated manufacturing, distribution, and management know-how.

These two technologies are also important because they address
opportunities that many see as threats. Their existence is not a secret,
but their potential is. For example, increased environmental awareness is not a threat to the nation's manufacturing competitiveness, but
a major opportunity to grow new businesses. And, although remanufacturing is commonly viewed as a source of low-quality goods,
America's remanufacturing know-how can be used to produce high-
quality goods at a cost competitive with global competitors at the
same time that it contributes to a cleaner planet.

Part 4 also serves as an illustration of how the country's administrative heritage, in combination with its access to outsider thinking and
technology, can produce powerful competitive advantages. Post suggests that there are two essential requirements for American firms that
wish to seize the environmental opportunities before them. The first
requirement is an inventive capacity, which the chapter on invention
argues the United States has historically had. The second requirement
is the capacity to think differently and entrepreneurially, the weapons
that the authors in Part 3 believe the nation's outsiders bring.

Lund's analysis of remanufacturing suggests that the essential
ingredients for deploying the nation's remanufacturing know-how
include important and highly developed manufacturing management
skills—important attributes from our administrative heritage. His case
studies and comments also show that remanufacturing depends on
entrepreneurialism and a willingness to do hard and dirty work.

Part 4 illustrates the creative synergy available by combining
America's administrative heritage and outsider population, with the
country's technological base. That synergy generates important
opportunities for the future. The American edge can, thus, be simply

stated as a formula: Heritage + Outsiders + Technology = Opportunity.

Exploiting the Edge

We set out to balance an unbalanced debate about where American manufacturing should look for competitive advantage in the future. We did so in the belief that the nation's loss of confidence in its competitive abilities was resulting in a systematic undervaluation of its assets and an overvaluation of the practices of manufacturers abroad.

In the 1950s and 1960s American industry ignored many of its own discoveries because it was too arrogant to change its ways. Now, the country's manufacturers have been humbled because competitors from other countries used these discoveries against them. Things are different now; arrogance is not a problem. The enemy today is loss of confidence. The country still has the ability to produce discoveries of enormous importance—that is the American edge. But unless individuals and companies value these discoveries and use them first, they may again find their own secret weapons being used against them.

It is ironic that American manufacturing has such a pessimistic view when it has been so successful in recent years. However, it is very understandable that the massive dislocations of jobs and industries produce an aura of gloom. The country's manufacturing sector is going through a sea change similar to the change agriculture went through 50 to 100 years ago. The lament of 1930 was "woe is me, there goes the family farm." The lament of the 1990s is "woe is me, there goes the community's factory." These are wrenching changes for individuals, families, communities, and the nation. But the long-run result of the changes in agriculture was the creation of the most productive food-producing country in the world and the avoidance of starvation for millions. A few people can feed the world, even though the demand for food has risen at an enormously fast rate.

The long-run result of the changes in manufacturing will parallel the changes in agriculture. A few people will be able to supply the world, even though the demand for goods will rise dramatically. The world's political systems will be challenged to an extraordinary degree to adjust to these changes. But that is not what this book is about. What it is about is creating a vision of how America can be a place that has more than its share of the remaining manufacturing jobs in the future. It will not ensure this share by copying others. It will ensure its share by beating the others in applying its own discoveries.

The chapters in this book are eloquent in establishing that the basis for the nation's advantages are not genetically encoded in individuals who happen to be born here. They do not flow from secret ingredients in America's water. They are the product of history, political structures, and economic policies and of the beliefs of individuals intricately intertwined into the fabric of society. The country must, therefore, preserve the foundation upon which it is based.

Preservation of the American edge rests on the country's ability to sustain the forces that value multiple inputs and perspectives and further the development of knowledge-processing capabilities. It is true that some of the qualities that the United States had in earlier times are diminishing absolutely or relatively due to modern trends elsewhere. In addition, there is a danger that the foundation may be eroding due to shifts in public sentiment or government policy, particularly in the areas of being open to outside perspectives and seeking more sources of input than others around the globe.

To prohibit any further deterioration of the American heritage, public policy must focus on maintaining open access to people and ideas. The risks of barriers to immigration or to the open exchange of information between companies and countries must be investigated; there is a need to encourage greater industry cooperation, such as has been done in the semiconductor industry with Sematech. Public policy can also further the integration of new ideas by fostering greater interaction between government, academic, and industrial leaders.

The nation's manufacturers and their managers and workers also have a responsibility to preserve and sharpen the American edge. Their duty is to value the American edge and use it creatively, not as a cookbook procedure. As we noted in the preface, those readers who thought they were going to get 10 secret things to do tomorrow that will give them results in two weeks will be sadly disappointed in this book. Using the edge means valuing what the country has and what its people produce.

We began this chapter with a vignette that described how Mimi Vandermolen and the Ford Motor Company are using the American edge. We will end with a set of vignettes that describe four people in a manufacturing organization who are equally intent on releasing the potential for the American edge.

> Kee Young is an employee working on a production line at one of Pitney Bowes' Mailing Systems manufacturing plants. He is not just any employee. He is one of about 25 percent of all employees who volunteered to be a part of the company's future. Like a large proportion of the work force at this plant he is foreign-born, has difficulty reading and writing in English, and is intelligent and hard working.

When Kee Young signed up to be a part of the company's future he knew what it meant. It meant that he had to join the company's "work force transition" program and that meant studying and mastering new technologies, such as statistics, production engineering techniques, and how to work with computers, in order to integrate these technologies into his work. He also knew that he would have to work in a different way—as a member of a small business team, rather than isolated by "job code" on a production line. In order for his team to obtain the advantages of their multiple perspectives, he also knew that he and many of his workmates would have to improve their ability to speak and read in English.

Ann Pol is Vice President for New Product Development at Pitney Bowes' Mailing Systems. An Irish immigrant, she rose to her present position through a number of jobs in production, human resources, and other functions. Like many immigrants, she believes, more fervently than her American-born counterparts, that America is the place where the best manufacturing can be done.

Her part in using the American edge is to focus on the functional integration of engineering, manufacturing, and marketing knowledge. She has focused her attention on helping the different parts of the organization *value* the multiple sources of information and perspectives available to each of them and in building teams that will process the knowledge. She has found that when the teams respect and use each other's knowledge, the time-to-market problem solves itself.

Fred Purdue is Vice President of Manufacturing at Pitney Bowes' Mailing Systems. One of the new breed of manufacturing executives that was described in the chapter on production managers, he and his working group *discovered* the work force transition program. A third-generation American, his current focus is on using the American edge to globally integrate the company's manufacturing operations. He is carefully leveraging the multiple sources of inputs and perspectives from the company's overseas managers and also from potential allies. He does not want a "melting pot" vision of global operations that forces the American view on all locations. He is striving to integrate the best from partners and global operations to create new advantages.

Hiro Hirandani is President of Pitney Bowes' Mailing Systems. An Indian by birth, he has held a number of international positions as well as positions in numerous functional areas. He is exploiting the American edge by using his understanding of global business and cultures to lead the company to a dominant position in global markets.

The stories of these four individuals are an appropriate ending for this book because they illustrate our most important conclusion:

exploiting the American edge means valuing it. The stories also show the potential available for U.S. manufacturers to continue to lead the world with innovative ideas and technology. Society as a whole cannot exploit the edge. It is only individuals, who value what America has to offer and then take actions within their own companies, who are able to realize the potential of the American edge.

References

1. Greg Bowens, "Mimi Vandermolen: Women Drivers Have a Friend at Ford," *Business Week,* November 16, 1992, p. 66.

2. Thomas Kuhn, *The Structure of Scientific Revolutions,* University of Chicago Press, Chicago, 1962.

Index

About the Editors

Janice A. Klein is a visiting associate professor in operations management and human resource management at MIT's Sloan School of Management and author of *Revitalizing Manufacturing: Text and Cases.*

Jeffrey G. Miller is a professor of operations management at Boston University. His previous books include *Benchmarking Global Manufacturing.*